THE WHOLE STORY

A Walk Around The World

THE WHOLE STORY

A Walk Around The World

Ffyona Campbell

ORION

First published in Great Britain in 1996 by
Orion
An imprint of Orion Books Ltd
Orion House, 5 Upper St Martin's Lane, London WC2H 9EA

A CIP catalogue record for this book is available
from the British Library

ISBN 0 75280 109 0

Printed in Great Britain by Butler & Tanner, Frome

For the spirits of my ancestors,
who watch over me and who come in many forms

ACKNOWLEDGEMENTS

There are some very special people I would like to thank for keeping my secret safe. They know who they are. I can't tell them how much it meant to me, or what I would have done to them if they hadn't.

I would like to thank all the people who supported me while I wrote and who worked on this book: my editor Yvette Goulden, who never gave up hope of a manuscript despite living through two previous deadlines without a scrap of paper in front of her and who gave me the confidence to write the story myself; Nick McDowell who inspired me to question further; Louise Page who remained unfazed; Katie Pope for brightening the days; Selina Walker and Andrea Henry who copy-edited at the last minute and saved me many blushes; the designer, Leigh Jones, and illustrator, Ceri Staziker; Dr Ken Kingsbury for hope; Mr Stallard for removing the disc; 'Great Aunt' Sara Parfitt for sticking with me; Mark Thomson for a strong decision; Emma Rogers for keeping me organised regardless of the changes of plan; Carolyn Malham for transcribing the tapes despite the noise; Neil and Lynn Hanson for understanding; Sarah Parker for the massages, both real and telepathic, which allowed me to sit; the people of Stoke Fleming and Dartmouth for standing by my parents with such humour during the British walk and in anticipation of their continuing support during the storm over this book; Andy Pirie for pushing comics on me when I needed some relief; Nan for guidance towards the centre; my father; my mother, for all that she is.

PREFACE

On 14 October 1994, Ffyona Campbell walked to the signpost at John O'Groats in Scotland, eleven years and some 20,000 miles after starting out on her journey at the age of sixteen.

The Guinness Book of Records defines a walk around the world as beginning and finishing in the same place, crossing four continents and covering a total of at least 16,000 miles. Two men had done it before her; Ffyona would be the first woman.

After walking the length of Britain at the age of sixteen, a journey of 1,000 miles which she completed in fifty days at an average of twenty-five miles a day, Ffyona set off to walk across America from New York to Los Angeles two years later at the age of eighteen, supported by a two-man back-up team.

At the age of twenty-one, she walked across Australia, a distance of 3,200 miles, in the record time of ninety-five days at a rate of fifty miles a day with a solo support driver.

In 1991, at the age of twenty-four, Ffyona set off from Cape Town, heading for the Mediterranean. Supported by two men in a Land Rover, she walked thirty-one miles a day for two years.

Ffyona started the last leg of the journey in April 1994, from Algeciras in Spain and walked through Europe, reaching the shores of Britain at Dover. For the last 800 miles, she was accompanied by walkers from Raleigh International, a youth development charity.

Put bacteria in a test-tube, with food and oxygen, and they will grow explosively, doubling in number every twenty minutes or so, until they form a solid, visible mass. But finally multiplication will cease as they become poisoned by their own waste products. In the centre of the mass will be a core of dead and dying bacteria, cut off from the food and oxygen of their environment by the solid barrier of their neighbours. The number of living bacteria will fall almost to zero, unless the waste products are washed away.

The Doomsday Book, Gordon Rattray-Taylor

I

The trees were golden once but now the wind is blowing away the leaves, revealing dark and twisted skeletons underneath. It is inevitable and there's nothing I can do to stop it.

My spine is in spasm; it never fully recovered after I stopped walking and sat down. I stand now, drying up the plates and shift from one foot to the other to ease the strain.

The washing water has not drained away. Bits of food and gas bubble to the surface. I am mildly fascinated. I have never seen a blocked drain before, never lived anywhere long enough to know that if you stuff muck down the plug, one day you'll have to fish it out.

I select a newspaper article, one which describes me as a heroine. I wind it into a tight tube around a roll of tin foil five inches long, and chase the bad stuff with it. I find this darkly amusing.

I could go to the doctor, tell him how tired I am and ask him for something to make me want to live again. But a friend I'll call J knows the doctor can't help so he brought me some smack up from London. He knows I have passed a deadline for a book I can't write, but he doesn't know why.

He tells me I am an inspiration to him.

I recoil.

He tells me I am an inspiration to others then.

I recoil further.

The heroin is making me miserable. I was told it was good, but it turns out to be full of impurities. And it's not working for J either.

He says to me, let's play a game then.

Truth or dare, I tell him.

OK, he says, I dare you to tell me the truth.

About what?

About why you can't write your book.

You want me to tell you the story?
The whole story.
What's the alternative?

2

I didn't steal things as a child because I wanted them, I stole because it was a buzz and because I never really got caught. My parents might find out, but nothing happened to make me stop. They might make me take it back, like the time I stole money from a woman down the road a few weeks after we'd moved into the neighbourhood. She was outside with my big sister Shuna and I was in her kitchen. Her purse was on the table. I got such a rush from opening it, taking out the money, putting it in my pocket and closing the purse before she came in.

I hid the coins in my little camel skin handbag and I couldn't help jangling it around in front of Shuna as we walked home, asking her to guess how much I had in there. When she ignored me, I jangled it in front of my parents. They looked inside, of course, and demanded to know where I'd got it. I told them eventually, after exercising my imagination about fairies leaving it for me in the night, and they called the woman and said they were sending me over with it, on my own. I got to the gate and chickened out, leaving it under a stone. I ran home and lied. But nothing happened because we moved and I never saw the woman again.

At the age of five, I went to my third new school. The kids asked me where I was from. I didn't like this question because the answer I was given by my father wasn't quite right and the real answer was too complicated. I was born in Totnes; we lived in Dartmouth but then moved to Cornwall I think, and then to North Carolina in the States where my father was posted for two years on an exchange with the American Marines. Being a Royal Marine helicopter pilot, of which there are few, his knowledge was in great demand. We'd come back to Britain and lived again in Cornwall, then moved somewhere else in Cornwall, then to somewhere in Hampshire. My father said we were Scottish, but I'd never been there. That's what I told the kids: 'I'm from Scotland.' But by the time I'd worked out where I was from they were off on some other topic, asking me if I remembered something which had happened last year but then stopping with the words, 'Oh, but you weren't here larsh year!'

At each new school my parents sent me off with a new pencil case with a pencil, rubber and ruler. I couldn't handle these things; I kept losing them but never thought to look for them. Besides, there'd always be more. I'd ask someone to lend me theirs but I'd lose them too. If they didn't like me, I didn't care, I'd be moving on and I'd never see them again. At the next school, after the usual round of where are you from? questions, I'd tell them I was from a sect of vegetarians which would excuse me from having to eat the gristle 'n' gravy at lunch time. And they might remember a vegetarian they'd had in the school once, but get bored with me, because, 'Oh, you weren't here larsh year.'

Shuna was my god. She was two years older than I and she knew everything. When she consistently won at Cluedo, solving the mystery of who'd killed whom with what instrument in which room, while I made my stab-in-the-dark guesses without any idea of deduction, I thought she was a magician. However, there was one game in which I was master – Pairs. We'd turn all the cards face down on the table, then try to pick two which matched. I won because I could remember what was where. At times, when Shuna was feeling particularly sure of herself, like when she'd got me to tidy up the room simply by picking up a toy I wanted and holding it out of my reach till I did the jobs, she'd have a stab at playing Pairs. But she never took a single game off me. She'd quickly follow her defeat with an act of magic, I'd forget my victory and she would be restored to her position of immortality.

I considered it my job to make Shuna laugh. The highest reward I could get was to make her laugh till she peed the bed. I did this mostly through mimicry of people we met. I could imitate virtually anyone and all I had to do was begin twitching my upper lip, or stand with my hands on my hips and my pelvis thrust forward, for Shuna to get it. And once I'd got her hooked, I'd become even more subtle, finishing my performance with the slightest flick of my buttock and she'd be howling out of control.

During the day, I entertained her with my maxim of never turning down a dare. They were usually successful – ringing on doorbells and running away, or venturing into the garden of the haunted house to come back with a full skirt of strawberries. But once, a dare to go into a boys' garden at the bottom of the estate went very badly wrong. They caught me, tied me to the washing line post with their elastic belts and the four of them danced around me, howling like Red Indians, tugging at my clothes and threatening to strip me. I thought I was a gonner, until I heard the most blood curdling scream. Shuna charged into the garden, her face red with fury, whirling a tent mallet round and round her head with a whole bunch of local girls behind her. She cut me loose, took a hostage and dragged him to the top of the hill. Simon Muckley blubbered all the way, but my big sister showed no mercy and tied him to a lamppost.

When my grandmother was alive and came to stay for Christmas, I'd once asked her how people show they love each other. She told me I must give them whatever I held most dear. At the time, my most precious possession was my big Ted and after a particularly vicious fight with Shuna, I'd wrapped him up and given him to her. I couldn't sleep without him though, and she'd given him back.

Mostly, when we argued, there'd be a time of ignoring each other until we made eye contact and made up. This we would do in silence, taking out our little jewellery boxes and solemnly selecting a piece which suited the measure of the argument. We would exchange these treasures, close the lids and carry on with the war.

Sometimes, when the wars downstairs frightened us, we would reconfirm the pact that we'd made that no matter what happened, we would stand by each other. At times of insecurity, we'd ask each other where our loyalties would lie if anyone came into our lives: 'If you were in a lifeboat with me out on the ocean and your husband and child were in there with us but there were only two life jackets and you had to have one of them, who would you choose to give the other one to?' At first, we said we'd give the life jacket to our sister. But then our husband and child would die and we didn't think this was right. So we decided we'd give both life jackets to our husband and child so that Shuna and I could die together.

Our favourite film was *Escape to Witch Mountain*. We'd spend all our pocket money each week on seeing it at the cinema, until, after three weeks, it moved on. It was about a brother and sister who ran away from an orphanage because they knew they had to get somewhere but they didn't know where it was. Along the way, through their telepathic powers, they worked out that they were actually from another planet and were trying to make their way to a space craft landing site where they would return to their people.

After another four house moves within a year, we were told we were moving to Scotland. Out father had left the Marines and joined British Airways and would be flying to the North Sea oil rigs. We'd live in Shetland, the most northerly group of islands. I felt something very good was about to happen, that at last we'd find out where we came from and find our people.

But on our first day at school, the kids rejected us for being English. And just at the point where I failed to secure my heritage, I almost lost my only guide when my big sister collapsed.

The last thing Shuna said before slipping into a coma was, 'Don't worry Daddy, I'll be OK.' She'd started to go blind while we were shopping in the town, then she'd thrown up and now she was virtually gone. She only woke up twice during that week. Once was on the air-ambulance flight from Shetland: the dressing on her drip had come off, she put it back on herself and lost consciousness again. The second time was in a triangular emergency room in Aberdeen. The doctor asked her questions; she didn't reply. He asked her to add two plus two and she woke up and said, 'What do I want to do that for?' And under she went again.

My mother asked practical questions like, 'Will you need to shave her head?' She just accepted the doctor's nod. I wasn't going to stand for this. I wanted to shake her. I told the doctor it wouldn't be possible, my sister loved her hair. They said they'd just shave a small patch then.

Everyone had suddenly become huge and distant. We didn't talk about my sister's brain haemorrhage until the night before her operation. We sat in the stifling heat of the hotel dining room. I could have what I liked from the menu: macaroni cheese. My mother didn't like the plastic portions of butter. My father looked down his action list, held his pen in his left hand and said, 'Your big sister might not make it tomorrow. Have a think about what you would like written on her tombstone.' I felt he was ruining her chances by even thinking of the worst. I wanted him to clap his hands and believe in fairies like me.

I didn't know it then, but he was clinging on to that clipboard for dear life.

Another new school, this time on my own. I had no answer to their first question, 'Where do you come from?' No answer to their next question, 'D'you know what a vagina is?' I wanted to go and see Shuna in hospital after school but Mummy was tired when she got back having spent the day with her and it was forty miles away.

I missed her. Little did I know, I would never play with my big sister in the same way again. Though she came home at last, appeared as a bundle of blankets and a funny cheesy smell on the sofa when I got in from school one day, she was fragile, she needed my protection now. She couldn't sleep at night so we'd lie awake together in the dark, and I'd make up stories about three characters called Big Mouth, Medium Mouth and Little Mouth, but my desire to let the story take a comic twist had to be put in check. If she honoured me with the highest accolade and laughed till she peed, we couldn't get up and change her sheets like we used to.

At school she bumped into furniture and her right side was cut by the sharp plaster on the corridor walls because she couldn't see in the peripheral of her right eye (I always sat on her right at meal times so I could nick her chips). And they bullied her. When I heard of this, I got her to point out the kids to me and no matter how big they were, or how strong their accent, I'd tell them that if they messed with my sister, they'd have to contend with me. I wanted them to give me the opportunity; I needed a punch bag too.

One afternoon as the bell rang, my form teacher pulled me over to her desk and waited till everyone had gone. She always wore a red Slazenger sweatshirt; I'd stare at the logo trying to make out what it said whenever she spoke to me. She asked me how come I always finished my sums first and never got one wrong. I told her I'd done long addition before, at one of my previous schools. Then she asked about my sister. It startled me; I'd never met an adult before who knew anything about me. I said she was fine. Then the teacher made a very bad mistake. She introduced the notion of self-pity to me by asking me if I felt left out. Coupled with the attention Shuna was given because she was weaker now, I now assumed that love and being included were based on pity.

We moved back to Shetland on April Fool's Day, this time into a bungalow on a new housing estate. Not long after, Shuna began having problems at school. She was in the secondary five miles away from me; she was getting bullied, sexually accosted and the standard of work required was far below what she was capable of. Both of us were moved up a year but that didn't help her deal with the other children. My parents decided to send her to a girls' boarding school in Aberdeenshire where the classes were smaller and the teachers could give the extra help she needed. This was the second time, after they'd taken her from me at the hospital in Lerwick, that they robbed me of her. I felt their power and I felt the despair of being utterly helpless to intervene. I was the one who could protect her, not strangers hundreds of miles away on another island.

So they sent her away and my life was empty. As always, I tried to join in with the other kids, but the years of being a new girl every six months or so had left me awkward and confused. When I arrived I'd be myself but they rejected me. So I changed, donning different characters in the hope of finding one they would like. When that didn't work, I stayed away from them, knowing I'd be moving on and maybe at the next school I'd find kids like me. But I didn't stay anywhere long enough to discover territory. Had I done so, I might have seen other new kids arriving and noticed that rejection is often the first thing they experience. Without territory, I had nothing to fight for or defend; I had no sense of where I came from, no sense of pride or responsibility to uphold the reputation of a people I respected. And now that Shuna was gone, I had nobody to learn from. In fact I had absolutely no idea that any of this existed. All I knew was that I was OK underneath, that somehow I would find my way back to my people and in the meantime, I would treat others as they treated me.

The only person I could be myself with was my sister. I needed to reach out to her, she was my only link to the diminishing possibilities of fun. I found that if I walked up onto the windswept moorland, I could pretend she was there with me. I'd chatter with her and find things to amuse her. From a distance, I might have looked like an actor doing his or her bit before the animators have drawn in their cartoon counterpart. I'd walk up there for hours, till one day I found myself at the store of Robins Bray near my school, five miles from home. They sold matchbox-sized figurines for 50p. A fortnight later, I walked up there again with two weeks' pocket money, rehearsing how I would ask the woman for the one I wanted, imagining it in my hand, straining the horizon for sight of the little stone shop. And when I got there, bought it and walked home, I felt better for having a ritual for my sister.

When my father learned of how far I'd walked he praised me. 'Well done, tough guy,' he'd always say. He'd say it when we were out on long walks as small children and I'd soldiered on just to hear his words. Sometimes, if we'd been very good and not complained while camping with ice inside our tents or finding our way through thunderstorms, he'd say we'd earned our Royal Marine green beret. This was the ultimate achievement and I lived for it. But it confused me. I didn't know whether my inclination towards doing dares and masculine things was a natural one or praise related, confusing because I didn't know which one was supposed to be right. On top of all the other mixed messages of who I was and what I should strive to be, I wasn't sure whether my resentment for being only half a boy and not a whole one was actually real or completely fake. Before I was born they'd named me Bruce Richard Murray. When my mother became pregnant again after me, they gave this name to the unborn baby. It turned out to be a boy, but he died before he was born.

Without Shuna and without anyone at school accepting me for who I really was, I was now under the undiluted influence of my father, and unconsciously he started to direct me by what he most respected in a person. But my father didn't realise that he was the only one guiding me and that, of course, I might misunderstand him.

However, I found a sense of self when I drew. There was something absolutely true and right to strive for when drawing and I could feel it. I knew when a line wasn't quite right and if there's a wrong there must be a right. From my eye, through my arm, into my hand, down my pencil, and out in a perfect replica. I didn't have to pretend to be anyone else: this was my world and nothing confusing had, until this point, ever contaminated it.

One day my father came home and told me that British Airways had launched a painting competition for children in Scotland to commemorate some milestone in their history. He suggested I enter it. My first reaction was that I didn't really want to draw anything to order, but then I thought maybe if I drew a helicopter, he might look favourably upon me.

I decided on painting the scene of a recent search and rescue operation. He paid me a lot of attention over this and took me down to the hangars and introduced me to the mechanics who propped me up on a balcony where I could sketch the actual Sikorsky 61 which had rescued several men from a fishing trawler off the nearby Vee Skerry rocks. It was very cold in there and I found the helicopter incredibly boring, but I stuck it out until I'd finished various angles, then I walked home.

I won the competition for my age group and went down to Glasgow to collect my prize with my mother. I didn't meet any of the crew who had flown in that rescue operation until sixteen years later on the day that I finished walking around the world. One of them managed the hotel at John O'Groats.

A year later we moved to Aberdeenshire and were reunited as a family of four. But we had no home again. For the first month we house-sat for someone abroad, then in the summer we moved onto a housing estate in Elrick, a suburb of Aberdeen.

There were two bedrooms for Shuna and me to choose from now, but both of us wanted the smallest one. It was given to Shuna because she was the eldest; 'eldest perks', they called it, when there was only one of something going. When I was picking my nose, I'd use each finger in turn, starting with the biggest one and finishing the grooming with the smallest. One day I looked at the little finger and told it I was very sorry but no matter how good it was at getting into the crevasses, the smallest would always come last. My little finger waggled back, protesting the injustice, especially when I was completely honest with it on occasions and whispered, 'You're actually the best, but the others would feel left out.'

Mummy had made us summer dresses but Shuna always wore hers with a double-ply winter cardigan. When she took it off at night, she looked chubby underneath. It made her cry. I tried to cheer her up by racing around the garden, but she couldn't do the things I could: her balance had gone. She started having coffee with Mummy in the kitchen and they'd stop talking when I came in. It seemed these were private discussions which I wouldn't understand.

A new school and the same old promise: 'You'll be here till you finish your education.' Yeah, yeah, yeah. We arrived late in the summer term, both of us famous within the class as the new girl, always known for being a stranger. Again I'd hear the words, 'Oh, but you weren't here larsh year.' I'd heard them so often, said in so many different accents, that I wondered where on earth I had been. I didn't care how I treated anyone; after fourteen school moves, I knew I'd never see them again.

We spent the holiday of 1979 driving around within a circle. My father had taken a map of Aberdeenshire, stuck the point of a compass on the airport where he flew from and drew a circle with a radius of forty minutes' travelling time, for him anyway, in which to look for houses.

Mummy, Shuna and I sat in the car, driving from an office with directions in hand, competing to see who could spot the building with the FOR SALE sign, my mother cursing when people said, 'You can't miss it', and then at the estate agents for erasing the power pylons from the photo. She had her brief to find a 'gentleman's residence'; she had her vision and her hopes, and she wouldn't give up. But she wasn't stupidly stubborn: my mother would compromise, would take a step sideways if it was her only chance of taking one forward.

We ended up in a one-man farmhouse, at a pepper corn rent if my parents would renovate it. It gave them breathing space to look for a place to buy, that is if you could breathe in there for all the paint stripper. Eventually, they found a house. After twenty-five moves in twelve years, Reivesley was the first place which offered the possibility of doing all those things which had been put off with the words, 'When we get to . . . ' But Reivesley was derelict. It had no mains water, no electricity, virtually no roof.

My parents applied themselves with fervour to their 'island' project, digging foundations and wells, knocking down and building up, removing and renovating while creating a semi-self-sufficient farm in the background. Money was tight, schedules tighter with the coming of each winter. The more they achieved, the more there were occasions to celebrate. But as we raised our glasses, just the four of us, trying to build a home out of bricks and sweat, it struck me that my parents had found a new way to avoid admitting that our lives were completely empty of other people. In the isolation, two miles from the nearest village, two hours' bus journey to the school, it sometimes felt like they were building us a prison. But we didn't need cells: we were building those ourselves.

One afternoon I walked past the daffodils my father had planted with a plumb line, and into the steading which he used as a workshop. I watched him stripping down an old pine door. He'd removed the paint till he was left with those tiny flecks deep in the grooves and notches. I watched him working out the little white niggles with a bit of wire wool and Nitromors. So thorough, he was unable to pass over even the tiniest flake of paint in the deepest groove for more than a few seconds before it screamed at his conscience and back he went with his wool.

'That'll look lovely when it's varnished,' I said.

'Oh, this is just the beginning,' he said. 'Then you sand, wet to raise the grain, let it dry and sand again. Then you apply the undercoat.' I wondered why he bothered with the flecks in the deepest grooves if he was going to paint it, but I knew better than to ask him. My father had a temper. Though it never actually surfaced, you could see him simmer, his skin would be stretched over his nose and begin to turn white. That was the time to scarper, to tiptoe around the sleeping monster.

And though they painted the window frames grey to match the grey of the stone and slate, they painted the front door bright red; caution red I often thought.

Whilst my father worked out his frustration on his pieces of wood, my mother in her way met the loneliness of loyalty, in following her husband around the country, through her music. She played the piano when she couldn't stand the silence of the control room any longer. I hated the sound of it. I started to walk then, really walk, trying to sort out what was true from what was screwed up, gathering my armour, reassuring myself that I had what it took to return and face the situation. When I did and felt stronger for it, it struck me that the longer I walked, the more I could work out what was going wrong. And I decided then that if I walked around the world, I'd come home and find everything was right again.

But locked in our own little cells, none of us noticed how often Shuna was dismissed to her room, didn't notice that these arguments coincided with the presence of food, didn't see her body under all those heavy layers of jumpers. Till one afternoon, when our parents were out, we had a terrible fight. Shuna stormed upstairs in tears and I heard her smashing stuff in her room. Then it all went quiet. Too quiet. I climbed the stairs, feeling instant remorse, and knocked on her door. No answer. I opened the door and saw her sitting on the floor amongst shards of broken mirror. She held a piece in her hand and she rocked as she drew it rhythmically across her wrist. I called the doctor. Shuna was making damn sure that her cell was a time capsule, without any nourishment or stimulation, keeping her childlike and protected. Inside anorexia nervosa, her routines had become rituals, carrying severe punishment if broken, and she lived in a detached fascination with her shrinking body. At the age of fifteen, she weighed a little over five stone. Like an animal desperate to be free, she was refusing to eat in captivity.

The following summer my father had the offer of sailing a boat down the Caledonian Canal. He needed a break, wanted to take the whole family, but Shuna and Mummy preferred to stay at home so he took me with him. In the first few days we didn't speak much (out of shyness) but found our way through well-timed mugs of tea, synchronised sail rigging and an easing off of the 'stay with me' rules. After two weeks I came back to admiring praise from my mother at just how well I was growing up. I had made a start, a false start as it turned out. Under financial pressure, my father didn't have time after that and we never did anything together again.

I'd had a taste of challenge but instead of moving on to the next one, I found myself in a chamber of sensory deprivation. There were no kids to hang out with after the two-hour journey from school; I couldn't find any books or comics or characters on TV to identify with, none of them were like me, none of them dealt with constant moving or with isolation. As far as I could see, these were aliens, sent for me to laugh at, but never to laugh *with*.

My body was changing and with it came a deep and unquenchable frustration which I didn't understand. As the eldest, Shuna should have developed first and as our parents they wanted to protect her from feeling abnormal. To do this they had to curb my own growth and they did it by refusing to accept that I had needs beyond hers.

But I refused to retreat. And when I didn't get the encouragement or direction or communication I needed, I went savage.

For three and a half years I fought against them and the pettiness of the girls' school they sent me to. They tried to punish me by taking away things, but the more they tried to put me down, the more resilient I became. I felt they ganged up on me. They told me I was to blame for the rift in the family, but I refused to apologise or I felt I'd be admitting fault for everything that went wrong. When they told me I was abnormal for wanting to go out on Saturday nights with a girlfriend, they forced me underground. I lied to them and deceived them to protect myself and I refused to believe there was anything wrong with me. I had to get out of the prison; I had to know that the walls weren't permanent and to test this, I baited them, provoked them, found their weaknesses then thrust in the knife and twisted it. The more I fought back, the less pain I felt.

At school I got my kicks out of subtlety: I'd test the measure of their pettiness by how far they would punish me for the smallest of things. The ultimate piss take on my headmistress came when she threatened me with expulsion simply because I hadn't done up the top button of my shirt.

But I knew I'd have the last laugh because they couldn't keep me there after I was sixteen. And one day, I would simply pack my bag and walk away. But all my experiences of moving house and moving school without coming across anyone or anything from my past had led me to believe that the world is infinite, that the world is flat, not round. And I wanted to see how far I could go.

3

Still wet from the bridge jumping celebrations into the snow melt water of the river Dee on my first day of freedom, I stuffed a brown duffel bag with the clothes I had only worn in front of the mirror and lugged it down the spiral staircase from my attic to the front door. I didn't notice that a few extra, pretty heavy items had somehow slipped in and it would take me years to offload them – hang-ups, guilt and a full tank of rocket fuel.

Freedom: I didn't have to run away any more, at last I was sixteen and could leave home without my parents' consent. There was no need to discuss it: we were all agreed that my desire to 'get out' was best for everyone. But I wasn't stupid, I stayed till the last exam – Highers, the Scottish equivalent of A levels.

We'd left the 'gentleman's residence' once it was finished and moved to another house and another school in Aboyne, Aberdeenshire, six months before, so there was nobody to say goodbye to and with that first step into the outside world, I shot off.

I had £50 in my pocket – a cashed-in Premium Bond – and flew down to London using my 'daughter of staff' discount plane ticket on British Airways at a cost of £10. I knew I needed to get some money together, get some breathing space before working down the list I'd made of what I wanted to do when I got out.

I got a job as a nanny – more like a person to be around so that the twelve-year-old son of a model and her fashion designer partner wouldn't be a latch key kid. The first morning of the job, with Ashley packed off to school and the washing up done, Jenny turned to me and said, 'Right now, would you like to look around Covent Garden?' Ha! I don't have to go to school!

Each minute was a confirmation of freedom and then there was the weekend! I'd wanted to hit the open road ever since my father wouldn't give me a pocket money advance on a bus fare down to

Newcastle from Aberdeen to see a boyfriend I'd met at a local dance. He'd agreed to let me cycle (probably hoping I'd be too worn out to be a bad girl when I got there) and, despite hammering up the Cairngorm mountains in top gear (because I couldn't figure them out), I'd felt alive and independent.

The first weekend arrived and saw me hitching down to the New Forest to look for a cave to stay in for the weekend. I couldn't find a cave but made camp by a stream. I shot up a tree when a herd of wild ponies came charging through. I couldn't make myself comfortable up there so I headed back to the nearby village thinking it must be near morning and I could get a bite to eat. A couple of cops picked me up as a suspected runaway and let me doss in a cell for the night. When I told them I was a nanny in London and gave them my employer's name and number as confirmation, they thought I'd said, 'My nanny's in London', and called my employers down to a local station at 3 a.m.

I worked my butt off that week to make it up to them but by Friday I had a new plan. I'd always wanted to spend a couple of days in a ruined castle on an island. So, with a new friend, Philip, I hitched down to St Michael's Mount in Cornwall, where I'd lived for a few months as a child. We got there just in time to run across the causeway before the tide came in and cut off the island. But the big rock was slightly more inhabited than I remembered. The last ferry signalled its imminent departure and the boatman called to us to get on. I said we were staying with friends. 'Well, that's fine but whatever you do, don't go up to the castle.' Red rag to a bull.

The ferry left, the moon came out: time to set off to explore. There was a light on up in the black walls, perhaps an exhibition light, I was sure it was ruined. Up and over the rocks and fences, encouraging Philip, we reached the great oak door and tried the handle. Locked. It might be worth knocking; we might get a bed. Footsteps on the other side.

'Who's there?'

'Sorry to trouble you, um, we've just hitched down from London to see the castle and . . .'

'What do you want?'

'Would it be possible for us to spend the night?'

'Get off the island or we'll call the police.'

But the last ferry had gone and so had the enchantment of the place. The mainland didn't look very far, in fact we could see the dark square shapes of the shop buildings quite clearly in the moonlight. We stripped off and stuffed everything into two plastic bags and started to swim, using the edge of the causeway pavement as a guide.

After a while I became aware that Philip wasn't swimming any-where near me. I called out cheerily to him but he puffed back, 'I'll stay here, I'll tread water, you go for help.' A mixture of irritation and guilt sprung me into action. I swam back to him, tipped him on his back, hand under his chin and started to swim. I kept kicking him from underneath, which was unintentional but it might have kept him awake and I talked to him, telling him to look at how beautiful the blackened castle appeared against the huge, cratered full moon. His body shivered and jerked. I told him it's all in the mind; I told him just relax; I told him we'll be there soon. I kept turning my head to get a fix on the shore but the tide and the currents were pulling me off course. The moon slipped further away from the edge of the castle but we weren't making any progress.

I didn't know my body could do this.

And when my foot finally kicked hard rock, I was surprised at how I could pull out not only our saturated bags but the convulsing Philip as well. His bare feet didn't bleed on the glass broken on the rocks.

We were turned away by the first pub, probably because Philip had adorned the wall with vomit, but once the second door I banged on opened, there was a flurry of activity: hands were grabbing us in – blankets, logs on the fire, brandy, hot bath water and a grey and frightened face staring up at me without any lips. Philip hadn't rest-ed there long when the local bobby arrived, pulled him out of the bath and started rubbing him down amid a chorus of Cornish about the right thing to do with a hypothermia victim.

I got my fair share of it for being so stupid. There used to be swim-ming races from the island till the currents took their toll. We'd been very lucky. But our shoes, sweatshirts and wallets had slipped out of the bags – I'd felt them but couldn't do anything. So there was no money to pay for the room. Highly embarrassed, I said I had a place to sleep outside and could we pay for Philip's room when we got back to London? They refused to allow me outside and made up a bed of blankets on the floor. I slept lightly, keeping an ear out for Philip. On the road back to London, I harboured deep humiliation that I had been so dependent on adults for help.

Payday came and after my share of the room, I had £1.80 left. Enough to buy my sister a drink. I spent Saturday hitching up to St

Andrew's University where Shuna was in her second year, looking forward to surprising her but, after eleven hours on the road, I found she'd gone to our parents' house in Aboyne for the weekend. And I wasn't about to go there again for a while. I didn't understand the close relationship she had with them and somehow felt betrayed by her. But the worst of it was the loss of my hitching partner, who ran under a lawn mower on the golf course. My albino hamster was a trusty friend: I'd left home with him and he provided me with security up in the cab when I showed the truckies my white, tailless, but sharp-toothed little 'rat'.

There was no purpose to these forays except to get out and explore and with the sense of incompletion after each of them, I was conscious of needing something more defined to channel my energy into. I was always conscious of a time limit, always in a hurry possibly because I didn't quite grasp the eternity of my freedom, anxious that I would be sent back to the prison. I didn't want to go to university though I'd passed my Highers well. I couldn't understand how anyone would go to school voluntarily but I had a vague notion of going to art college.

In the summer of 1983, I took out my hit list. Looking at it in 1996, the contents seem quite bizarre: objectives from two very different character traits, neither of which were mine. I didn't know what effect the constant house and school moves had had on me. Strange places, being a stranger, made me clam up and rush home to the people I knew. I learned by watching my parents and only my parents so it was quite logical, I suppose, to emerge from them as a juxtaposition of two conflicting and rather less than perfect identities. I see this list now and how it was formed: I rejected my own talents and had taken my scant understanding of the worth of man and woman and simply married them together.

I must've scrubbed out swimming the Channel after the St Michael's Mount escapade; item number two would have to wait till I had the physical tone to take my clothes off in front of a camera, but item number three provided a physical challenge, a direction and time to think about what I was going to do with my life: *to walk the length of Britain*.

As soon as I said it aloud, I started asking questions. How far is it? How long will it take? How far can I go in a day? Where will I sleep? What do I need? How much will it cost? When shall I do it? I scribbled it down on paper, sectioning off different concerns like routes and funding and kit and weather. Suddenly there was form in my head, a coming together of desires into a tangible aim, something to build and carry out which was all mine.

Shuna finished university for the summer and I met her at High Street Kensington tube station. Her first reaction was to buy me a pair of shoes for wearing around town since I hadn't replaced the ones which were now floating out into the Atlantic Ocean. I told her about the plan: to walk from John O'Groats to Land's End (better to walk downhill I decided) eating baked beans and cabbage (cheap fuel) and raise money for an EMI scanner. Ever since Shuna's life had been saved by a brain scanning machine on loan to Aberdeen hospital, I had wanted to raise money for a permanent one. But a little research found I was too late. However, on the flight down, Shuna had seen an article in *Cosmopolitan* about the Royal Marsden Cancer Hospital's appeal for a CAT scanner.

That sunny, slightly humid afternoon, Shuna and I set off for the Marsden to offer my services. We expected to see the building at the second junction and got quite irritated when road after road, junction after junction, we couldn't find it. In fact we'd got off at the wrong stop and walked two miles extra, long miles when you expect to see what you're looking for round the next corner.

The secretary to the fundraising director turned down my offer. She said it wouldn't be something they'd like to lend their name to in case something happened to me. I've often wondered whether she turned me down because of the state I was in having just walked from the tube station. Shuna and I took the piss all the way back to Kensington.

Their lack of enthusiasm had a decidedly strange effect on me – I found myself spurred on even harder. The telephone rang.

'My name is Alan Massam. I'm calling from the *Evening Standard* newspaper. We've been following the progress of the Royal Marsden's fundraising appeal and . . .'

'You can stop right there. They don't want me to raise money for them.'

'Well, I wonder if you'd like to have lunch to discuss it?' *Lunch*? I'd never been out for lunch.

'OK.'

I met the fifty-year-old Alan Massam in an Indian restaurant off Fleet Street. He was very fat and tired. I spent the whole time trying to figure out what he wanted. He didn't talk in straight sentences, but hummed around the edges. Too subtle for me, I wished he could just say what he wanted and let me answer. Was he trying to persuade me to raise money for them? But they'd already said no. He said that could be discussed. What did he want from it? Well, he thought there was something in the story. What does that mean? I don't know, maybe we might be interested in running a story about this amazing sixteen-year-old who was going to walk the length of Britain for the hospital.

'I'm doing it anyway,' I said, 'with or without the fundraising.'

A couple of days later, he called again to say that the Marsden would like me to raise money for them and that the *Standard* would like to sponsor me.

'Per mile?'

'No, pay for your bed and breakfast, food and toothpaste.'

'I see. And you get a story?'

'We send a reporter to follow your progress.'

'I'm not sure about that.'

I thought about this for a while and conceded that having a guy, a young blond preferably, might make the whole thing a lot of fun. 'OK.'

Massam thought it would be a good idea for me to go and see John Hillaby, Britain's most prolific long-distance walker. Since the furthest I'd ever walked in a day was twenty-five miles when I was seven but didn't have to get up to do it again the next day, I thought it a good idea too.

John and his wife Katie each greeted me with a hug. I wasn't used to physical contact. I had a list of questions but John waved them away and began to talk. He grilled me a bit first on how far I would walk a day and when he realised that I really was a novice with a capital N, he started at the beginning.

'Decide on where you're going to begin and finish. Get some Ordnance Survey maps – you know about OS maps, don't you? Yes, good. Don't waste your money on buying them, go to the library. Forget the roads, take the cross-country routes; you don't want all those cars.'

Much of what John said next, about watching natural history, fell on deaf ears. I didn't want to wander, I wanted to burn. And when we went out for a walk and talked about a different kind of gait and about never, never thinking of the end, I wanted logistics. He told me to break the distance down into weeks, taking at least one day off in every six to have something to aim for. Twenty-five miles a day was about right, but break into it gradually.

I set about planning the route. My way was to draw a line from

John O'Groats to Land's End and look for the smallest roads closest to that line. The rusksack which John had secured for me from Karrimore I stuffed with telephone directories and walked laps around Hyde Park in training. I set a date for the beginning of August, just one month away, so that I'd be walking in Scotland in the summer and the south of England in the autumn. At twenty-five miles a day, six days a week, it would take me fifty days. I decided to divert to Ben Nevis and Snowdon because, well, why not.

I gave my notice. Jenny was enthusiastic about my project and gave me a present to take with me – a small golden hamster to replace the one I'd lost. I called her Eros Jenny: Eros after the god of love and not, as a reporter once asked me, because it's the *Evening Standard*'s emblem. I had a medical test and did an interview for the Marsden's hospital radio. I got quite irritated with the interviewer because he kept asking me questions he already knew the answer to. But then, just as everything was working out fine, Alan Massam rang to say the *Standard* had been informed by John Hillaby that I wasn't ready. What? And that if I didn't postpone the walk by two weeks, they would have to review the situation about sponsorship.

'OK, let's get one thing clear: I am not going to postpone the walk; I don't believe Hillaby said that and if you pull out of this sponsorship I'll go down Fleet Street and tell all of them how you reneged on your commitment.'

I surprised myself by how far that talk went – all the way to the editor, who actually called my mother for advice on handling me. She was pretty cool about it: 'I've had Ffyona for sixteen years', she said. 'It's your turn now.'

It was Annie, the reporter, who suggested taking a stick of white chalk to mark the end of the day's walk. I hadn't thought of it so puritanically. In fact, I wasn't at all sure that I could do this walk. I found myself swept along a bit by the handful of interviews – it was my first taste of recognition *before* you do something and it had the effect of making me think I'd already done it.

On the way to John O'Groats with a reporter and a photographer in tow, I couldn't resist stopping off at my parents' house for the first time since I'd left home. But I felt, and maybe I needed to, that they still viewed me with the old scepticism, the old disbelief which I suppose was justified after the years of being completely untrustworthy. They told me years later they'd in fact pulled off the deal with the *Standard* by persuading the editor to continue with the project. But

First
— British Walk —
1983

John O'Groats
Wick
Inverness
Fort William
Glasgow
Carlisle
Kendal
Lancaster
Preston
Chester
Shrewsbury
Worcester
Gloucester
Bristol
Okehampton
Taunton
Land's End

N

I saw that brief visit to their house was more of a refuelling stop than anything else and I left with full tanks of rocket fuel.

I'd plaited and twisted my hair into dreds, pulled on shorts and a sweatshirt which said SPONSOR ME and checked myself in the mirror of the hotel in Wick. I looked frightful: completely out of shape. OK, fatso, let's see what you look like in fifty days' time! Good inspiration and something tangibly positive which would come out of the walk. Little did I know. I thought I wouldn't have to watch what I ate so I tucked into steaks every night and bars of chocolate at every corner shop.

I still didn't know who the reporter would be who would drop in on me once a day. The reporter and photographer, Annie and Stuart, who accompanied me to John O'Groats were just there for the send-off and the first few days. There was a signpost at the second most northerly point in Britain which marked the miles down to Land's End – 874. With the diversion to the mountains, the walk would total around a thousand but I didn't mind the error – it was just an incomprehensible distance. You could get letters from the local shop to slip your name on the arms of the signpost to have your picture taken. Stuart took my picture there in front of my name.

At 7.17 a.m. on 16 August 1983, I picked my way over the seaweed rocks and dipped my toe in the North Sea. It begins. I turned round and saw, instead of the mass of experiences which I'd imagined this walk to be, some people and sheep with similar expressions under the grey, threatening to rain kind of sky, and a triangle of road. My job, for the next fifty days, was to walk towards the tip of the triangle.

I waved goodbye to Stuart who went off to wire the photos, walked 200 yards and stopped at the Seaview Hotel for a round of toast and marmalade. Then I went back to the sign, kissed my fingers and touched it.

I spent much of the next five hours and twenty-six minutes pulling my raincoat on and off, singing 'Oh you never go to heaven' and 'There's a hole in my bucket' to cheer myself up when the drizzle and the hot spots on my feet tried to get me down. By the time I reached Wick, I felt very pleased with myself. Annie greeted me at the bed and breakfast with a casual hello. So casual, it was as if this was nothing, that the day's walking in comparison to what I was about to do, was no achievement at all. To hell with you, I thought, and topped up the fuel tanks.

My first thoughts on waking up the next morning were a general recap of where I was: I've left home, I'm on the walk, I'm on day two . . . I am about to find out that I can't move. The thought of Annie getting hold of this information and sending it back was just the threat of humiliation I needed to throw off the sheets, flip myself over with my arms onto the floor and walk my hands to the bathroom like a crayfish, giggling at the absurdity of being completely paralysed from the waist down.

Virtually glowing with Deep Heat I bent myself onto a chair for breakfast and took out my map. Clearing my cup and glass out of the way, I opened it up and found John O'Groats beside a jutting out bit near the top. Scanning around the bottom for Wick I got a sudden rush that I'd taken the wrong map because it wasn't marked. This was ridiculous: I'd been map-reading for days; in fact for five hours in the car from Aberdeen I'd found our position and whizzed my finger along the roads as we went. I got an even worse rush when I eventually found my position, also a five-hour journey, about an inch south of John O'Groats.

The pace of impatience which had got me to the start was now my greatest enemy. In future I protected myself from the frustration of my speed by scanning the map close to where I had left the day before. When I found my position much further than I expected, I was delighted at my progress.

Once the single road stretch from John O'Groats became a series of junctions and crossroads, I took the map out several times during the day but forced myself not to let the eye wander, or I'd get panicky about how far I still had to go. But there were times when the map wasn't entirely accurate. I raged when I found I'd gone the wrong way.

'Excuse me, I think I'm a bit lost.' I'd reached a definite fork in the road which wasn't on the map.

'Where are you going?' A question which didn't bug me now that I had an answer.

'Dunbeath.'

'Well, now,' said the middle-aged woman, looking at the map and then at the fork in the road. 'I really don't know. You'd better ask a man.'

Oh, for goodness sake! There were no other pedestrians so I went into a pub on the corner and asked the barman.

'Are you in a car?'

'No. Why?'

'It's a long way.'

'I don't want to know how far it is, just which direction.' This tone of voice stopped the conversation around me. A lad not much older than I was looking at my rucksack's badge: John O'Groats to Land's End for Cancer. He sniggered something.

'Sorry, was that right or left?'

He sniggered again, 'You'll never do it.'

I stormed out, crimson in the face and made my own decision.

Early morning of the sixth day was cool and clear and I felt light and strong. I passed an English girl and her German boyfriend packing up camp in a layby. She had been badly mauled by midges so I handed her the tube of Anthisan cream which Katie Hillaby had given me. We chatted for a bit till she'd rubbed it all in and I waved goodbye, turning back to a deliciously crisp bright morning.

I'd enjoyed the sunshine at first, but as the day wore on I felt like I was walking uphill even on the flat. My right knee started to click and a blister stung my heel at each footfall. I whined. I felt my temperature rise out of irritation; I whined again. I hunted for a mental stick and began lashing myself on up the road with, 'You'll never make it, you'd better ask a man, you'll never make it, you'd better ask a man, you'll never make it . . .' And suddenly there *was* a man. He was leaning across the passenger seat of a car.

'Are ya needin' a ride?'

I looked at the vacant seat he offered. I thought of the window rolled down, the cool air, the whizzing along. The tiny, hammered voice which had whined a few minutes ago lapped it up and made a suggestion: your knee's playing up, it would be sensible. Yes, I suppose it would be. And you haven't got any water. No. And nobody would know.

'D'ya need a lift?' His accent was the same as the boy at the bar.

'Thanks,' I said very quickly before I could change my mind, 'but I'm walking.' And with that I stepped away from the car and walked on up the road. I felt very, very pleased with myself that I hadn't cheated. Just as I rounded the corner I saw a woman walking towards me. I hadn't found my road protocol and was embarrassed, not knowing whether to look at her or look beyond her. I felt she was looking at me so I looked up and bored straight back. It was Annie the reporter! Thank God I hadn't cheated.

By the time we arrived at Bonor Bridge, my knee was making rather loud noises and hurting a fair bit but a quick stop at the clinic patched it up with a bandage and even though the doctor suggested I reconsider my project, what was really on our minds was a nice cup of tea.

Annie and I, red faced and smelly, ordered tea in the modern conservatory and stretched our hamstrings under the table.

'I must admit, Ffyona,' she said, 'I didn't realise how hard it is even to walk seven miles.'

'Neither did I. This has been the worst day so far.' Could it get worse?

The door opened and Alan Massam walked in.

'What are *you* doing here?'

'I'm the lucky one who's been selected to accompany you to Land's End.'

'But you don't think I'm ready. You wanted me to postpone the walk.'

'I was on holiday. I've had to cut my holiday short.'

'So all that stuff about Hillaby was rubbish?'

'There's something wrong with your knee, isn't there?'

It must have been very difficult for Massam to keep up the pretence to people we met along the way. He'd go ahead, find a B&B, tell them about this amazing girl, come back, throw me my lunch out the window then go and write glowing reports on my progress to encourage readers to send in donations. I saw him as the reincarnation of everyone who had ever put me down and I found that when I was having a hard time on the road in the rain, I only had to imagine his face and I'd get through. I encouraged myself through lashings. I hated him; I hated my father; I hated anyone who said the word NO.

I wanted this walk to be exclusively mine. There'd be none of the 'new girl' hang-ups, no sense of arriving in someone else's domain, isolated from their chatter because, 'Oh, you weren't here larsh year.' This would be my place. It might be their village but it was my road.

Only months before, I felt I had been put down by every adult I knew, parents and teachers. But now, quite suddenly, in direct contrast to how I was used to being treated, strangers were in awe of me. Adults actually arrived in cars to take my picture and interview me. And the great thing was, I could get away with being rude to them and they'd come back for more. I had no fear of recrimination because no matter how rude I was or how much I laughed at them, there was an endless supply of people who thought I was amazing. And I just assumed that this was how people related to each other.

There were many times, though, when I wanted to cheat. Left

alone all day, I had the opportunity. However, I was frightened that Massam might turn up as I was getting in or out of a car, so I didn't. I hadn't really set off on this journey expecting to walk all the way, and Annie's suggestion of marking the road with a piece of chalk had alarmed me. But, at the end of each day, when I reached the next B&B and felt a sense of pride, I started to be very defensive of my new maxim to walk every step of the way. In fact, there were drivers who said, 'Come on, jump in, we won't tell.' And I'd let rip at them. There were times when Massam himself suggested skipping out a bit to get to an interview on time, but I wouldn't do it. I became incredibly pedantic about where the marker was put and how it was put and how I touched it that night and again the next morning. These were my rituals. I had always known myself to be a liar, but here I was encouraging myself to be truthful, truthful to me. And as the journey went on, I began actually to believe in myself.

But the country wasn't quite long enough because just at this point, the end started to come into sight.

The day before I reached Land's End, Massam asked me a favour. 'Look,' he said, 'I need to get the pictures of your arrival in tomorrow's paper but it'll be too late if we do it as you arrive. It's very important to us to be the paper which carries the first photo. We'd like to drive you ahead to Land's End this afternoon, take a picture of you arriving, wire it, then drive you back here and you can do it properly in the morning.'

The thought of walking in to Land's End had been about the only positive image I'd carried with me and remained true to; the idea of faking it was appalling. On the other hand, the *Standard* had supported me, had made it possible to raise £25,000 for the hospital and this article was very important to them.

I agreed.

The real thing was a terrible anticlimax. Shuna was waiting there for me. She sprayed me with champagne. Everyone was asking me how I felt. I didn't feel anything because I knew what it all looked like and I knew it was coming – except when I called home from the red payphone to tell my parents I'd made it. My father's voice made me react. He said, 'When are you going to stop swanning around and get a job?' Crushing and very confusing. It was only years later that I found out it was just a joke.

There were masses of people staring at me at Land's End and when I got back to London, people pointed me out on the street and whispered. But when I went to the Royal Marsden to deliver the cheque and the fundraisers took me round, I got a shock. As I was walking across the courtyard, surrounded by suits and PR shoulder pads, I heard someone calling my name; not Ffyona, but 'Fi!' I looked up and saw a young man with a chemotherapy style hairdo leaning out of the window. He had a smile on his face which I'd never seen in my direction before and he was actually making me smile back. Hello, I know you too.

4

From the end of the British walk onwards, I reached new levels of feeling like a freak. I was on TV chat shows, on the radio, in the newspapers and I felt like I'd turned the city of London into the territory I knew best – one where I knew no one and many of them knew me but as a stranger. It was the bed I knew how to make.

I stayed with my great aunt in London for the second week of October 1983, but when I got word that a friend of an old boyfriend was living not far away, I gave him a call and he offered me a place to doss in his flat. He prefers to be called by the number 87, which he feels has special significance for him.

If I thought I was strange, 87 was from another planet. He wore purple, ate a lot of cereal, rode a motor-bike, was heavily into left-wing politics and had stuck the foam stoppers from pill bottles in a collage all over the walls to make them look spongy. He was working in a pub down the road, saving for a trip to Australia and over the weeks, as I worked on my portfolio for art college, we ate terrible food because neither of us could cook and we got into punk just as everyone else was getting out. But when I pierced 87's ear with an ice cube and a needle, he squawked so much that I wet my pants and had to leave him, midway through the operation, to go to the loo. There was no lock on the door and on the odd occasion when one of us took a bath, we'd try to humiliate the bather by simply standing in the doorway and refusing to go out.

A school friend of his, Charlie, had got the idea to go travelling in Australia for six months before going to Sandhurst. So they went and I stayed and worked in Boots the Chemist during the day and at a pizza joint in the evening and met them in Sydney a few weeks later with £100 in my pocket. I was still sixteen and figured I'd give myself a year out before going to art college. I wondered at the time what happens to people who spend more than a year travelling but since I didn't know any oldies I couldn't tell.

Though 87 was only eighteen years old, he was streets ahead of Charlie and me, knowing how to find work, how to negotiate wages, how to tell a dodgy dude from a good one. We did the usual slave labour bit, picking garlic for mafioso types. We followed the trail of rumours to the land of easy picking and laid-on showers and sick pay to find it was a crock; and up in Queensland we went into Aborigine bars looking for weed and cruised around in the back of their cars testing the stuff and trying not to choke. We swam on the Great Barrier Reef, first near the shore of an island where the water was still but the coral unimpressive then out in the deeper, bluer, more turbulent water, where the reef was teaming and vibrant with life.

My three-month visa was about to run out. I had a ninety per cent staff discount standby ticket on BA and hitched down to Sydney but the flights were full. In fact, because they were increasing the fares at the end of the month, they were fully booked for seven days. I had my $20 departure tax, a pack of twenty-five cigarettes, but that was it. I couldn't get my visa extended to cover the wait but if I paid $200 I could get a standby seat on Qantas immediately. I called my parents to ask if I could borrow the money for a full fare and pay them back when I returned to London. Humiliating, since I'd sworn that I'd never ask them for money. They were away on holiday and my step-grandfather answered the phone. He relayed the message to my father in a grass and mud hut on the Serengeti. My father relayed back that there was no money and I could bloody well get myself out of the mess. He also said that I wasn't allowed in the house when I got back because I'd used some of my mother's cosmetics. Serves me right. I stayed at the airport, nicked sweets from the kiosk, bummed smokes and bugged the check-in staff all through the day for the jump seat.

After about four days one of the airport staff asked if I wanted to stay at her place. Somehow it was arranged so that I could leave the airport even though my visa had expired. We had a terrific time and she gave me a pair of shoes in case there was the chance of being upgraded to first class as can happen with staff stand-by if economy is full. As it turned out, an aircraft was late getting in from Singapore because of mechanical trouble. Some passengers didn't want to fly and I got on. I laid into the drinks trolley big time, didn't know you get pissed much quicker up there. It was the best birthday and the longest: my seventeenth lasted about thirty hours.

I hitched up to St Andrews to stay with Shuna for a week. She was finding people like her and she was really enjoying herself. I tried to hitch back to London but I couldn't get a lift so I turned and hitched up to Aberdeenshire to get my bike from my parents' house. Being February it was freezing cold so I needed some warm jumpers too. My step-grandfather wouldn't let me into the main house, but, after a bit of plain talking at how silly this was, standing there in the snow, he allowed me to enter their little house at the back. I got some clothes and my bike and cycled down to London. I wasn't puritanical about it: I took lifts if they were offered.

I took the cheapest bedsit I could find. For £9 a week I got a bed with a Baby Belling stove, a space to stand up in and a bathroom which was shared with twenty-eight other people. The caretaker was a simple woman who rocked and cooed on her feet when you spoke to her and you always knew when she'd cleaned the bathroom. I didn't know that you have to pay out a month's rent in advance but you don't get paid till the end of the month. I got an overdraft of £100 from the bank, paid my rent, signed up with a temp agency and went out on day jobs. I'm not sure if getting a temp to do the filing is a demonstration of faith in human nature or naive stupidity. These were dark, damp days as my tan began to fade and the grind set in. But it was a very different kind of grind from being out on the road, walking twenty miles in the rain: I didn't have the push and then the high, the desperation and then the relief and I didn't have a map any more, didn't know where I was going, couldn't see how far I'd already come. I was getting fat and isolated and I knew I was going down. The bigger the downer, the bigger the project I needed to aim for to get me out of it.

I wanted to go to art college, but I needed something in the meantime. There wasn't time to walk across America, the next continent along in my childhood fantasy of walking around the world. In Australia, picking fruit, I'd had a sense of the migrant life, how rumours spread of the greener grass elsewhere, and it reminded me of Steinbeck's The Grapes of Wrath story I'd studied at school. I wanted to re-create something of their journey by cycling across America from North Carolina, following the Cherokee Trail of Tears until I hit Route 66 to California. I wanted to do it on bikes of the twenties, dressed in their clothing and using their cooking methods.

But I didn't want to go alone; bumming around Oz was much more fun with someone else and I had just the person in mind. Gordon Jell was a strapping lad from Northumberland whom I'd met one summer holiday with some friends of Charlie's. I hitched up to see him. He got very excited about coming with me, but only once everything was in place – the money, the route, the kit. Fine: I wasn't used to sharing the work on my projects.

After a bit of research I found that the Royal Marsden had a sister hospital in New York called the Memorial Sloan-Kettering Cancer Center. I wrote to them with my idea, explaining that I'd like to raise money for them through the local papers *en route*. I punched out hundreds of sponsorship letters on my manual typewriter, sending them to corporations I found who advertised the most in American magazines, which I got from the Chamber of Commerce. There was only one phone for the block, a pay phone on the floor below me, but anyone who was there during the day was either too stoned or too hungover to bother with messages. I walked or cycled everywhere to save money for stamps, bought veggies from the market just before they closed up for the day, picked the lock on my electricity meter so I could spend the contents and send the same 50p piece through the slot each time, bought a couple of tester pots of paint and coloured the bedsit and each piece of furniture brilliant yellow.

After five months of 'unfortunately our budget is already allocated' letters, which only spurred me on even further, I received an answer to my letter from the Sloan-Kettering. They turned down my offer to raise money for them. I'm not going to twist their arm, I thought. I binned the whole project and left with my sketch pad and a girlfriend, Val, to hitch around Europe.

We bought the cheapest form of Eurorail and hitched in cars, trucks and trains to supplement its restrictions. A grand way of hitching on trains, we found, was to wait till the ticket inspector came round then ask him when we were getting into Zurich, for example, knowing that Zurich was in the opposite direction. He'd wave his hands in concern, the full hassle of our predicament hitting him as he'd realise we'd have to wait till the end of the line before there was a chance of making a connection to a Zurich-bound train. And, of course, he didn't bother to check our tickets as they were for a different journey.

We hitched through Italy in cars, always aware of the danger. But I wanted to see what would happen if we took a dodgy lift. I got the chance when a couple of guys were giving us the eye at a cheese and meat stall on a mountain road. One had a scar down his throat and the other, who only had one eye, kept bumping into the hanging meats. Sure enough, when we stuck out our thumbs they stopped. Val was into it. The driver wouldn't keep his eyes on the road, wouldn't keep his head facing forward. We got the industrial demo on brakes and steering over the mountains and through the tunnels. We'd had enough when they pulled into a small village on the pretence of buying smokes. We knew the cigarette shops were closed at this time of day so we got out, thanked them, refused their offer of beer and headed off down the road to find a good hitching spot. But they drove after us. I realised I'd dropped my scalpel in the back seat of the car; I had it in my belt with a pen lid on it and I used it for sharpening pencils. They opened the door, I looked, but it wasn't there. Didn't matter. We thanked them with that false cheerfulness I've spent a lifetime trying to temper (because it's so obvious that you're frightened) and walked on under a railway bridge and along the sea road. Out of sight of the village, they pulled over up ahead. We stopped. One of them got out and walked down to us. With his right hand he offered us a smoke. I refused. In his left hand, tucked out of sight of the road, was my scalpel. 'Get in the car,' he said. We said, 'No.'

He came closer. 'Get in the car.'

'No.'

At that moment, a little old man pulled up in a Fiat in response to our extended thumbs.

'Napoli?'

No, he was just going a kilometre down the road. That's fine by us. It was terrific! I wanted more of this; I wanted to be scared and to get out of it. And it was very real, a real need, not a twisted one. For the rest of the journey, our senses grew sharper as our money got less; we laughed more than we'd laughed in the comfort of the safety zone in England, and it was good to know that if we fell there was no safety net but ourselves to catch us.

I returned to London and stayed with Shuna in Lincoln's Inn Fields. She was house-sitting for a lawyer's family she'd worked for in the summer. It was bizarre: though we sat on chintz furniture, drew back velvet curtains and slept in four-poster beds, we lived on three slices of a hardboiled egg and a handful of Cheerios a day. I went back to the bedsit to collect any mail and found a couple of rent rebate cheques and payment from some TV and radio interviews I'd given after the UK walk. I went shopping and returned with bags of groceries, feeling for all the world like a hunter returning triumphant to her cubs.

When the summer was over, I went to stay with a friend in Wandsworth. But, after a disagreement over the sleeping arrangements, I walked out. I had no place to live, no money, no job and no one to call on. I liked these times, when I'd look at the situation quite objectively and say, 'Look where you are. Now get yourself out.' A week later I was working for a commodity broking house and living in a Hooray Henry flat, albeit a wild one. There were no official exams to pass at this place; if you could sell on the phone you could command a portfolio. It had an air of school discipline with its gloss paint halfway up the wall in the corridors and bells and break and it was highly charged with bullish nineteen-year-olds in bright red braces shouting deals under the tables into telephones, only lifting their heads to check on the prices and snort another line of coke. They competed with car crashes and orgies and they churned and burned their clients as much as themselves.

After a couple of months I got on a plane to India. I had to get away just to hear my own voice. Madonna's song 'Material Girl' played on the inflight entertainment. I wanted time to think. I had the chance of getting my own portfolio and becoming an account executive if I went for it. I didn't want to turn down the opportunity to better myself but I wasn't sure if the hype was any part of me. Though I was bonking the top broker, it was more because I was fascinated by him as a mentor. Ever since my older sister had become my younger sister after her brain haemorrhage, I had never been inspired to look up to anyone and watch, even if there had been someone there.

The broker, Stephen, introduced me to something I'd never considered before – other people's motivation. He said the secret of his success as a self-made millionaire at the age of twenty-three was to understand 'want'. He said he never sold anyone any commodities, he simply nudged them into selling it to themselves. The way he saw it, people were inspired by one of two things and he told me a story to explain it: if you put a bunch of healthy fleas into a jam jar which they can easily jump out of, then put on the lid, the fleas will keep jumping up and hitting their heads. After a while, they'll jump just short of the lid because they don't want to get a headache. If you take the lid off, the fleas won't be able to jump out any more. There are two ways you can get them to jump out: either put a Bunsen burner underneath, or put in a normal flea which jumps out straight away and the others will follow it. People, he said, are either motivated by force or by inspiration.

In all the clamour of forty brokers trying to make money, Stephen stood out from the others because of his principles, his manners and because he wasn't motivated by money. I knew this beyond doubt when chatting to the receptionist and the subject moved round to him. 'I'll tell you something about Stephen,' she said. 'You know he's having his house done up? Well, the end of the week, the builders want their money and they want cash. It comes to about a grand. So Stephen goes out and gets a grand in cash, puts it in an envelope and asks me to call a courier. Biker collects the package. About a half-hour later I get a call from the courier company saying he's been in an accident and the package is lost. I call Stephen. I'm a bit worried how he's going to take this. "Stephen," I says, "I've got some bad news for you. That package you sent has been lost. Biker had a crash." And the first thing he said was, "Is he OK?"'

I spent two days in New Delhi, not a good place to hear your own voice, and it left me stunned. I had been approached hundreds of times with offers of everything from tours of the Taj to dope to requests for donations for the mutilated, but there was something quite different here from some of their brothers in London who crawl along beside you on the street, slipping dirty talk at you. These people were laughing. But they weren't laughing at me; it seemed like they were laughing at their burden. And their manners were so refined, I felt clumsy and insincere. Though there were similarities in the decibels between these streets and all the bullishness I had just left, here there was an air of serenity.

I didn't for a moment think of reaching for it. These people were different from me; their depth of humour belonged to them, as alien to me as their love of spices or their body language. I had never tried to learn from anyone because I couldn't identify with them; never had a meeting of the minds over even the most trivial of things like hair dye, because my words were simply an echo of those around me in my yearning to fit in. Though I'd recently glimpsed the idea of a teacher and something I wanted to learn, it went beyond the sphere of what I'd been led to believe at Reivesley – the most desirable human being is the one who works alone, puts his or her head down and grinds. Though I'd fought against this mentality, I hadn't replaced it with a new way of thinking. But I didn't want things to change any more, I didn't want to go home to a different bedroom, I wanted it to remain exactly the same. And now that there was a threat to it, to the territory of my foundation, I panicked.

I made a decision to work until I was offered promotion, just to know that I was capable of it, then give in my notice and walk across America.

I went hang-gliding with Rory McCarthy, who'd recently set the world altitude record. During the hours of waiting till the wind was just right for my first flight, I went for a walk along the top of Devil's Dyke, away from the waiting pilots and the picnickers and the ramblers, following the rabbit trails towards the fluorescent light, always brightest just beside the darkest edge of a cloud shadow. And I felt a rhythm inside me as I moved and swayed among the rocky outcrops which was no mimic of anyone near me, but something which was mine in my animal body which felt right, like riding a perfect corner freewheeling on my bike or drawing a perfect curve. And my face relaxed its clown-like grin and my fingertips tingled and my torso felt huge and comforting and my legs felt long and nimble and my feet felt deft, as though they had a purpose quite separate from my mind, so subtle, just a hint of what was to come if I followed.

They say that if an outline of an expedition can't fit on the back of an envelope, it's too complicated. I ran through my aim and how I would achieve it – to walk from New York to Los Angeles. I'd get my overheads sponsored, find a charity I empathised with and have proper back-up. I liked the idea of sharing the journey with someone, someone who wasn't there before me, but in there with me. The sponsor would get their returns through the local media coverage along the way as a form of advertising. The charity would benefit from a donations coupon we'd asked to be printed alongside the story, as with the *Evening Standard*. To keep costs down I'd need a camper van in which to sleep and make food, and two men, one to drive it and the other to drive another vehicle ahead to the next town to alert the local media. 3,500 miles at twenty-five miles a day, six days a week would take me almost six months. I'd cross the desert in winter, so I'd need to begin around June from New York, hitting Los Angeles in December. It was now November 1984 and I was seventeen.

The day came when I was offered promotion. Before turning it down, I called the director and went in to see him. W, I'll call him, looked like what he was – a hippy who'd got wise to the system. He'd started out trading while travelling, drawn to opportunities like a cat to a squeak, and as he grew more cunning he went for bigger game. Some fifteen years after setting out in the world with his pack, he now sat in a leather-bound office with hints in the tassels on the rugs of where he'd spent his apprenticeship. Even now he'll leave his million-pound penthouse flat and take off for the East with his pack. He doesn't take a credit card, just a shoestring budget and journeys in search of his own mentors.

W was highly enthusiastic about my journey, about the adventures I would have, making me even more excited. He was reassuring me that I must follow my own way and he gave me a grand to start up the sponsorship search. I walked out of his office, vowing that when I saw him again, it would be to tell him I had walked across America.

I couldn't afford to live in the Battersea flat. Jo, the only other girl there, was moving into a small flat above her work at a dress hire shop called One Night Stand in Belgravia. Jo was a punk. She didn't take shit from anyone and she invited me to stay with her.

I needed the charity to be in place before I went to look for sponsorship. It gave the trip its purpose without getting into the psycho bull about my personal needs for making a journey. I had felt very proud when I met the cancer patients at the Royal Marsden and I wanted to feel like that again. But when the head of the fundraising programme for Cancer Research took me out for a very expensive lunch at the Queen's Club and got pissed on port, I scrapped that idea and turned instead to where I saw that sense of humility and kinship and pride: Band Aid.

All I knew of Africans then was that they lived in despair, hand to mouth in the mud and dirt and they seemed to have no hope or else they'd be able to get up. It appealed to my anger to walk across America showing pictures of such travesty, thrusting starvation in their fat, contented faces, making them look. But all I knew of the world then was what the media told me and God forbid that the media should be anyone's mentor or wise man.

I went along to the Live Aid offices. Amongst the jumble of phones and posters and ankle warmers and laughter, I felt the excitement of something happening. I outlined my plan to walk across America and then, because of the power in that place, I let go and went the whole hog. 'Actually, I was thinking of walking around the world.' They thought it would be terrific! They ran through the plans for the Live Aid concert and how there'd be one in the States but they weren't sure where and with the satellite link-ups there'd be massive awareness to draw on as my walk went on after the event. They immediately organised a sanction, piled me up with headed paper, leaflets, press releases, photos, till I had to stop them: Jo would be mad for the space it'd take up.

It sounds corny but I doubt I was the only one who walked out of those offices feeling like I could walk around the world.

I rang the *Evening Standard* to put in a piece about what I was doing next with the hope of attracting sponsorship. I'd found a couple of guys to do back-up but the motivation I had simply inspired in them to get on with their own dreams took over and they blew out. The *Standard*'s piece brought a call from an insurance broker who wanted to know what insurance I had and if I came in to the office, he might be able to pitch his company to cover the cost. I met Chris and was immediately impressed with his vitality. Even in the relative calm of the lunch hour, he looked like he'd drown if he stood still. Within an hour, the twenty-five year old had agreed to join my team. One of his colleagues, Brian, who was twenty-four and a former racing driver, wanted to get out of broking and Chris was sure he'd join us as the back-up driver.

Jo's place was getting too small for all of this so, having seen the virtually derelict former offices of Lyons in Hammersmith, I called them to ask if we could use them as a base for a month. They called me back within the hour with a big yes, and provided free use of the photocopier and phones and fax. The three of us met up there, Chris running around like a blue-arsed fly and Brian, darker, more masculine. There was an immediate sexual tension between us. And I wasn't sure whether I wanted it to go away.

As Chris and I called companies in Britain and America for sponsorship, Brian organised equipment and Shuna came by to run errands and go out for food. After a month we still hadn't found a sponsor. We had to start the walk at the end of June. There were only five weeks to go.

I went out for a meal with Stephen. We ended up in a bath in some hotel and he turned to me and said, 'Look at your situation: you've got nothing – you've got no money, no possibilities of sponsorship, no back-up van, no flights and you're starting the walk in five weeks' time? Don't you know it takes months for companies to make those kinds of decisions?'

I got out of the bath, dressed, kissed him, said goodbye and decided to leave for Philadelphia.

The night before I left for America, Jo started having a go at me over utterly trivial things. As we were going downstairs to get another bottle, she turned and hit me. I hit her back. She lashed out. I lashed back, till we were both exhausted and matted and bruised. Then Jo burst into tears. I couldn't see what was wrong. She'd have her flat back; she'd just been promoted to manager; she had plenty of friends. But she was really crying. I tried to comfort her but she pushed me away, shouting, 'Don't you understand?'

'No, I don't. What?'

'I'm frightened for you.'

It jolted me. I hadn't experienced a friendship before which was based on anything but practical needs. It was way beyond my comprehension.

Brian and Chris and I had £500 between us. We packed up, said our goodbyes and arrived at Gatwick in time for the press conference which Virgin Atlantic Airlines public relations had organised in return for giving us the flights. Once they'd got their photos, we found there were no seats for us. We waited two days to get on a flight, during which time Chris left his briefcase in the loo. Security took it away.

We had nothing organised the other end except a contact name with the Live Aid group who were organising the American concert in Philadelphia. We landed in the dark. I went to one of those car hire request phones and asked to speak to the manager. He agreed to lend us a car for two weeks. We drove to a hotel and asked if we could stay the night. No problem. Next day we split up. Brian's job was to pitch for hotels and Chris and I got on the public pay phones and started calling companies. The strongest lead I had was with a company whose offices were nearby. I'll call it The Company. They were my first call. I spoke to a marketing manager whom I'll call Rob and asked if we could meet. He told me later he'd agreed only because he knew I wouldn't stop bothering him.

At the meeting Chris led the way. He'd been to college and he knew the marketing jargon. It emerged through the discussion that they were, in fact, looking for a promotion to help them change their current image. Health fanatics, as they called them, were giving The Company a hard time over their E number preservatives. A new, healthy line had been introduced and they needed a vehicle to promote it. Chris improvised ideas, drawing a picture of me as an athlete, inspiring young people at 'grass roots' level in the local media across the country. But, they said, this doesn't fit well with images of people dying of starvation. But we said it did: if we are concerned about the health of our own people, this would be a stark reminder of what others didn't have and how we could lend them a hand.

We decided the walk would have a much better chance of bringing in donations if we began from New York just after the Live Aid concert. Chris had a brainwave of trying to get us on stage at the concert so that the media would be more interested in us as we continued our journey. He called a friend in London who called Geldof. Geldof said yes and put the phone down. The Live Aid team in Philadelphia gave us a thirty-second slot just after the Mayor would announce 13 July to be a holiday in the city each year.

Now we had a concrete date to aim for and a greater possibility of decent media interest, we went back to The Company and told them they must make a decision by 1 July.

Chris and I carried on putting irons in the fire with other companies while Brian got a job in a clothing shop to provide us with money for the phone boxes. Tempers frayed whenever we lifted our heads and looked at the time. We would not consider returning to Britain as failures but at times it seemed virtually a certainty. I've often found that seeing your predicament from the outside is soul destroying; better to know where you're going and keep your head down till you know you're on course, then look up, look back and celebrate how far you've come.

Sharing beds meant that Brian and I had to use more self-control than we could afford. Finally, when Chris was out, we let go and bonked all afternoon. When he came back the dynamics had changed irrevocably. I'd never been in this situation before; if I didn't like how something turned out, I'd just move on. Now I was stuck. I frantically searched my mind for scraps of a character to pull together and cover up before he came in, but it's hard enough to make an outfit without a pattern, let alone one which fits. Brian was embarrassed and ashamed too and he made it up to Chris by spending more time with him. At eighteen I wasn't old enough to go into bars in the States, so this was where they headed, the two of them, after the days on the phone. I wasn't old enough, either, to know that though it takes two to tango, the woman is often blamed because she is the one who is supposed to have the self-control.

Suddenly I found I was the odd one out again, worse than at school because this was my walk. I felt resentful and humiliated. One night, in a hotel where Brian had scored two adjoining rooms for us, they locked theirs, went out and came back with a couple of girls. I heard the whole thing.

It became very difficult to organise meetings with The Company now that we weren't talking to each other.

A penultimate meeting was called. They laid out their concerns about the cost of the back-up vehicles but we knew we could get them. Charlie, one of their team, waved his hand saying, 'Don't worry guys, I'll get you the van and the car by next week.' So, we left it up to him. A week later, Charlie had nothing and couldn't even remember saying it. Rob shook his head. We convinced him to let us have a go; the whole thing hinged on this.

Chris and I worked the list of manufacturers, dealers, rental agencies and anything we could think of, but nobody would do it. The market was too weak to stand a vehicle out of use and the publicity would be nominal, they said. We came back with assurances quoted from the Marketing Society that a sponsored event covered in the press is three times more eye-catching than straight advertising and it carries more weight if a product is linked with someone real. But it didn't work; they needed dollars this summer not the possibility of more next year and if this was a walk what good would it do them as suppliers of vehicles?

I went up to the pool for a work-out when I couldn't get anyone on the phone over lunch and tried to think of a different angle. What about getting a loan with the sponsorship money as collateral and buying a second-hand van which wouldn't depreciate. If we then sold it in time to repay the loan, all we'd have to pay was the interest. It was 12.35 p.m. on 1 July when I was called to the phone. It was Chris. 'Rob has just called.' I couldn't tell from his tone of voice: it was flat and tired.

'The man from The Company says yes.'

'Congratulations Chris, we did it! Thank God for The Company! Thank God for Rob!'

He hung up. As it turned out, Rob himself pulled in a couple of favours and got the lease on a thirty-three-foot camper van and a Ford Bronco.

I rushed down to his room to hug him, but he was leaving. They wanted to see him without me. 'Let's all get together tonight and have a meal. I'm sorry for all the misery. We've done it now. Let's make a fresh start.' But Chris just snorted, picked up his jacket and left. Hardly surprising really. Chris didn't know yet what I could do.

That night Brian and Chris rented a car and drove to Atlantic City. They gambled and drank champagne and stayed the night. When I saw them again, Brian had a new gold watch, Chris a gold chain. But they hadn't won a cent. I confronted them.

'This money is not ours. It's sponsorship. It's to cover the cost of the walk and you have no right to go gambling it or drinking it away on champagne.'

'You're just being a little bitch. This is our walk just as much as it's yours. We worked for this; we left our jobs and we're going to celebrate in the way that we want. So, what are you going to do about it?'

Had I laughed, I might have learned something. But, even at the age of eighteen, I was still a little girl. I was enjoying grown-up pleasures but the way I'd learned to deal with problems was to sulk, to wind myself up in the moral high ground without taking an honest look at the state of my own behaviour. Honesty had always been so confused and admitting I was wrong at home seemed to mean I was accepting responsibility for everything that went wrong. I felt I'd be trodden on if I gave an inch, and my fear simply added more distance to honesty. I'd had no experience of anyone going through this mess and watching how they handled it, no idea even that it happened to anyone else.

My first reaction was to get rid of them, but The Company would no doubt withdraw. I felt my defence for the walk take on a greater passion: this was my territory, I was here first and if they stayed, I'd make them suffer. I felt the vicious fury of being trapped and I kept lashing out to find a chink, any chink, just to know these walls were not a prison, that they could be broken. But, of course, Brian and Chris only strengthened their unity.

I went out and bought a kitten. I called him Driftwood and he was mine, to love, protect and care for.

The Live Aid concert was now only four days away and The Company had still not produced a contract. We knew if the concert passed we'd miss our greatest advantage. Chris took the brunt of the worry in his solo meetings and I hated him for it, but I didn't know then that The Company didn't feel comfortable with me in meetings because I never smiled.

Finally, at 1 p.m. on Friday 11 July 1985, too late for any negotiation, Rob met us in the lobby of the hotel with half a dozen copies of our agreement. It laid out our jobs. Chris was to arrange press conferences and to liaise with The Company's PR girl, whom I'll call Amanda, from a PR outfit in Chicago, to increase awareness of The Company's new range of products as being healthy and nutritious and to do his best to ensure the Live Aid donations address appeared in each article. I was to walk twenty-five miles a day, six days a week and to articulate the message of The Company and Live Aid in all interviews; and Brian was to support Chris and me to the best of his ability. But there were a couple of things that I didn't agree with. The

41

Company was concerned that something would happen to me as I walked along the roads and they naturally didn't want the unlikely possibility of their logo on a rape victim or smeared with blood across the front pages. So they demanded our assurance that Brian would drive the van directly behind me at all times.

I couldn't bear the irritation of a van up my ass for eight hours a day, the driver staring at my behind, but their lawyers insisted. The contract also said that they would suggest sponsorship to their subsidiary in Australia only if Brian and Chris remained on the team. They wouldn't budge on this either, so I signed, as did they.

On the morning of the concert we dressed in T-shirts and shorts. They weren't emblazoned with The Company's logo as we'd feared, just a dignified two-inch scribble in the left-hand corner of our T-shirts. Together, we'd written a script for my thirty-second slot, which I practised and practised till it was completely flat. I figured with all the excitement of the moment it would come out properly, just as long as I didn't forget it. Now, I wrote it out and stuck it in my cap.

We took the subway over to the stadium. If we'd been blind we could have found our way by feeling, there was such a charge in the air and it grew stronger the closer we got, so strong it felt like something had to explode. And it was infectious, infectious emotional energy.

At the stage door we were given our ID badges as 'artists' and shown round to the back to get our make-up done. It felt like some kind of wonderland back there: in another country we were surrounded by people we knew but, like a nightmare, they didn't know us. At the Hard Rock Café mock-up, an aging member of the Beach Boys tried to chat me up. Bizarre, as I'd listened to their songs while babysitting in the bleak Aberdonian winters; now here was one of them giving me the eye. The Thompson Twins were wandering around like life-sized cartoon characters at Disney World – I'd been used to seeing them four inches high – and in the make-up room, Dionne Warwick sat me down, tied my hair back and layered on the foundation. 'Oh, before you go, must put some on your ears. Can't have you going out without make-up on your ears.'

Above the corridor which led up to the stage, a huge sign was painted: PLEASE LEAVE YOUR EGOS BEHIND. But it seemed unnecessary, except perhaps, for people like us, whose egos were developing by the minute.

Brian heard that a telephone company had sponsored the phone bill, so I made a quick call to Shuna to let the family know that we'd be on. Brian called his friends and I left to wander around. I returned about an hour later to find he was still on the phone, talking about what he'd done after leaving school. It seemed like he was calling around everyone he'd ever met. The others in there didn't know who the hell this bloke was but he seemed to command such an air of self-righteousness that they figured he was someone important. I tapped him on the shoulder and pointed to my watch. He pushed me away, a vicious expression on his face which turned completely into good-laddishness when he answered his school friend's next question. I felt disgusted and embarrassed.

I went down into the crowd which, as the time grew nearer for the concert to begin, could only be done once if I wasn't to get caught on the wrong side. It was so hot out there without any shade, but the local fire engines came in and sprayed the audience. It seemed like nothing could bother them, nothing could stop them from having a good time and I immediately felt a part of it – people who looked like me, were dressed like me, were feeling excited like me. It was an extraordinary day to feel a sense of belonging for the first time, to be amongst a crowd who were anything but territorial.

And then the moment came. A runner found us, directed us to the dark corridor with its steps up on to the stage, a table on the right with three books to be signed. I kept breathing deeply against the desire to turn and run, all senses heightened, noises and smells suddenly brilliant and merging together, trying to block out images of tripping flat on my face, trying to remember the first line. Someone held me in position as the Mayor, surrounded by his workers, spoke to the crowd, but it was a cheerless interval: the audience wanted to rock. I felt stupid. What was I doing here? A flash of regret at all the commercial crap I'd let the walk become. I felt cheap, ashamed. Then the announcer swung on, working the space as the group cleared. He announced my name, I think, I couldn't really hear and suddenly Brian and Chris and I were running into the space, big clean windy space, in front of a massive living pointillist painting. I took the microphone and the announcer whispered, 'I'd introduce you anywhere', and I felt all those pointillist pieces fidgeting and I desperately didn't want to do this. Oh Christ, who am I going to be?

So I shouted: 'Hello everyone, I'm Ffyona Campbell and together with my two-man team I'm about to start an expedition to walk from New York to Los Angeles for Live Aid. We'll then carry on and walk around the world. Lend us your support. We welcome your encouragement. Follow us around the world!' I raised my fist in triumph, expected there to be a cheer or something but there were a few idle claps. I swung round to pass on the microphone baton but there was nobody there. I ran off the stage as fast as I could. Faces stared at me as I went down the steps, beetroot.

5

I didn't dip my toe in the Atlantic Ocean. Instead, the walk began on 16 August 1985 from the Ralph Bunch Park across the United Nations building in front of all the flags and the bag ladies. Brian wasn't there. He couldn't drive the monster into town; he'd meet us on the outskirts. Chris was there, smartly dressed, Rob and Amanda and a handful of photographers and they were all looking at me, expecting some radical change in attitude and, I suppose, so was I.

I faked the start: the prima donna wasn't me; but then what the hell was? I giggled and jiggled and pretended I felt something when they asked, sure I must, worried that I didn't. I knew it was all wrong but I'd never felt a right to aim for. This is what it looked like on TV when people were in the spotlight, so all I had to do was to imitate them, right? Isn't that what everybody does?

A man from India had recently walked through town. He'd carried a banner: Walking Around the World for Peace. His name was Prem Kumar. Prem is Hindi for love and he had no back-up. He walked and people came to him, took him in and fed him and in turn he spoke to them. In my mind I had a vision of doing that too, but I knew I could keep up that character for as long as the others I'd tried out – about as long as I could hold in my tummy.

But I wasn't an athlete either, wobbling along in my synthetic shorts; even Amanda looked more athletic than me. After a couple of blocks they got in their car and followed me, and Chris followed in the Bronco. I got a sense then that this was it, I was on my own now, each step taking me away from the unity of a group. But I'd had nothing to contribute. Now that I was doing my job, they'd see I had some worth. I felt a rush of fear then; they were all here because I said I could do something, something amazing. But I didn't know if I could actually do it. Then again, I figured, I don't know that I can't. Look at it this way: you know you can walk 1,000 miles

— USA Walk —
1985-6

Los Angeles
Phoenix
Fort Sumner
Clovis
Amarillo
Oklahoma City
Tulsa
Springfield
St Louis
Indianapolis
Cleveland
Philadelphia
New York

N

because you've done it; America is three and a half times more than that. Sound frightening? Not really. When you started at John O'Groats saying you could walk twenty-five miles a day for fifty days, when you'd only walked twenty-five miles once, your pledge was fifty times more than you knew you could do. But you did it. By comparison, this is far more possible. Remember how you'd got into a routine and the miles got done systematically? That's how it will be. The beginning always sucks, the end always sucks, the middle is strong and even and becomes easy as you forget any other way of life. Remember what Hillaby said: 'Never, never think of the end.' Don't know what you're getting so wound up about, you're just going for a walk.

As I plodded through the bustle of the streets, the same old frustration came back: I was used to rushing around at high speed and now there seemed to be an invisible gel in the air which was holding me back. My shins hurt as I tried to push my legs forward even faster to keep in time with the beat of the city noise, but they began to stiffen. All I'd done was to walk too quickly without warming up first. I tried to relax. Easy does it; you'll find your own rhythm out of the city. When I knew the photographer was ahead, I kept tripping and my arms went out of sync with my legs. I hated being examined, but after all the episodes of being a freak I should have found a way to overcome it; but I didn't want to accept it was really happening, I wanted it to go away.

Chris drove behind in the traffic, his elbow resting on the window ledge, his hand in a fist thumping the underside of his chin. I knew his mind was racing as always and he must be feeling frustrated too. We kept each other in view but I couldn't wait for him when he stopped at the lights, or I wouldn't get out of town that night. He'd waggle his finger when he found me again. I'd shrug. Sorry pal, all you have to do is move your foot down by half an inch and you've covered 200 yards.

As the blocks around us petered out and more of the sky came into view, the horizons became a brownish backdrop to the flashing stars and triangles and flags of the car dealerships and motels and fast food huts. I felt my first rush of finding the treasure: in a parking lot amongst the sedans and Oldsmobiles sat my house, the motor home. Food! I climbed the steps, aware of stiffening muscles, and opened the door. Inside felt like a cool capsule of safety, a personal tardis in the mayhem. Brian brushed past me to welcome Chris and I heard their buddy laughter. I picked up my kitten, let him nestle under my chin as I explored the drawers and cupboards with my free hand. His bag of food and bowls were under the sink. There was milk in the fridge. I placed Driftwood down on the plastic sheet beside the gangway and poured out his food. This would be his eating place.

Chris opened the door, making us jump, and called up from the pavement, 'We're going for a beer.'

'Can you bring one back for me?'

'Yeah, sure.'

Great, I won't see them for a couple of hours; I can unpack and make a place. Like my mother before me.

Thirty-three feet of vehicle were arranged in sections, each with a sliding partition. Everything matched in shades of tan and chocolate brown with flowers or stripes. From the front with its wide slanted window there were two seats, more like armchairs, which could be rotated 180 degrees to the section behind it. This was Brian's domain. Above them was a flat padded panel which could be pulled down to make a bed with its own curtains. This was where Chris would sleep. I found the duvets and covers, sheets and pillows and made up his bed. A step down from the driver's seats was a sofa on the left, which could also pull out to a double bed, and another swivel chair with a table beside it. Next to the table was the gangway down to the door. On the right was the kitchen sink top with pump-action taps, a microwave, a fridge and a cooker. I sorted the utensils and crockery and cooking pots and food more logically in the fitted cabinets above and below. On the other side was the dining-room with a table at right angles to the wall with a bench along each side which could also be folded down into a bed. Going towards the back through a narrow corridor, there was a concertina door which I pulled back and found a shower and on the other side a sliding door to a loo with basin and fitted cabinets and mirror. I put my wash things in one cabinet and Brian's wash bag on the unit top so he could sort them out as he liked. Further back, through a sliding door, was the bedroom with a bed on each side, cabinets above and two wardrobes. Curtains could be pulled all around. I made the beds and folded my clothes in the cabinets. I drew the line at arranging Brian's things, so I left his bags on his bed.

The motor home was brand new, very flash and far more than we needed even for three people to live in for six months. I hoped it wouldn't give the wrong impression. We'd had a banner made for the walk logo and the donations address with banking details was taped to the outside. We'd wanted a donations telephone number because this arrangement was stupid. We knew nobody would come along and write down a five-line address with fourteen digits, then write out a cheque, then find an envelope, then find a stamp, then take it down to the post office. The credit card over the phone system worked so well because it capitalised on the spontaneous gesture. But Rob was under pressure to keep the costs down, having allocated a huge budget to their PR company to turn the project into sales for their new range. He said we'd see how we got on with the address, then think again. But, we said, we've only got a month of high density population, then we'll be heading into the farming land. At this time Bob Dylan had launched a new campaign, Farm Aid, to help out the small-scale farmers in the Midwest who were being forced out of business by larger conglomerates. But Rob intimated that we should stop giving him flak about his budget or else he'd have to reconsider the whole project. It was ironic really that he kept calling emergency meetings with Chris over the next five months to decide on whether or not to continue funding the project, because we were raising so little money.

Now that Brian could drive behind me, Chris went ahead to meet the press and the dignitaries who had agreed to get involved with the project after an initial contact by Amanda in Chicago. Our first big reception was in the town of Camden, New Jersey, four days into the walk. At the end of walking on the third day, Chris came back to say we'd need to be there by 11 a.m. the following morning. This was impossible; I'd need the whole day.

'Well, you said you could do it,' snorted Chris.

'I said I needed four days: that's four full days not three and a half.'

'What d'you expect me to do about it? Call the Mayor of Camden and say sorry, the prima donna can't make it? Hey Brindle [as he called Brian] fancy a game of Pacman?'

When they left, I felt like bursting into tears. Come on, buck up. There'll be a solution. I played with Driftwood, dangling string in front of him while doing some calculations. I expect Chris didn't understand that for twenty minutes sitting down with his foot resting on a pedal I'd spend seven hours in hard work-out. Appreciation of distance depends on the effort you have to put into it. If we were to be there at 11 a.m., I must start walking at 4 a.m. I left a note for them, drew the curtains and went to bed, letting Driftwood snuggle under the covers.

Brian was always very good at getting up (especially remarkable since he wasn't a natural early riser) and starting the fry up. I hadn't learned yet that protein makes you feel sluggish as the body needs energy to digest it. It's better to have it in the evening so digestion takes place at night, then eat an immediate energy giver like fruit first thing in the morning.

At 3.30 a.m. we bumped around in the bright light, aware of our noises in the quiet street. I set off half an hour later at 4 a.m. It was breezy and dark outside, with the sprinkling of street lights making the parked cars look showroom shiny. I knew this feeling well from the British walk: a sense of possession. I am here first; this is my road.

By 9 a.m. I felt lightheaded. I needed something to eat but we were in an industrial area and there were no fast food huts. All we had on board was soup. I walked beside Brian's window. He wound it down, stuck his elbow on the ledge. Driftwood, who had been sitting on the dashboard, now tested the rod of the wing mirror and bobbed his head up and down when he saw his reflection.

'I need some food. Can you pull over and heat up some soup for me please?'

'We haven't got time. We'll be late.'

'What? I need something to eat.'

'Look, you silly bitch, they've got TV cameras scheduled and the Mayor can only come for a few minutes. And you're going to screw things up.'

'I don't give a damn. I won't get there at all if I don't eat something. Now fucking well pull over and do your job.'

'Stupid bitch.'

He overtook me and I thought he was going to pull over up ahead, but he didn't. He just kept driving about a hundred feet in front of me at four miles an hour. When I ran after him, he sped up. When I stopped, he stopped. When I started walking, he pulled away. I couldn't do anything against this. If I stopped I'd be wasting time; I couldn't catch him and I needed food. I felt a huge welling up of red hot heat from the pit of my stomach through my chest through my neck and into my face. I wanted to get him by the scruff of the neck and smash his head down onto the dashboard again and again.

Eventually he pulled over and made the soup. I ate it and got back out on the road, feeling his eyes boring into my back. I couldn't escape him; I couldn't win. He was in charge of my food and my water. No doubt he would tell Chris what I had done. Christ! I'm stuck. I hate them. I can't do anything about this. This is like

Reivesley all over again. I'm trapped! I walked faster and faster but I couldn't get away from him, he stuck on my tail like glue. He had the vehicle, he had my food and water, he had the power. He knew it.

We reached the town hall only twenty minutes late, just as the arterial tibia muscle of my left leg began ripping off the bone from walking too fast. It would heal, but I didn't know that.

Mayor Randy Primas greeted me on the steps. He made a speech and presented me with the key to the city. I stepped onto the platform with the microphones of the TV and radio stations propped on the podium's edge and thanked the Mayor and thanked The Company and told them how very grateful we were to have their support because it meant we could do something, all of us, which would help those who are less fortunate than ourselves. I told them while they enjoyed their nutritious foods, not to forget how lucky they were.

They gave us a cheque for $3,000. It was very good.

Chris spent most of the days up ahead, trying to persuade dignitaries or clubs to get involved. He'd then find a location, usually a conference room in a hotel, then call Amanda's contacts in the press and set it all up, including making sure there were refreshments, the right number of chairs, press packs etc., all from pay phones with no chance of anyone calling him back as our budget couldn't cover a mobile.

We were all tired at day's end but each of us had a different kind of fatigue. Chris would still be buzzing from the million action sheets he'd written out and delegated and new relationships formed and pumping each person with enthusiasm. He wanted to unwind by whizzing around, burning it off. Brian was virtually asleep from driving for seven hours at four miles an hour, without using his brain or his body, and I was physically tired but mentally brain dead. Brian and I found Chris's dynamics hard to bear; in a way we were jealous of him, his energy only reminded us of what our jobs were lacking.

The corn was high and golden as it had been since New Jersey, but in the valleys I noticed it had not caught the sun, just the mist and the dew, and was wet and undernourished. It reminded me of the Biblical sowing of the seeds: some landed on good fertile land and grew straight and well but others landed on stony ground and did not grow. I didn't find this analogy very inspiring – kind of says you're fucked for life if you get a raw deal through no fault of your own. So I thought of it another way: the chick who struggles the longest to get out of its shell will emerge with stronger muscles than his brother who virtually walked out. To stand by and watch this struggle without helping would not be cruel; it would only be cruel if you reached down and pulled the shell off the struggling chick whose muscles would then be weaker and his fight for life greatly diminished.

Through Pennsylvania and the humidity of the July heat, chugging off the road, I walked into Amish country. When I heard these people were living in preindustrial ways I thought they were a hippy group who'd chosen this way of life. When a policewoman pulled us over to check if we'd broken down, as so many people did, she told us the Amish are a sect of the Anabaptist Church who came over from what is now Holland in the eighteenth century and who had not changed their way of life despite the progress of the communities around them. They make their living selling vegetables and fruits on the road and trading in cattle and horses. They wear their traditional clothes and live by a strict law of the church. She told us they are heavy drinkers and she often has to reprimand young boys for drag racing their horse-drawn carts. When she said this I felt a surge of anger and leaped to their defence: 'Why are you curbing what is a natural desire?'

She looked startled. 'Well, it's dangerous.'

'What's wrong with danger?'

'Oh, don't be silly. You can't stand by and watch a boy injure himself.'

'No, better to be a walking zombie.'

I saw a couple of teenage girls driving a buggy looking like Laura Ingalls from *Little House on the Prairie*. I couldn't see their faces for their bonnets till one of them turned her head and looked at me. She had such a clear complexion, such wide innocent eyes and she looked a very different kind of clean – hand scrubbed cotton skirts, scrubbed skin. I couldn't imagine her breaking out in greasy zits or letting off body odour. She must be as clean as you can get in America, clean of pollutants, clean of chemicals inside and out. This, I thought, is what the white human being is supposed to look like, even better looking than a touched-up photo of a cosmetics model.

After ten miles the next morning I climbed into the motor home to do an interview with a reporter from the Columbian *Times*. It was the first time I'd been into the van that day and I called the cat. He didn't come. He had played games with us before and would suddenly appear out of the woodwork after half an hour. So the reporter

and I hunted around in dark corners, under covers, between cush-
ions, but he wasn't in his usual hiding places. I began to feel
dreadfully frightened. When the reporter had gone, Chris said,
'Don't blame Brian, it's your cat.'

I wanted to go back to our camp site to look for the cat, but Chris
had arranged for me to meet the Mayor of Columbia. I knew I had
to stay; mayors were very important. He arrived and wanted to walk
with me. He chatted away about his ancestors coming from Bath and
his proposed visit to the Virgin Islands; I kept thinking that every
sentence of his was a death sentence for my cat. Even when he left
and we could drive back, someone else came up wanting to donate,
then another wanting me to talk at his school, then some kids wanting autographs. I was quite proud of myself for keeping my cool. At
the end of another fifteen miles, Brian parked up the motor home
and turned to me. 'Well done,' he said.

He heaved the motor-bike that had been lent to us in case the RV
broke down off the front of the van and we rode back to the camp
ground. I kept seeing horrible images of the little thing mewing for
us, pitifully, lost amongst all the traffic, which was stupid, I was just
winding myself up. I guessed that unless someone had found him
quite soon after we left there was little chance.

We stopped in York at the fruit market where we'd begun the day's
walk. In the darkness of the morning, it was possible that the kitten
had leaped out to prowl around, unaware of our intentions to drive
off. I rushed into the market, asking everybody if they'd seen a little
black-and-white cat, but the reaction was the same: 'Nobody ain't
seen nothing.' I ran down to the river next to the market and called
and searched, looking for hiding places where a kitten might shelter,
frightened from the noise of the traffic. I found nothing. I climbed on
the motor-bike and we drove to the camp site of the previous night.
I went to the registration office. They hadn't seen him but allowed
me to look around the camp. I went to the place we had camped and
called and searched. Brian looked in the tobacco house. It was so
peaceful there, surely nobody could have hurt my cat.

There was a clean-shaven man sitting outside his motor home
wearing a white striped open-necked shirt and brown trousers. He
was old and well kept and he was positioned next to where we had
camped. I asked him if he had seen or heard anything of a black-and-
white kitten. He said yes.

'YES? Where is he?'

His tone of voice made me think he was scolding me for being so careless and leaving the little thing lying around. Then he said, 'The cat is dead. You ran over it with your motor home when you left this morning. I found it in the tracks of the tyres. I'm sorry. I put it in a paper bag and threw it away.'

'Where?'

He gave me directions several times. I walked in the direction of the trash dumper completely stunned. Brian approached on the bike. He stopped. 'The cat's dead,' I said. I couldn't say anything else; I was so numbed I couldn't even feel.

Brian leaped off the bike and cried, 'How?'

'You ran over it this morning.'

He hugged me hard. 'Oh God, I didn't know. I'm so sorry.'

The man approached. He explained it was best that we knew. He had spent weeks looking for lost pets. I asked if he was killed instantly. His head was completely smashed. We buried Driftwood under some trees at the border of the RV park and the next field. The man kept apologising. I thanked him. Ironic, really, that the very thing which had saved the walk had killed the little animal.

The basis of the press interviews were the same: who, what, why, when, how? Even after 200 interviews I was still being asked who are you and what are you doing. It seemed that no matter how much I explained it, I was still at square one because each person I met was a stranger. It gave me the impression that I wasn't getting anywhere. My conversations with others were limited to pointing me out as being odd and this confirmed a notion in me that I was not the same. And without similarity they could not empathise with me.

After three weeks on the road, giving four or five interviews a day, which took several precious hours out of my walking day and forced me to start at 5 a.m. to get the twenty-five miles done, the donations still weren't coming in. In virtually every town we'd met the mayors and local dignitaries but, even when I tossed away the softly softly approach and went graphic, laying it on the table with, 'Pity is all very well but it doesn't save lives; we need your money', I was still met with polite nods and claps but no clamour to swell the coffers. Perhaps it was me: perhaps they sensed my own anger was being channelled through the words; perhaps they needed photos (which The Company wouldn't allow us to show); perhaps they were just donated-out.

Rob kept threatening Chris that he'd pull out if more money wasn't raised. The Company didn't want to be associated with a fundraising failure. Even though the money they gave us to pay for the walk was completely separate, by law, from the money which came in as donations, it would put them in the embarrassing position of having to justify their sponsorship instead of giving it as a donation to the charity. They might be accused of funding a charity walk as a promotions campaign. But Rob wasn't prepared to set up a donations telephone number. He would, though, get some posters printed and some donations envelopes, which we'd asked for so that we could distribute them as we went.

Each time Chris returned from one of these meetings, he put the pressure on me to do more interviews, but there simply wasn't any more time in the day, let alone patience. There comes a point during a marathon, after the morning's enthusiasm and excitement has been worked off, when you put the blinkers on and go for it. Like deciding to tidy up your room, you start with gusto because if you wander from one item to the next, nothing gets done and you'll give up. You're on a roll and someone comes into the room and wants to chat. You're polite the first four or five times, but when the clock's ticking and you've got to get it done there is only a certain amount of patience even a saint can give at that time. From the outside, of course, nobody can ever see your pressure, and a person walking down the road seems to exude that they have all the time in the world. If you tap on their shoulder for a chat and you're the twenty-fifth person that day, you might get upset at the reaction. I'd get angry and I'd get graphic and it didn't work. Chris witnessed these occasions, remembered them more than all the times I had been polite, and he shook his head in disgust. It took me years and years to work out that nobody can appreciate your job until they have a go themselves, and that went for my appreciation of back-up too. And even longer to realise if you aim to be good one hundred per cent of the time and end up with fifty-one per cent you're doing pretty well.

There were several times when I simply put my foot down and said, 'I can't do this interview', and went inside the motor home. I was getting physically exhausted, feeling washed out and the emotional pendulum during the hours of walking to keep at bay the frustration of my pace against the traffic was made worse by having to put on a smiley face when someone entered my tight world of concentration.

Because I was the only one behaving this way, I harboured a secret acknowledgement that I really was a little bitch. But I was the only one walking. That confusion goes with the territory of isolation: if you have no one to measure your behaviour against, you never know if you're doing badly or doing just fine or what, in fact, to strive for. It got to a point where I was screaming my defence and it was met with snorts of disgust.

When Chris arrived with his demands I think Brian began to resent him too. When there were just the two of us, we learned each other's mood swings and we compensated for them. But Chris seemed to want to return home to the same set-up he'd left and perhaps he felt betrayed by our union. So he tried, successfully in the beginning, to break us up.

After the death of Driftwood, I turned my attention to tidying up the motor home. Not only did it give me something to do and a sense of putting things in order but, as I cleaned out the fridge and made a shopping list of what we needed, I was taking care of something again. After the years of protecting myself, this was a very new feeling for me. And, just as Stephen had said, Brian responded to the inspiration with as much fervour as he had with force, only in a different direction: we cleaned together, we shopped together, we cooked together, we laughed together. And, after a while, we were sleeping together.

For 150 miles during the week I'd look forward to our only night off on the eve of the rest day. Unexpectedly, Chris barged in around 7 p.m., ignoring me and thumping Brian on the back. 'Come on, matey, let's go out on the town.' I reverted instantly at this intrusion and the brick walls shot up. Brian saw this, was very easily led and turned away from it, towards the effervescent Chris who was on the make. They showered, jabbering away at each other about the girls they'd pick up, pulled out clothes from where I'd folded them, dolled on the aftershave and the gold jewellery and took a wodge of cash from the food kitty. Brian came out of the bedroom wearing one of my jackets and, when I protested, his sweeping hand almost made contact with my face. They got into the Bronco, turned on the music, revved the engine and sped away.

I threw up. This was Reivesley all over again. I reverted to force. I cleaned myself up, found some quarters and my address book and went out to the camp ground phone box. I called Amanda at home in Chicago. I took the moral high ground that they were spending the walk's money. Amanda suggested that instead of paying us automatically every two weeks through money transfer at a Western Union outlet, they would release the money only when receipts had been submitted and approved. I felt better. But I didn't know then that all of this would come back at me – what affects those you are dependent upon, affects you much more.

The next day, after their banter over sniffing girls' seats at the disco and taking the piss out of the DJ, who called the dancers 'spunk-heads', Chris sent in the final shaft.

'We work very hard for you, very very hard for you. You've said that you must get sponsorship for the Australia walk within a week of finishing the America walk or you won't comply with *Guinness Book of Records* rules to make this a continuous walk. Right?'

'So?' Wish I'd known at the time that this wasn't true. I'd stuck it in my mind to get me moving, as I did with everything I decided to do, by setting a time frame.

'Brian and I are prepared to find sponsorship for you. You said when we joined you that any endorsements or advertising work that you get after the America walk would be split three ways [my attempt to make them feel like we were a team]. So, we've decided to put our resources together, that's two-thirds of what you make, and represent you as your agents in getting promotions work and sponsorship and handling your books and talk shows and marketing you. Actually, we'll need expenses on top of that, we'll need an office, secretary, phones . . . I mean you can't expect us to represent you from a pay phone, can you?'

'You can't expect us to pay our expenses out of pocket,' chipped in Brian.

'Actually, I think to cover those expenses, we'll need more like ninety-five per cent. We're not being out of line with this figure. Look at any agency and you'll see they take at least ninety-five per cent. [Which isn't true, but I didn't know that.] So, what do you say?'

'I'll think about it.'

'We're only giving you this offer once. You'll have to make your decision within the next week because these negotiations take months, but I'm prepared to add to my work load now to make sure things work out for you. I can't say fairer than that.'

Because I had been told for years that I was to blame, I assumed that they were being reasonable and I was being ungrateful. But I did not agree or disagree then, I thought about it. Despite the hundreds of people telling me that I was fantastic, what I really needed was a person who knew me, simply to nod their heads or raise an eyebrow, guiding me along the road. But I thought this need was weak. It didn't look like anyone else needed a guide. I'd chosen a road which had no guides; nobody had been there before me. One night, Brian told me that if at the end of it all he and Chris had made loads of money from me and I had nothing, he'd give me some of his. I realised I was being taken for the ride of my life and turned them down flat. If breaking up the walk to find more sponsorship meant the loss of the record as the first woman to walk around the world, I didn't care. I would not be manipulated.

We spent an evening with our clothing sponsor in Cincinnati. We'd had to leave the walk and drive down there but it was worth it to meet the people who had been so sympathetic to our individual needs. They'd send us packages along the way with new items they'd made up and I was especially grateful to them for adapting their sports range to suit the needs of a body doing one motion all day. In the high humidity, the relentless rubbing can become pretty uncomfortable.

Chris fell in love with the receptionist at first sight. Over the next few days Brian ribbed him mercilessly about it, but we had no idea what impression he'd had on her. By the end of the week, he took off for a two-day break to stay with her. When Brian called him, he said he was going to stay there for a few more days; he would be more productive with a telephone where people could call him back and he didn't have to worry about finding a pay phone and parking the car.

I was relieved at this. But it became harder to meet Chris's arrangements when he was even less aware of our needs. He'd set up press conferences in towns twenty-five miles apart but didn't take into consideration the time it took to walk between the two and the hours each demanded. We had to drive ahead, then drive back to carry on walking, but that meant we were falling behind. My lethargy was getting pretty bad; I'd wake up and feel exhausted. I couldn't keep my food down and I felt weepy.

I didn't know what special requirements the body needed after 1,000 miles; perhaps things change at this point and since we were 1,200 miles into the trip all this was unknown territory.

Finally Brian took me to a doctor. I explained what I was doing and how I felt and he ran various tests. One of them came back positive.

Pregnant.

I felt a rush of excitement. But then I put it in check: I did not love its father; at the age of eighteen I could not support it; having been on the move all my life I knew nothing about permanence and I couldn't even take care of a little kitten let alone a baby.

'Can you do an abortion?'

'You'll need to wait until the fetus is a certain size or the suction method might miss it.' He did some calculations and set a date for 3 December. Either he made a genuine mistake, or he did it deliberately in a state which was anti-abortion, because when the day came and I arrived at the abortion clinic, I was over four months' pregnant. It could have been done as early as six weeks.

Brian hugged me when I told him and even harder when I told him of my decision. He felt I had made the right one.

Now that I knew this lack of energy and sickness was not going to go away with any vitamin supplements or a change of diet, I felt it was a new battle: I had never fought one against the power of my own body. I was falling further behind schedule. Even though I was spending more time walking, I walked slower and covered less distance. The miles were piling up against press conferences we had to drive to, driving back to carry on till it got to a point where we were two or three days behind the receptions we attended. We called Chris and asked him to cancel and rearrange. Word got back to The Company of the cancellations. They threatened Chris they'd pull out. They thought we were not pulling our weight. I couldn't tell them why or they'd pull out immediately to protect their image and I felt a failure when Chris sniggered at how slow I had become.

Brian kept urging me to forget the few miles we'd have to drive back and just carry on from the press conference we'd done, but I wouldn't do it. My endurance ability was the only true thing about me. I had formed this; this was separate from all the confusion of right and wrong and who I should be. I'd made a promise to myself to do this walk; it was the only thing in my life which I had some control over to keep my dignity.

On the road one evening, I'd screamed at Brian over something trivial and he roared away up the hill and over the top. I felt completely beaten. If it was up to me I knew I could fight anyone who tried to stop me, but I couldn't fight myself. When I wanted to charge on, I threw up; when I tried to get a grip I'd start crying and I couldn't shake it off; I built up walls but they dissolved. For God's sake, women have fought battles when pregnant, why the hell can't you? Where's your strength now when there's a problem? But I couldn't answer that. Perhaps I would have had more patience and found more energy if my motivation had come directly from what I'd seen of the Africans' plight. As it was, I couldn't put a finger on why I was doing this; I couldn't revert to one simple line whenever things got too tough. No want, no willpower. I just knew, deep down, that I couldn't win. If I could not walk a marathon a day The Company would pull out, but even if I could push myself through it, there was still no guarantee that I could complete the walk because The Company could simply pull the plug on funding at any time. The success of the walk seemed to depend more on passifying a corporation than the ability to walk across America.

This power over me went very deep. It had entered my own place, dominated my own place: someone else was controlling me. If I got in the van and skipped out miles, I'd have a sponsor but no walk. If I gave up there would be failure, egg on my face and all the people who had brushed me off when I said I would walk across America would have won. I could not see a way forward, so I chose a way out.

When I walked up a hill on the road to Terre Haute, somewhere past Indianapolis, felt the evening wind on my face and saw the motor home silhouetted against the deep orange sunset, I did not know that when I stepped into it, drove to the press conference and did not drive back, that I would carry an even greater shame. I did not know how this would come back to haunt me nor what it would drive me to in later years, nor how it would mean I could never trust anyone or see them clearly for what they were doing, good or bad, because I had destroyed the only truth around which my reasoning and my sense of right and wrong had pivoted.

The moment I said to Brian, 'Let's do it,' I felt the gel in the air dissolve, all the push and grind disappear, all the angst and misery lifted and I started to laugh. And Brian was laughing too. Though I assured him that it would be this once, just thirty miles to make up the time and from there on I would make sure I kept to a schedule which I could manage, it happened again. When things got too hard, I just got in the van till I was walking very little at all, just on the approach to a town to do the interviews. A little bit further past the town and I'd jump in again, all through Illinois and Missouri and Oklahoma and Texas. Nobody knew, nobody was hurt, I rationalised, every aspect of the peripheral demands on me were satisfied: I wasn't rude to anyone, I got on with Brian, The Company was happy with my performance and now that I was less stressed, I spoke more rationally and money actually came in. Perversely, when I cheated, I actually liked myself for the first time in my life.

Walking, while everyone else was driving, brought out the worst in me, and I'd hated myself. Now I was singing. I made a place in the motor home, took care of Brian, cooked wonderful food, swept up, went shopping, had wild sex with him, heard him say that he was madly in love with me and felt that I was really home, that I had something to contribute and I was needed. Perhaps the hormones in me then simply added to this and I'd never felt happier or more wholly feminine.

And I lied to protect this place.

On the morning of Thursday 3 December at 5.30 a.m. I got up and showered and washed my hair then put on my yellow woollen dress to prepare for the oncoming pain. Brian hugged me. But I didn't want him to. Hugging made me collapse inside. I pushed him away quite gently and squeezed his hand, giving him a wink and a smile. We found the building at last; it was hidden behind some trees and the sign was obscured by flowers and shrubs.

I walked up to the reception desk and said, 'Good morning. My name is Miss F. Campbell and I have a 7.30 appointment.'

The woman said, 'What?'

'What do you mean "what"?'

'Wait in the waiting room and fill out a consent form.'

The room was packed with young women. The ones with their mothers looked the most vulnerable. Perhaps they were there to try to take away their daughter's pain, but, like lifting off the shell of the struggling chick, they'd only be hurting her more if she walked out of there without building her own emotional muscles. If I were a predator, I would have gone for them, despite the mother hen.

During my counselling they took a test to see how far pregnant I was. The nurse came back in and showed the doctor the results.

'You are seventeen weeks pregnant. We only do terminations up to the fifteenth week. But we can try. It'll cost you more. Instead of $340, we'll have to charge you $470.'

Opportunist pigs, I thought. I bet they say that to all the girls.

'OK.'

We watched a film of what would happen and were then issued with appointment times. Mine was 2.45 p.m. We went back to the RV; I read a magazine. Whenever Brian tried to comfort me by putting a hand on mine I felt myself cracking up.

By 2.50 p.m. I was dressed in a white gown and was lying on the operating table. I knew that I must keep my head, so when the nurses asked me where I came from, I didn't spit out that I didn't come from anywhere; instead I told them 'from Scotland, the land of the haggis'.

'What's a haggis?' asked one of the nurses as she checked my blood pressure. So began the story of the small furry animal while the Argentinian doctor clamped my vagina open so that he could feel the size of the fetus. It felt like a forced deep entry. Then came the prick-pull feeling of a crochet hook on the walls of my vagina – this was the local anaesthetic. I felt a gentle pull on my womb. The operation began. The doctor made the comment that there was a large lump to be removed. My baby was big.

'. . . and all the males have a short left leg so they can run around the hills anticlockwise and the females have a short right leg . . . '

The instrument broke and a gasp of 'oh shit' from the doctor. Everything went quiet. He pulled the tool out, mended it, sent it in again and carried on.

'. . . so they run around clockwise. This helps when they want to meet and have a chat. If you want to catch a haggis, all you have to do is push him over and he'll roll down the hill where you can collect him and carry him easily to your car.' I felt drips of wetness around the area. I asked if it was the lubricating gel melting.

'It's blood, dear, you're bleeding quite a lot.' Actually, I was pissing blood throughout the operation and continued to do so for eight days. When it was done I rested a minute and then got up and dressed to wait for Brian in the recovery area. The nurses were fussing but I'd had enough. I wanted to get out of there.

That night I cramped. I dealt with it practically, got up, drank water, changed my sanitary towel several times, put more blankets on the bed. The following day, I felt much better but the most painful side effects hadn't even begun. We were in Clovis, New Mexico. We parked the RV up at a garage to get the motor-bike fixed. I watched Brian through the window as he walked over the concrete deck. He greeted the mechanic. They were jovial; they chatted; they laughed. I suddenly felt sullen. I felt like I was six years old at the door of the convent boarding school, beside the ivy, and my parents in their smart clothes were saying, 'Come on lovey, cheer up, you'll make lots of friends and we'll be back in seven short weeks. Come on, buck up. You're a big girl now and you're very strong. And you've got your new writing kit, you can send us letters every week.'

But all I was thinking was, 'I will never think of you when you walk out those gates. And I swear I will never leave one of my own out in the cold.'

And now, that's exactly what I had done.

I didn't want to stop crying. Some time later that night I got off the sofa, worn out and dehydrated, and cleaned myself up. I put on a clean nightie and got into bed beside Brian. He rested his head on my chest but, even though his hair was dry, he was making me wet. I lifted his head and saw that it was milk. I didn't cry. I simply thought, 'It's better this way, or my child would be conscious when I'd have to leave it.'

The next day the weather was perfect and the land was gloriously flat on the first day that I got out of the motor home, never to ride in it or cheat again and started walking, twenty-two miles before Fort Sumner, where Billy the Kid is buried. Chris returned and slept all day. We stopped for lunch and there was a knock at the door. It was a man bearing a single red rose in a white vase with a card saying, 'Thanks from millions.' He had been searching for us on the highways of the Midwest for several days.

Only now, as I write this eleven years later, do I understand who that man was and why he had come.

The weather that day was a freak break in the sub-zero temperatures which swung down from the Arctic along the west coast and across the southern belt of the States. We'd experienced minus ten degrees during the nights and rarely a day above zero. Now that I was walking fully again, I needed winter clothing. But the fortnightly instalment had not come through at the Western Union up in Alberquerque. The receipts had been sent, including the one for the abortion, which was discreetly written out as a medical expense. Chris flew back on his return ticket to Cincinnati because, he said, there was no media to contact across the desert and he could start organising the arrival in Los Angeles far better from a desk with a phone. Even though I objected to the use of sponsorship money to fly back to see his girlfriend, I wasn't in any position to question him and besides, the dynamics were better this way.

One morning after a night which was so cold it felt like there was snow at the bottom of the bed, I stepped out to begin the day as Brian started the engine to follow me. But it was dead. All three batteries had gone. The petrol was frozen; the water was frozen; the waste pipe was frozen. And we were twenty miles from the nearest phone. But the motor-bike worked. We couldn't get help until the money came through from The Company, so Brian rode off to Alberquerque to wait for it to come in. I carried on walking, taking water and the last of the food with me. Brian would pick me up later in the day.

The road was so frozen that I could only slide along it. I wondered, strangely, if this would affect the record – that I was sliding instead of walking. It didn't occur to me that I had cheated on and off for 1,200 miles. In fact, I'd locked away those thoughts so deeply that I did not acknowledge it at all.

When Brian eventually roared up to me, my first thought was whether he had some food, forgetting that he hadn't eaten a thing all day himself. But there was nothing. The money hadn't come through even though The Company said they'd wired it. He took me back to our frozen motor home. We had nothing to eat except a small box of Oxo cubes. No water; no heat to cook them on. Had I actually walked that distance, I would have built up a bank of self-reliance and resourcefulness and would have gathered some wood, lit a fire and made Oxo soup. As it was, I was too busy hunting around for someone to blame and we went hungry. Without food, it was pointless to carry on walking until we had some money. It was the right decision, in light of the snow storm outside, and the next morning we made a treacherous journey on the motor-bike to Albuquerque. After four days of doing this, the money finally came through. The raised cheque had been sitting at the bottom of someone's in-tray because she didn't know what to do with it.

We bought food, winter clothing and had the motor home towed to Clovis to get it thawed out.

I set off again, from the place where I'd stopped near Fort Sumner. It felt good to be out there, breezing through the miles, feeling the rhythm which came from a virtually untouched desert. I felt sensual again. With the shortened days, I walked through the dusk and into night to keep up the distance as we had to arrive in LA on 5 January.

One night, walking beside the monster, chatting with Brian, we were talking about the receipts. He let something slip: 'Yeah, it's been really hard to cover up the money we've been sending home.'

'What? What money? How much?'

'About $200 a month.'

'What for?'

'To pay my mortgage. Don't get on your high horse. You've just had a $470 abortion.'

'That's different.'

'Somehow I think The Company would see it as being very different too.'

64

'You fucking deceitful shit. No wonder that money didn't come through.'

'Who are you calling a deceitful shit? You fat slag.'

He roared off into the night. I expected him to calm down in a while and come back, but he didn't. I had no idea where the nearest town was and even though a few cars passed me I was not about to hitch in the night. It was pretty cold and very dark but I could feel what I was passing by the temperature of the air: where it was warmer I'd pass high rocks, then colder where they fell away to a ravine in the mesa. I started to get worried: worried about Brian having an accident, worried about freezing up, so I started to run, the sanitary pad rubbing away.

Some time later, I saw lights on the horizon. It took an infuriatingly long time to reach them. It was a village. I expected to see the motor home parked up outside the bar, but there was nothing. I went in and asked if there was an RV park in town.

'No. Nearest one is twenty-five miles away.' Had anyone seen a Fleetwood motor home? No. They saw that I was in some distress so they pointed me in the direction of the police station. There I explained that I'd had an argument with my boyfriend and he'd driven away – I couldn't think of how else to explain losing a thirty-three-foot motor home.

We got in the police car and began driving up and down the road. Nothing. The cop knew this area well and said there weren't any other roads. By pure chance, we spotted Brian speeding in the opposite direction, heading for Los Angeles. The cop put on his lights, pulled him over, but didn't book him for speeding. When he'd gone and we'd parked up off the road, Brian insisted that I apologise. I wouldn't. He thumped my face, demanding an apology. I was furious and lashed out at him. He ducked out the door. I locked it behind him then ran around in a blind panic locking the windows. I'd just secured the last of them when I turned round. Brian was inside standing right behind me. I screamed.

He reached out and took his helmet then unlocked the door and roared away on the bike. I closed and locked the sunroof hatch where he'd come in and started pumping myself up with self-righteousness. The more often I did this, the further I buried my own deceit.

When he finally came back, I had no solid rock to stand on. I fell into subservience and apologised.

Over the Rockie Mountains, across the plains of Joshua Tree, past pink adobi houses and electricity generating windmills, I walked with my chin in the air. Chris had come back and was buzzing around again, trying to get people enthused in LA to welcome me and, if we announced how little we'd raised, perhaps someone would come forward with a massive donation. But nobody, not even the BBC, was interested. They said, 'She hasn't achieved enough.'

Haven't achieved enough? What the fuck do they want? I was incensed, strutting out every day, waving my banner of righteous indignation about media scum and how millions of people were dying because even walking across the USA wasn't enough to get people to sit up and take note and be moved at the commitment someone else had made to lend a hand.

Even though nobody else knew what I had done, or hadn't done, somehow they wouldn't come to the party.

The Company didn't want any media attention at the end because we had raised so little money. Though we didn't know exactly how little because the donations went straight to the Live Aid Trust, we had a fair idea that it wasn't much more than $10,000. The trip had cost The Company $50,000. Even though their sponsorship came from a promotions budget, which is how they saw the worth of the walk, they didn't want the media demanding to know why, if they were supporting a good cause, The Company hadn't simply donated that amount instead of funding the walk. It would suggest that The Company was using the Africans' plight to promote themselves.

Chris wouldn't accept defeat in the face of all this lack of interest. He kept trying and when he wouldn't give in he was sent a massive thump. He had a car accident. The Bronco was totalled but the battery of the car he hit exploded into the face of the woman driver. She was blinded. Fortunately she made a complete recovery in hospital. At least the hand that sent the thump is somewhat selective. Now Chris had no transport to run around and drum up activity and, of course, Rob refused to pay for a hire car.

As I walked the last day through Los Angeles, Brian and Chris were called to an emergency meeting with The Company at a hotel in town. I expect they wanted to make damn sure the motor home was not in sight in case any media turned up. I walked alone down Pico Boulevard, drumming up my martyrdom till I saw the blue triangle between the sandy coloured buildings. Down the concrete landing strip and onto the white sand with its sea breezes. I took off my shoes, felt the heat on the wet soles, chugged out across the sand and, on the water's edge, I knelt down and cried.

But I couldn't really feel. I'd wiped it all out, all that it was and all that it could have been. So I acted as I cried.

After all, wasn't that what everyone else was doing?

6

J stood there on the moor with his mouth open.

'You mean, you cheated?'

I didn't reply. I had nothing more to say. I'd spilled my guts. Thudding now on uneven ground, jarring my spine.

There was a shiny Coke can in the tufty grass. I picked it up, put it in my basket. Its contents spilled out on the weave. It was black. It stank. It burned my nostrils. I moved past J, he caught a whiff and roared, 'Get rid of it!'

Over the rubbly track, up the grassy bank and down the other side, steeply through the stunted ash to the rocky bottom. There was a cavern in the hillside, dark and damp, an endless pit deep down into the catacombs of the underworld. I tossed the can into the hole. But the stench remained on my hands.

Further down into the ravine, a small stream trickled in a dried out river bed. We followed along the rocky bank, over the metal catchment mesh, under the stony bridge, through the slimy pools onto the mossy boulders and out the other side. The stream was wider here. I slipped down on my haunches and rinsed my hands. I glanced around for some soapwort till I realised I couldn't remember what it looks like. J was plopping pebbles under the illusion that they were skimming across the surface.

I gathered mushrooms. I was no longer selective.

The bank opened out to a grazing plain; the earth clods were rounder with cup-shaped hollows. Tucked inside, I saw a rabbit.

He did not move. I stamped above him. He jerked. Scuttled further back. I squatted down over him. His eyelids were glued together.

'Mixxie rabbit, J.'

'I'm not doing it.'

'Why not? You're a man, aren't you?'

'Fuck that. Let's go up to the cottage and get ya gun.'

'No, if we go we won't come back.'

Heavy stones take several blows; each swing needs more of what I did not have. Rabbit twitched; his head was down. I slipped my fingers under him and pulled him out of the hole. He shuffled then lay still in the crook of my arms. He was hot. I stroked back his silken ears. He was suffering slow death where adrenaline could not kill his pain. Man had denied him his final rush, the highest rush of adrenaline to carry him out of his body.

The only thing preventing him right now from peace, was my fear. Fear of not doing it properly, inflicting more pain, chickening out, running away, leaving him a blood pulp still twitching. I had the means to put him out of his own misery.

'Are you really going to kill it?' I stroked the ears. 'C'mon Fleabee, forget it. Let's go.'

I lifted up the rabbit to my face where I could smell him. But all I could smell was my own stench. I stroked him. I wished I could walk away from him. I didn't want to hurt him. It would take more courage, though, to take his pain away than to leave him to die in agony. I whispered to him, 'It'll be better next time.'

I stepped into the stream, bent down and plunged him under the water. He struggled. I gripped his rib cage. He was thrashing, didn't know there was still so much fight left in him. He lay still. I held him there a bit. Then lifted him up. He struggled again, I plunged him under. He was fighting me, scrabbling, thousands of bubbles. I desperately wanted to stop. Again he was still. I held him down, counting to sixty. I lifted him up. Oh God! Please die will you! I plunged him down again. Down to the bottom and stood there.

I could feel the change.

Back at the cottage J was next door watching *Shallow Grave* on video while assembling the paraphernalia on the coffee table. My word processor was over by the window, softly whirring. Like wiping away the condensation on the bathroom mirror, I saw through the fug a very distinctive V-shape in front of me. I was standing on the apex of the V and there were two paths to choose from: either I could walk towards the door to the sitting-room and get a hit, or I could walk towards my WP, switch it off and leave. From somewhere inside my cluttered head, a single line came into focus: 'Choose the hardest path. You'll regret it if you don't and if you fail at least you've tried.' Alison Hargreaves's words, our finest mountaineer, before she was killed in an avalanche on K2.

I didn't tarry. I knew if I thought about it I wouldn't do it. I walked over to the computer, switched it off, unplugged all the leads, wound them up, pulled out the carrying bag and packed each piece into the fitted sections. I gathered up all the papers with their dopey scribblings, all the mail answered or not and the faxes read or not and dumped them in a box. I pulled all of the hoover out of the under-stair cupboard, but as I tried to shove it between the chair legs I stopped. Come on, do it properly; you must do things properly now. I pulled the chairs out of the way and hoovered under the table. I bent to pick up a pen and my back let off a blasted rebuke. Come on, bend your knees, stand up with your thighs. You must protect your back now because you *will* be alive this time next year. I went out and got the wheelbarrow, filled it with wood, bobbing up and down with my thighs, pushed it through the door into the dining-room, restocked the basket, then wheeled it out. I went into the kitchen, pulled out the dustpan and brush and opened the iron doors of the stove.

'Hey, Fi? What you doing?' J shuffled into the dining-room in his socks. In one hand he offered me a joint, in the other he waved a foil wand, raising his eyebrows and flicking his head invitingly towards the sitting room. I was kneeling down. I took up the brush and swept out the hearth.

'I'm going.'

'What?'

'I can't stand the shame.'

'Come on, sit down, let's talk about this. Why don't you finish your book and then go?'

'I can't write the bloody book. What am I supposed to write? Oh what a hero I am that I never gave up? And what the hell do I know of the world for Chrissakes? Wasn't I the one with my head down, plodding along the road?'

'Hey, just cool it will you?' He pulled on the joint, holding his head down. Keeping it in he stretched out to pass it on to me.

'Didn't anyone ever tell you, J, that drugs are not the answer?'

'Yeah but,' he wheezed, sucked in deeply then let it out and moved his body round to flick the crumbling ash, 'running away isn't either.'

As I routinely went from room to room, stripping the sheets, noting down the food I'd used from the store cupboard, putting things back where they'd been, I made my escape list. The biggest thing I had to get out of was writing the book.

Yvette Goulden, my editor at Orion, agreed to put back publication for the third time. I wasn't at all sure that I would ever come back but something told me not to burn my bridges. I'd need to tell Neil Hanson that I wanted to write the book on my own. He'd postponed another book he was working on to help me with mine and he needed the money – his wife Lynn was expecting their second child. But Neil was down in London doing a publishers' 'meet 'n' greet' for his next project with Mark Lucas our agent. I left messages to call me but their schedules were too tight. He'd be back on Thursday. Do I pack up and leave a note in true FC fashion, or do I waste three days staying here and explain face to face? I started to justify leaving now and writing a note, that he was a good guy and he'd understand. But then this other person in my head quite calmly reminded me that every decision you make must be accountable for, not to others because they'll have their own reasons for trying to undermine your confidence, but as evidence when you wake up at 4 a.m. and the inner critics begin their courtroom drama. Thursday it is then.

I put my motor-bike in the barn, wrote out a bunch of Friends of the Earth redirection stickers for my mail, then took a box of chocolates over to Neil and Lynn when he got back. I really didn't want to do this to them but in a way I resented liking them: it added an intangible obstruction to the process of moving on which I could not cross off my action list. Neil made it worse by being so decent about it. I went round to see his cousin's wife next door to leave cheques for the phone at their cottage I'd rented. All this incestuous stuff felt like I'd been walking down a country path, quite happily, minding my own business, when I was grabbed by the arm of a bramble, then another, till I was stuck in the hedge.

I drove for six hours through the rain to London without mushrooms. The sense of control was a novelty.

It took me two days to pack up the hundreds of pounds' worth of comfort-buying junk in my rented warehouse on the river and call a removal guy who stacked the stuff into a storage depot. I went to see Emma Rogers, my booker, who took care of all the appearance requests and talks. I left several signed cheques with her for bills, parking tickets, speeding fines and court cases, then called all the engagements I had, apologised, said there was nothing I could do, but I'd try to make it up to them.

I left a box of receipts with my accountant, went to see my bank manager for a loan against future royalties, then bought travel insurance and a ticket on the next available flight out.

I took the depot padlock key round to 87's, but he was at work.

I was glad of this. Saying goodbye requires a certain charisma which, as I stood there on Tuesday morning, I did not possess. 87 was now a veteran of the motor-bike courier circuit in London. For ten years he'd been riding around in circles chasing his pennies, but what he lacked in sense of direction (which is an ongoing source of amusement between us) he made up for in speed and agility. Amazingly, in all that time of doing U-turns he'd never had a serious accident. I hated hearing him remind me of it. He needed a piece of wood. I cut the artificial sinew cord around my neck and threaded a new one I'd braided for him through my own piece of wood. This I slipped into the envelope. Like many seemingly stupid superstitions, this had a logical reason: every time he felt it tap on his chest, he would remember to respect the road.

It had taken me seven days to cut all the brambles. This, I thought, is the measure of growing older: I used to be able to escape the same day.

I got high with my sister and her flatmate on my last night and went to bed very early suffering from paranoia. I could hear them talking about me, as you think you do, but decided not to listen. No matter what was said, the inner critics were bound to extract what they wanted and replay the sound bites as indisputable facts. I knew my shame, that was enough.

Lastly, I went to see Nan. Nan is half native American Indian. I hadn't told her I was going, but when I was five minutes late she had a very strong sense that I'd left the country. We talked a while about other things. Her soothing presence, with her hands resting on her lap, sometimes lifting up to touch her neck, tilting her head when I knew a gem was coming from somewhere in her life, teased out the knots till the strands of my anxieties were more manageable. Nan is not my grandmother; all my grandparents are dead. But if I didn't have her to talk to, I'd have to turn to books and TV for advice.

There was once a wise man who had the power to guide sinners to absolution. Two men came to him who were consumed with the lies they had told. He asked them to 'gather a stone for each lie and bring them to me. Be very honest as you select them, think about the size of each one.' The first man set off and diligently over days thought of each lie he had told and picked up pebbles for porkies and rocks for stonkers. He brought back a barrowload and laid them out in front of the wise man. The second man returned several days later pushing an enormous boulder, far bigger than he was and they stood together, the first man feeling better by comparison. 'Now,' said the wise man, 'go and put them back exactly where you found them.'

'What can I bring you, Nan?'

'Bring me a stone,' she said.

7

I had liked airports. The fence between pastures. I had liked my life ordered in blocks, each block separated by a flight. And if you don't like one, just throw it away; there'll always be another. But that was when I had assumed the rocket fuel which drove me would never run out and that space was flat and infinite. Now that I was slowing down, looking for a place to land and settle, I had glanced back with horror: instead of flying around as a full form of all my experiences, I was actually a cloud of debris without any adhesive motive or understanding to pull all the pieces together. As I was, even if I saw Utopia below me, I could not land.

In the early days, I had changed my character every six months or so at each new school. When I left home, I changed with each person and each job. On a walk I would change with each driver and that was manageable; but when I had become well known and suddenly there were scores of people out there to please, I couldn't keep up with the demands and I felt like I was performing a stream of subliminal advertising images, flashing and changing every few seconds. Pretence takes a huge amount of energy and when at the end of the performance I had not reached my climax and been accepted, I just blew out. And although many celebrities I met said they had the same problem, at least they could go home to people who knew them as themselves.

I had to get away from every opportunity to act, go to a place where I was not known, where I was not followed or filmed or interpreted and just open my eyes to what I actually saw. I made a pact as I walked down the aisle of the plane to grab hold of my very first observation before I chopped it up to fit the character I was playing at the time. Since I was alone, with nobody providing a mould to squeeze into, I might be able to fit my pieces together as they were meant to be, to see what I had actually witnessed. And these truths would be me, would form the binding of the satellite debris which I trailed, so that I could be whole and I could land.

As I looked for my seat, I scanned the predominantly male, middle-eastern passengers hoping I wouldn't be seated next to one of them. They looked up at me, hoping the opposite. I found my seat at the back beside one of two other white females.

I sat down. We said hello. I asked her what she'd been up to in England. I listened to her stories of travelling around Europe as she flicked invisible bits off her blouse. Her fingernails were manicured and perfectly white but she had the most godawful spots on her face. She must hate those spots, I thought, and felt for her. No matter how much she cleaned her skin, they simply wouldn't go away. When she ran out of stories after an hour or so, instead of asking me what I was doing on the flight she put on her headphones. This is interesting, I thought. This is like being an observer of myself.

She pulled off her headphones almost immediately and I thought she was going to turn to me and apologise for being so rude. Instead she pulled over the hostess.

'My system's not working.' She didn't offer any suggestion as to what she wanted to do about it – just as I wouldn't've. The hostess tried but she couldn't get it to work. The girl pulled out the airline questionnaire and started filling it in quite forcefully. This is déjà vu. So often I had put strangers on pedestals because it's hard to see their failings, and I'd been intimidated by them. Now that I was making an effort really to watch, I could see quite clearly what was going on and what I could do about it. I got up and tried every console in every spare seat until, beside a white guy, I found one that worked. She went and sat in it; she did not thank me. I really didn't like her now. How quickly that happens!

I got comfortable in both seats. Five minutes later she was back.

'That man stinks,' she said. I moved over and she sat down. I wondered what she would do if I offered her a smoke. She took one. She took two more off me over the next two hours, but she did not offer me one of hers. Oh my God, this is me; I'm sitting next to myself. What happens next?

The in-flight video map flicked on to the screen. Normally I hate those things: I hate seeing how far we've got to go; but now that I was settling down to enjoy the real in-flight entertainment, I was quite pleased there was so much time. I wanted to know what happens to a girl on the move, meeting people she knows she'll never meet again. It doesn't register when you're young because the

world seems infinite and opens up more with air travel, allowing us
vagrants to move more easily from one pasture to the next, hunt-
ing for acceptance, gathering our injustices, because it can't be us,
there can't be something wrong with us. But what happens next?

I got impatient for her to do something else, but hey, why wait?
I had ten years of video tape in my head to watch and though it
had been edited by a sense of self-protective injustice at the time, I
felt the honesty hadn't been entirely erased and if I was brutal
about it, I might just see the bigger picture. So I settled back with
a smoke and a scotch, closed my eyes and rolled the tape on a film
called 'The Girl Who Thought The World Was Flat'.

Straight after the trans-America walk, Brian and I had stayed in
Santa Barbara with a group of expats he'd known from
Bracknell. Neither of us wanted to go back to Britain: it was
January and warm in California and I'd had enough of walking to
start drumming up sponsorship for the next leg. He hired a car and
taught me to drive. I passed a very easy test on an automatic which
allowed me to drive anything. After a week, when talk of my journey at parties only stopped conversation, I hired a stick shift trans-
mission and taught myself to drive it in a flash flood on the way to
Los Angeles. I needed a job, a place to live and a car of my own, but
I was broke. I stopped at a gas station on the outskirts of town,
thumbed through the yellow pages and got an appointment with a
nanny agency in Beverly Hills. Got to start somewhere.

Claudia was one of those very physical Californian babes who
seemed to be having an orgasm every time she said her name.
Perhaps it helped her to be good at her job because within an hour
she got me an interview with a screen writer I'll call Roger who had
written a couple of major films. He and his wife, I'll call her Sally,
had two children: Bobby aged five and Amy aged two and a half.

I drove through Beverly Hills along the wide, palm tree lined
boulevards and up into Brentwood where giant white houses stood
snottily and privately on high. I am down here and you are up there.
But by the end of the day, I thought, I will be up there with you.

I sat on the edge of the fifteen-seater sofa in the sunken living-
room, occasionally glancing out to the pool and jacuzzi and avoided
any mention of my walk. Employers don't like itchy feet in their
employees, especially when it comes to their kids. There was a scrabbling noise and Amy shuffled out of her room, clasping several dum-
mies in her sticky fingers. She was crumpled and confused and when

Roger scooped her up, she studied me from the safety of his arms then spun round and buried her head in his shoulder. He patted her bottom; it rustled with each tap.

When she looked at me again I didn't smile, I stared. She loved it and I got the job.

That night I stayed with a friend of a friend at Malcolm McLaren's house. There was one girl who was particularly strange. She'd start saying something with great enthusiasm, but then trail off to a whisper, then silence as she stared at the wall. I later found out that she'd been hitching around Mexico with a girlfriend till they caught a lift with a bunch of Americans who were returning home. At the border, a guard wanted to search the car. The driver refused. One of the guys in the back started screaming to 'do him'. He pulled out a gun and fired at the guard. They were caught very quickly; the car was searched and they were all arrested for massive heroin smuggling. She'd spent four years in a Mexican prison. She was raped every night.

On my first day Sally showed me round the house. She was warm and open but slightly vulnerable, slightly suspicious, stopping every so often to ask me to repeat something which could be taken either way till she was happy about where I was coming from. They'd been in marriage therapy since the day after their wedding. As she showed me her laundry system, she demonstrated how she liked the towels to be folded – in threes, starting from the outside edge. So, this is what it's come to? I've just walked across America and look what I'm doing now. Hey, don't knock it, this is a stepping stone and a very comfortable one too.

John Hillaby had sent me a contact name and address at Dent & Sons publishers in London. I wrote a synopsis of the journey, omitting any indication of my abortion or that I had cheated; in fact, I'd blocked it out so thoroughly from my memory I didn't even think about it. The basis of the conflict was between the almighty corporation threatening to pull out and the courageous walker, trying to do good for others. I sent it off and waited for their reply.

Neither of the children liked cleaning their teeth at night. So I got a couple of boxes which they could stand on to watch themselves in the mirror. I took my own toothbrush, held it like a microphone and announced, 'And now ladies and gentlemen, please put your hands together for a big Californian welcome, our very own Ammmazing Amy!' I clapped in rhythm while Bobby did percussion on his teeth as Amy jiggled in front of the mirror. We did the 'California Brushing

Song': 'I got those, can't get enough of those, brush brush blues . . .'
with the chorus of 'sh, sh-sh, sh, sh-sh-sh' from all of us with our
toothbrushes. They loved it: they'd race to get their boxes after bath-
time, which sped up the bedtime routine, allowing me time to get
ready and go out.

Nightlife in LA is good as long as you get an introduction into it.
My introduction came as the result of a bizarre set of circumstances
which seemed to begin when the price of soap in Guatamala almost
trebled overnight. Shuna had been staying with my uncle and his
family who ran tea and coffee plantations there. She was taking care
of their kids but when the government increased the prices to cover
their debt, the maids started stealing the soap. The staff were fired
and Shuna was in the antisocial position of having to do all the
housework. She didn't like it. I flew down there for a weekend to
persuade her to come back with me. It was a crazy trip, especially the
flight back, which made an unscheduled stop in Mexico City to
offload a stray piece of baggage. When they blew it up, they blew up
a bomb inside it. Everyone clapped when we finally landed in LA.

On the night Shuna arrived in LA, we went out on the razz and
met a bunch of UCLA students in Westwood. Sam was very different from the others, not only because of his incredible size – he'd
once been bullied as a child and had fought back by building up his
muscles – but because of his face, which seemed to look like different people in different lights. One minute he was the spitting image
of Sean Penn, the next he was David Letterman. As I got talking with
him, I found that he was a writer. Naively, I considered myself to be
one too as I'd just had a letter back from Dent asking for some sam-
ple chapters. He also wanted to act. A couple of nights later, on a
date together, we were walking past the cinemas and yogurt fast food
joints when I turned on him, quite out of the blue and said: 'I'm not
putting up with that shit. I've got my rights.'

He immediately caught on. 'I don't give a shit. You'll do as I say.'

'I will not. If you want to go sowing your oats all over town and
expect me to be waiting for you with your eggs and your bacon and
your shirts and hand over *my* free samples of Durex ribbed extra fine,
you've got another think coming.' And I stormed off. He ran after me,
grabbed my arm, swung me round and shouted in my face, 'Now look
here you stuck-up little sleaze bag, who was it who pulled you off the
streets in the first place?' I slapped his face; he slapped me back.

A police car pulled over, a uniform sprang out, pulled Sam off me
and asked 'Ma'am, is this guy bothering you?'

He later described our relationship as the most turbulent and dangerous of his life.

Bobby had been pissing in his cupboard at night. Every morning I'd find various containers in there full of urine. Roger and Sally figured they'd been putting him under too much negative pressure. When he got in from school there was a series of 'don'ts' – don't leave your boots there, don't play ball against the side of the house, don't stick pebbles up your sister's private parts. And this was his way of rebelling. So they decided not to end the sermon with a 'don't' but with 'but you can do this instead . . .' I was impressed with their concern for their children.

One night before going out, I put Bobby to bed and read him a story. Sally and Roger came in to kiss him good night while I slipped out to clean up the toothpaste spray in the bathroom. I overheard them talking to him. 'It's all right, there's nothing out there to be scared of, nothing's waiting to get you. We're here to protect you.' Then they turned out the light and closed the door. Christ! His imagination is immediately racing around drumming up images of what they're protecting him against. No wonder he's pissing in the cupboard: he's too scared to go to the loo.

The whole California therapy ethos dissolved right there for me and with it my interest in the job. I decided to leave and get another one.

I stayed with Sam while I went to interviews but when nothing turned up we decided to fly up to San Francisco to spend Christmas with his family. Even though they were Jewish and didn't celebrate the occasion, we knew we'd have a good time. At the check-in counter, I put my luggage on the conveyor belt, keeping my 'precious' bag with me which contained my jewellery, my passport, my Dictaphone diary tapes, my witness book and the negatives of the walks photos (I'd given the prints to Brian). I put it on the floor as I handed over my ticket. Minutes later, I bent to pick it up. It was gone. Stupidly, I didn't think of looking in the dustbins around the airport, where it would probably have been left after the jewellery and the passport had been taken. Looking back on it now, it seems like divine intervention. Without those tapes, of course, I couldn't write the book and put the lies in print.

I finally got a job, with Ted Danson. Funny really, that I'd watched him in *Cheers* on Saturday nights when I babysat in Aberdeenshire and wondered whether he was actually real. His wife Cassie had hired me to take care of their two daughters aged six and one and a half.

Now that the idea of writing a book had been scrapped, I turned my attention to another project. Ever since I was a little girl, I had wanted to live in a cave, wear skins and gather berries. On the day I'd finished the UK walk, Lucy Irvine had flown in from her year as a castaway, living from the land on the Torres Straites island of Tuin. I'd read her book and now that I was living on the edge of the Pacific, I wanted to put my dream into practice and find an island of my own. I didn't want to go alone so, like G. Kingsland, I advertised for a co-habit. The ad was supposed to come out on a Tuesday and I gave my phone number as my private line in my bedroom. The day before, on my day off, I drove up to Death Valley in the Arizona desert in a new car I'd bought to give it a spin. It was a stupid place to go to test drive a secondhand car because it's one of the hottest places on earth and miles from anywhere. I had two blow outs and ended up having to walk into Nevada to get help. When I got back, late that night, Cassie was sitting up waiting for me. The phone hadn't stopped ringing. The ad had come out on the wrong day. She'd answered every call. She was furious that I'd given out the number of a phone in their house (not that I'd stuck a line in the ad saying, 'Hey guys, this is the home of the Danson family') and she fired me.

I called Sam. He agreed to let me stay but at that time he was living in his fraternity house so I had to sneak in after lights out and disappear early in the morning. I hunted for jobs but nobody wanted to employ me. It didn't strike me that maybe word had got around at the agency that I couldn't hold a job. Sam moved into a flatshare with a Chinese acrobat who, even when he was slightly drunk and fell off buildings, never seemed to hurt himself because he 'landed athletically' and a heavily-tanned macho who handed out towels to bunny girls at the Heffner mansion swimming pool. It was around this time that Sam decided he didn't want me to go off for a year on an island with someone else; he wanted to come with me. And that was when he entered the dangerous world of my childhood.

Whenever I spoke of the island, I began with, 'When I get to the island I'm going to . . .' and he'd interject with, 'What are you saying?'

And I'd think, hang on, what do you want me to say here?

'I said when I get . . .'

'Don't you mean when *we* get to the island?'

'Yes.' Phew, that's what he wants. 'When *we* get to the island.'

But a few days later I'd make the mistake again. I couldn't understand how some people seemed to be able to keep up the pretence all the time and never put a foot wrong. Why couldn't I do that? While I was chastising myself over clumsy mistakes, Sam was grappling with the implications. He kept wanting to know if I cared for him, demanding me to repeat the words, 'Sam and I are going to the island *together*.' One time, when I kept making mistakes, he shoved my ice cream up my nose.

I stormed out after that in a blaze of self-righteous indignation and found myself on the beach without any money, a place to stay or a job. I quite liked it, repeated my challenge: look where you are; now get yourself out. Within a week I was sipping champagne in a jacuzzi looking out over the Beverly Hills with a brand new Ford Bronco in the drive and $200 in my purse. I'd got a job with a woman who'd married for money, had a kid to secure her income then divorced the old codger. She was having difficulties keeping her dignity. She kept telling me never to marry for money because she was so rich, guys were too intimidated to date her and she felt she had to kiss her ex's ass for every penny.

I took her son out for a pizza and got chatting with one of the waitresses. She was an Australian model/actress who had married to get into the country and we saw each other in the evenings sometimes and spoke on the phone each night.

During my spare time, I was making some headway in finding an island. I'd spoken to Lucy Irvine, who'd pointed me in the direction of Fiji where she knew there were thousands of uninhabited islands, some of which had fresh water. I'd spent several days in one of the best map libraries on earth, selecting an island through a process of elimination. I wrote to the Fijian Tourist Board with my suggested list and got a letter back from them with the name of the chiefs I'd need to contact for permission. I'd begun to gather my equipment and even though I'd advertised again, I hadn't met anyone suitable – that is, anyone I really fancied, if truth were known.

One night, Sam called me up and asked me to go out to dinner with him. He took me to a very special restaurant on the beach. After dinner, as we sat there in the evening breeze with the palm trees and the waves, he pulled out a poem he'd written entitled, 'If you will be my Queen' and he read, 'I am a humble man, my dreams are small and insignificant compared to yours of a kingdom, but I hold them sacred . . . tonight I'll feel like a King if you will accept a Queen's crown of diamonds . . .' and he reached into his jacket pocket. I jumped, for some reason expecting him to pull out a blunt instrument with which to bludgeon my head so that I could see the twinkling diamonds he was referring to. Instead, he laid a velvet box on the table. I opened it. Nestled inside was a ring encrusted with gems. I pulled it out. The diamonds reached all the way round. I suddenly felt like he was taking the piss; I don't know this scene. What do you want me to do? Who do you want me to be? Give me a clue? He looked so sincere, no hint of contempt. I didn't want him, but maybe I did. Somewhere in there, I found a movie scene and adopted it. I gasped, 'It's beautiful. I will be your Queen.' We went back to my place, crept in and made love. In the morning, my employer was walking past my bedroom and noticed my light was on. She opened the door to switch it off, saw us in bed together and fired me.

I went to stay with the Australian actress, whom I'll call Elaine, while I looked for another job. I arrived with my rucksack of clothes, a cooking pot, two fishing rods, a couple of hammocks and a large blow-up boat. She and her boyfriend, who was really her husband but nobody knew, worked all hours of the day and night at his father's prestigious pizza joint, at acting classes and modelling shoots. I didn't see them much and finally moved out when I got a job with an art deco dealer as a cleaner. There was a separate flat on the ground floor of the apartment he shared with his girlfriend which would be mine and a car they'd give me the next day. That night, I hitched up to the Hills to get all my stuff, but Elaine was out. I hitched over to the pizza restaurant. It was her night off, but they did give me a phone number. She was at a party in the valley. So I hitched down, each time getting lifts from middle-aged men who were concerned for my safety.

The music was too loud for them to hear the door bell, so I walked in. Like a scene right out of *Blue Velvet*, I had walked into the underworld. The dancers were on coke, dealers and henchmen with bulges under their jackets hung around looking cool and frightening, and as I walked around looking for Elaine to get the keys from her, ratlike people scuttled out of the corners where they'd been shooting up. I found her, rubbing her nose. I felt a mix of prudish wholesomeness and disgust. She grabbed my arm, saying she only did it because she'd put on weight and she couldn't work if she was fat. I got the keys and left. That was the last I saw of her until a few years ago, when I saw her on the cover of a gossip magazine, marrying a rock star.

It took me three journeys to move all my gear, the last one at 4 a.m., and I was just thanking my lucky stars that I'd pulled it off when I got to my apartment door and reached for my keys. They were gone. I must have dropped them somewhere over the Hills. These were the keys not only to my apartment, but to the one upstairs which contained some of the most valuable art deco in the world, as well as the keys to the gallery which contained the rest. It didn't go down well on my first day, especially since I'd tried to climb in my window, had been pulled out again by security, couldn't prove who I was and slept outside on the grass.

The dealer's girlfriend, an aging French madame, ordered me around like scum. I told her that I couldn't speak French so that I could eavesdrop on them, but I didn't like what I heard when they discussed me. It's quite true, people do say, 'It's hard to get good staff these days.' But if they knew what you were asked to do, like washing skid-marked underwear by hand, they might understand.

I'd clean the gallery once a week. One of the girls who worked there, Rebecca, had a particular aura about her. She was about twenty-five, six foot tall (which isn't unusual out there) and had eyes which seemed to look straight inside me. She used to work with the police, directing them towards graves of victims which she saw in her visions. I was a bit sceptical about this kind of stuff then, but she told me she felt I had the same ability. So, one Sunday, together with an actress called Catherine Oxenburg and a bunch of girls, we went to the Park of Self Realisation for their weekly Witching Ceremony. A bird 'led' us to a clearing in the bushes which was just big enough for all of us. We passed round totems and they chanted. Just at their climax the bird returned and pooped on them. This was received with such excitement that I left and never joined them again.

Over the next few days, I sent out requests for sponsorship for the island year. I decided we'd film it and Sam was taking lessons from a local film-maker. This would provide the company with some footage to use in advertising. Within two weeks, I got a bite. A vitamin company were interested in sponsoring the project and they'd be in town the following week. Sam and I went to see them.

All went well. They liked us and they offered us full sponsorship. I couldn't believe how quickly it was happening; either the Americans were much more clued up to the benefits of sponsorship or it was just a very good idea. I got that 'it's going too well something's got to go wrong' feeling and sure enough, a phone call came through disputing our ages. I'd said we were twenty-four and twenty-five instead of nineteen and twenty but, of course, they'd read a few of my press cuttings and worked out that I'd lied about my age. If I'd lied about that, what else was I lying about? When I explained, quite honestly, that I didn't think they'd go for it if they knew our real ages, the chairman understood – he'd started doing business at the age of fifteen and had to get a thirty-year-old actor to play him in meetings. We set a date for departure, 9 April 1987, when my US visa would run out, and agreed to meet on 2 April to sign the contracts and receive the full sponsorship.

Sam worked furiously at the filming aspect and I studied books on survival techniques so that we could live from the land for a year, gradually replacing the stores and tools we'd taken. I was confident we could do it, if we worked together, but in those last few weeks Sam's demands for reassurance started to turn nasty. He'd climb through my window at night and, like a cat homing in on a squeak, he'd pounce on me at the slightest hint that I was saying, rather than feeling, how much I was looking forward to being with him on the island. I just couldn't understand this. He was demanding something which I didn't know existed, not just a hint of it which I might be able to improvise, but more: he wanted the next line; he wanted an answer to 'do you want me?' When I failed, he'd pin me to the floor, fill my vision with his face and spit, 'When *we* get to the island, I'll kill you.'

But I wouldn't let go.

On 2 April, seven days from departure, we went to see our sponsors for the last time. After the small talk which I always hated and wanted to rush through to get to the point and go, the chairman put his hand on the contracts, leant back and said, 'Ffyona, tell me why we should sponsor this project.' The phone rang, he raised an eyebrow at me as he leant over to pick up the receiver. I had till the end of his call to figure out a reason. If I failed, they would pull out.

My mind whizzed around all the marketing bull which Chris had used, which sounded good and convincing, and when he put the receiver down and looked up at me, I said, 'I think it would be a good project for you and you've invested so much time it wouldn't make sense to pull out now.'

He just stared. He looked over at Sam and then back at me. Then he said, 'You're young. Let me offer you some advice: always speak from the heart.' And he picked up the contracts, tore them up and put them in the bin.

As I drove Sam back to Westwood along the freeway in silence, I didn't get a hint of warning that it was coming until it hit me: his fist on the side of my face. He did it again and I could hardly see where I was driving because my eye swelled up immediately. I pulled over at a gas station. Sam picked up my Filofax with all my contacts and stood on the forecourt grabbing at the pages and flinging them out on the wind in great arcs, laughing hysterically. I left him there.

I gave in my notice, poured a whole bottle of bleach into the madame's underwear bucket, packed up and bought a ticket home. Just before I left, a call came through from Sam's roommate: he had shaved his whole body of hair. He hadn't eaten or drunk anything for four days and he wouldn't speak.

I found him in a stinking mess on his bed, naked and bald and dehydrated. Is this you, I thought, or is this me?

I got him to break the trance and drink some water. Then I left and flew back to Britain.

I wiped out that block, and most of the one before it and decided they did not exist. Had I looked at them then, from a distance as I flew home, I might have seen what I could see now: Sam was hitting against an empty iron box and the bruises on his knuckles were exactly the same as my own.

8

I heard a rustle and, thinking the meal service had finally arrived, I opened my eyes, put down my scotch and glanced around. The girl beside me was pulling a twelve-inch sandwich from her bag. She turned her back to me, curled herself around it in the corner and fed the whole thing into her mouth. Then she dusted off the crumbs, screwed up the cellophane, slipped it into her bag and settled back with her book as though nothing had happened.

I arrived in the London drag again, not so much a drag of the weather for me, more like the drag of having to change again. But this chameleon ability turned to my advantage when I got a job as a telephone actress. I fell into it quite by accident – I'd been a receptionist for a while at a headhunting firm in the City. Rather like an employment agency only instead of advertising for the jobs on their books, they identified people already working in the field then called them up, got them in for lunch and tried to convince them to change jobs. They knew the importance of surprise, and instead of using height, they used ego.

Post Big Bang and the scramble for talent meant the firm's researcher just couldn't keep up with the demand for information. In a panic with all hands on deck, they asked me, the receptionist, to see if I could find out the names of people who did the job they were after. It was confidential information. Their researcher told me the ruses he used: ask to be put through to the department which does the job, then say you're a client of theirs and you're having a party and you'd like to send out some invitations but, as a special occasion, you'd like to personalise them and could he give you the names of people who did the job.

I tried this but found it didn't really work: they'd give you some, but they were busy. The researcher said this was normal. One of the executives heard me on the phone and reckoned I could be very good at it. I was surprised and a little shocked – I'd never heard someone suggest I might be good at something. The others scoffed at him; I was only the receptionist. This was all I needed.

I wanted to get *all* the names, I wanted them to be accurate, I didn't want to arouse suspicion that I was a headhunter, I wanted to move easily around the companies to get more information if it was needed and I didn't want any other headhunting firms to get this information after me. So, I started to think about who would need to know these names and, after a bit of honing, my alias was born.

'Oh 'ello, it's Stacy 'ere, Stacy Smiff from administration. How you boys doin'?'

'Hello, Stacy. What can we do for you?' Always a good sign if his tone was patronising.

'Well, I was just updating the internal telephone list and putting all the people in each department in alphabetical order when I got to your desk and I don't even have anyone apart from yourself listed at all. Is there anyone else doing UK equity sales to Japanese clients?' (I'd stutter over this line, get the intonation completely wrong as though I hadn't a clue what the company did.)

'Yes, there is, there's about six of us here.'

'Oh, I am sorry. I haven't been 'ere very long but the state that some of these records is in it's just diabolical. That's why they got me in.'

'Do you want to know who we are?'

'Yes, I would actually.'

'OK, got a pen? The head of the desk is . . .' And he'd give me all the names.

'You sure that's everyone? Nobody off on holidays, 'cause I got to get this really accurate.'

'That's everyone.'

'Thank you. Oh, one thing which Susan, my boss said for me to tell you, is that if anyone calls asking for names just out of the blue, don't give them out.' At this point I'd load my voice with melodrama and whisper, 'It might be a headhunter. [pause] You know me, if it's not me who calls, just put the phone down or something.'

'Yes, of course, Stacy. Nice to know there's a little angel looking after us.'

It worked so beautifully that soon I had a rapport going with many people on desks around the City. If for any reason I was tripped up, I simply found out where they had offices abroad, worked out the time difference so I'd pretend to be calling after work hours from my office in some other country and call up administration as a secretary preparing for a global personnel meeting. If they wanted to send me a fax with the names I wanted, I'd say I would've faxed them but, 'Darling, I'm out of fax paper. I mean this is New York, it's two in the morning, you can get wallpaper, you can get wrapping paper, you can get toilet paper, but you cannot get fax paper.'

There were memorable chases – a girl on a desk suspected me, got my extension number and said she'd call me back with the information. I called admin very quickly, asked for the name of a personnel person, called her back as that person and said to her, 'I don't want to alarm you but we've just had a girl on the phone asking for information about your desk and I think she's a headhunter.'

'I knew it!'

We'd have a bitch about headhunters then I'd ask her, 'While I've got you on the phone, who *is* on your desk? I couldn't find the information when she asked me so I suppose she did me a favour in pointing out a gap in the internal list.'

If they ever queried why I was using an external line, I'd bring in Bobby, the clumsy office flirt who always tried to chat me up and that morning he'd sat on my desk and knocked over my coffee onto my telephone system and 'It went all tststststs, so I had to call maintenance on an outside line but maintenance can't fix it till tomorrow so I must be costing the company a fortune having to make outside calls when all I want to do is call Carol in stationery for some staples.'

It reached a point where Stretch, the executive who'd bet on me as a success, wanted me moved off the reception desk to work beside him full time. He put his year's bonus on the line. With this kind of encouragement, I could get any information from anyone and, like being unable to turn down a dare as a child, I'd be game for anything. A client who'd heard of my reputation made a bet with Stretch, once I'd been moved onto his desk, that I couldn't find the whereabouts of his boss. He was in some kind of highly secretive meeting, somewhere in the world. Within two hours I called him back with the country, the town, the hotel, the room number and the information that he wouldn't be in his room at the moment because he had a 4.30 meeting but he would be back later before meeting so-and-so for a drink in the Peacock Lounge.

He couldn't figure it out and was so scared that he never honoured the bet by taking us out for lunch. He'd actually given me the

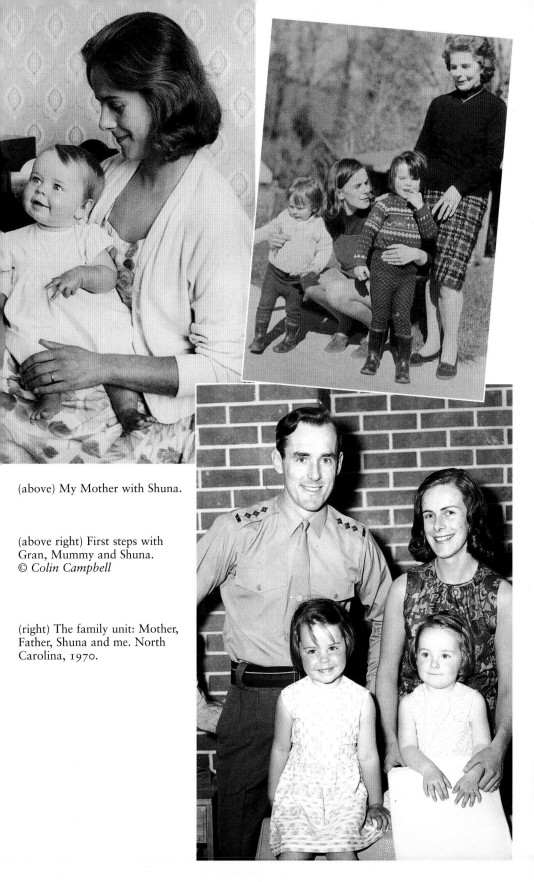

(above) My Mother with Shuna.

(above right) First steps with Gran, Mummy and Shuna.
© *Colin Campbell*

(right) The family unit: Mother, Father, Shuna and me. North Carolina, 1970.

(left) Early expectations. © *Colin Campbell*

(below) With Shuna, my big sister.
© *Colin Campbell*

(bottom) Following our Father from one flying job to the next. Essex. © *Colin Campbell*

(above) The painting competition picture. Aged 10.

(below) Reivesley before my parents renovated.

At Lands End.
© Mail Newspapers plc

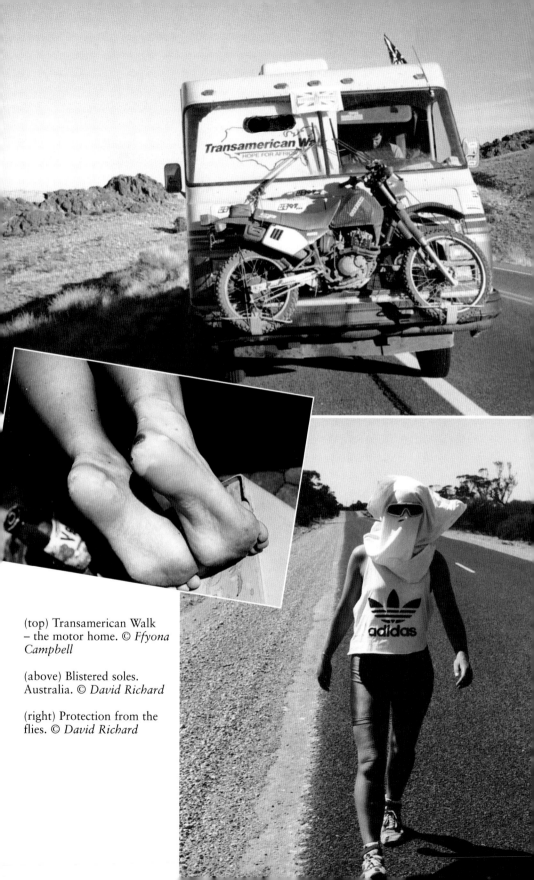

(top) Transamerican Walk
– the motor home. © *Ffyona
Campbell*

(above) Blistered soles.
Australia. © *David Richard*

(right) Protection from the
flies. © *David Richard*

(above) My first fire
without matches.
© *Raymond Mears*

(right) Daydreams come
true – writing a book on
a tropical island.
© *Ffyona Campbell*

(below) Ketut Sukanti
teaches me how to get
into a coconut. Bali.
© *Ketut Budiasa*

Scraping rawhide in the sun.
© *Raymond Mears*

The feeling of the woods.
© *Raymond Mears*

(above) Crossing the Karoo, South Africa. © *Charles Norwood*

(below) My fanatical road marking at day's end. South Africa. © *Charles Norwood*

information himself when I called him as the guy's wife and simply said, 'Where is he, Bob?'

Looking back at it now, perhaps I would have been better working for my country or something, gathering information as a spy, but at the time, I just enjoyed doing what I was good at without having to pretend to be good at it. The morals of the company's business didn't keep me awake at night. I squared it away in my own mind that people only move jobs for two reasons – money and challenge. The market wasn't based on loyalty any more: they could make you redundant at any time and if they weren't prepared to pay you enough and keep you challenged it made sense to keep your options open. We simply kept salaries high and kept managers on their toes to treat their employees right. As for the morals of my own ruses, I didn't even think about them – questioning myself hadn't occurred to me because I'd never been caught.

The humour of the chase brought me into the central group of the office; it gave me confidence around others, and the level of communication which comes with shared experience allowed me into a new circle of friends where I could understand the double talk and take the piss out of the no-hopers. On one hand this was comforting and fun, but on the other, their fear of making the wrong career move was, like any other fear at close range, highly contagious. Since there was no other indication around me that any other sphere existed, I began to feel this was all there is – all work and no home. The despair that came with this was very real. Though I could pretend my ass off to be someone else, when pretence entered the world of my direction, I'd start falling until I neared a 'pit point', a kind of anti-G spot which, when I hit it acted like a mental reflex and I'd be kicked straight out. This happened one empty Sunday morning in the room I rented and my arm flung out to the bookshelf and brought out my pocket atlas. As soon as I opened it, the blues and greens and pinks and lines and degrees and curves gave me a sudden rush of excitement. The stop-watch started ticking. I didn't have to take this shit; I had to get going!

Going west, the next continent I would hit would be Australia. Ever since I was a child, looking at the wall maps of the world, I'd been fascinated by the blank spaces. What's out there? What does it look like? There were a lot of blank spaces in Oz, especially through the middle. This would be a different journey; I would walk across the outback. But on the rip-off pittance I made at work I'd need to save for three years before I could go. I would need sponsorship. I wouldn't get one sponsor, but a bunch of them, putting in a small amount each so that none of them had control. As for a charity, Sport Aid '88 was coming up, a global fun-run benefiting children around the world, and that would do nicely. To avoid the heat of the desert in summer, I decided to begin in midwinter and walk through till spring. It was December 1987, I was twenty and I would begin the walk the following July.

But, after a few calls to companies, it became clear they wanted to know what was in it for them, what cities I was going through so they'd get the coverage. If I wanted to do this, I'd have to make concessions: either camels in three years' time, or roads and a few cities right now. I am an impatient animal by nature.

I wrote out a proposal for sponsorship of a walk from Sydney to Perth via Canberra, Melbourne and Adelaide and I sent it to all the companies I could find who were opening up branches in Australia who might want a promotional vehicle. It was a strange kind of life: getting up at 5 a.m. to walk ten miles into work as training, telling lies on the phone all day, walking ten miles home then getting on the phone to companies in Australia to persuade them to sponsor a walk for charity.

If I were to promote them, I'd need back-up. But I wouldn't go for two guys again, just one on his own and if I could get a hotel chain on board, they could organise the press conferences in the five cities, developing their relationship with the local media and leaving my driver free of it.

All the while I didn't stop and think, hang on, this is going to be the same as last time. I just wanted a focus, something to aim for to get me out and patterns, any patterns, seem safe when you're faced with chaos.

Most of this had to be put on hold when the company sent me to Hong Kong to set up their research base. It was easy hunting: few researchers had worked the market so I simply called up the reception desks, said I was a visiting employee on holiday from London and would they send over an internal telephone directory for me to take back. I got them all to courier one to a hotel over the road where I'd asked the concierge if they could accept a few parcels on my behalf. I wasn't staying there and when, at the end of the day, I went over to pick them up the concierge was standing behind forty-five parcels and he wanted some kind of ID. They were all addressed to Amanda Reynolds, my posh alias. I was about to go hunting down in the markets for some fake ID when a friend of one of my colleagues dropped in for a chat and agreed to come over and vouch for me – men being more impressive than women. It worked. The guy's name was David, he was attractive and aloof and perhaps because he didn't understand the measure of what he'd done, he brushed off my thanks. Now that I'd filled my mandate to get 1,000 names in three weeks by getting 15,000 in one day, I had time to play.

Hong Kong has a different kind of freedom: you can drink all night, sober up in a hotel over breakfast, go home for a shower then out to work to do it all again. I don't know how they keep it up because after three weeks of this I was knackered. On my last day, I went up the cable car to the Peak with a guy I'd hung out with and there we paid a visit to a fortune teller.

In a dusty cubicle, the air thick with incense, sat a wizened old Chinaman with a translator by his side. In his hands he held a tortoise shell into which he placed the dice, and for each of the three questions you could ask, he would shake and throw the dice then read what he saw. First, I asked him if I would complete my journey. He said he could see contentment after many years of confusion. Next I asked him if I had ever met or spoken to the man I would marry? He was quite abrupt at this one and suggested I didn't even think about marriage. Then I asked him how old I would be when I died. I dispute my memory at this point because I wanted him to say thirty, the time I'd always imagined I would run out of energy. What he actually said I don't remember, but I carried my version with me and like everything else in my life, it acted as a cattle prod.

Back in London I was greeted with two bouts of good news on the same day: the first was a call from a guy I'd invited to be my back-up driver saying yes, he was into it. The second was from the marketing manager at Johnnie Walker whisky, who said they'd like to offer me full sponsorship. I accepted his offer, put down the phone and screamed. It was happening. All I needed now was to get a back-up van on loan, plan my route and get really fit.

A few days later, I was sent my third piece of good news: Michelle Field, a freelance reporter who'd interviewed me for a magazine down under, called to ask if I would consider writing a book about my forthcoming journey. Michelle was a scout for Heinemann Australia, who had expressed an interest in seeing a synopsis and a few chapters of the ditched USA manuscript. I wrote an outline (quite difficult to do when the journey hasn't actually been made), rewrote some chapters, sent them off and crossed my fingers.

It seemed very strange to me that things were happening with very little effort, as if I hadn't put enough into them to make them hold. Something had to go wrong.

Sport Aid '88 set a date of 1 September for their global run. But that was in the Australian spring. If I started on that date I'd have to walk through the desert in summer. But, if I started before they launched I hadn't a hope of raising money for a charity which nobody knew about. I checked the annual temperature charts and found that my route, down in the south, would reach the bearable heat of twenty-eight degrees centigrade in summer. I didn't notice that these were mean figures, the average over a twenty-four-hour period, making the actual daily figure far higher. I called Sport Aid '88 and said I was into it, to begin on 1 September.

As the summer went by, I went through three drivers, each one making a commitment then backing out. With only a month to go, I was still retrawling and advertising until my godfather, Alan Hooper, a colonel in the Royal Marines, offered me one of his lads. At the same time, Rusty, my colleague in Hong Kong, called to say that David was interested. It was a toss-up between two different kinds of men. I knew instinctively that I should choose the Royal Marine: he would never let me down, he would protect me and he'd probably know exactly what I was going through out on the road. And yet I was more attracted to David. Stupidly, I gave in to the temptation of the voice which hinted at the fun to be had with him. So I called David, offered him the job and when he said yes, he actually meant it.

Just at this point, the marketing manager for Johnnie Walker whisky called me and said, 'Hello, Ffyona, I've been in contact with our Australia office who are running a promotional event which clashes with yours. I'm afraid we're going to have to pass on this opportunity.' It was a terrible blow. If I'd known there was any doubt I would've been developing new leads. As it was, I hadn't followed up any other companies since his confirmation of sponsorship. I refused to be beaten by trusting a marketing guy. Who the hell was he to control my journey?

The other guys in the head hunting office were terrific. They called contacts and gave me an introduction. From Stretch I was introduced to James Fergusson of James Capel, one of our clients. He chipped in £2,500. From Roger Leader I was introduced to Adidas, who offered me shoes and clothing and 'do you need any money?' And from Buff I was introduced to Neil Franchino who had just taken over Scholl. David left his job to work on sponsorship full time and pulled in another grand and got Hyatt Hotels on board as our hotel chain. Within two weeks I had £9,000. I needed £16,000 for a five-month walk. I refused to postpone the start; I was going anyway. £9,000 would mean a three-month walk. Fifty miles a day. Twice what I hadn't managed before, but I had conveniently forgotten about that.

9

The girl tells me she has run out of smokes.

And I have three left.

Do I care enough to teach her a lesson? Actually, that's not the point. The point is, is this attractive young woman who has just discovered the vast pastures of air travel actually aware that she needs to learn? And if she is, can she grasp the subtlety of what it is?

I pull out my copy of Feet of Clay, *the book I wrote about the walk across Australia. I'd torn off the photo cover so that nobody would recognise me. After a few painful paragraphs the penny drops, as they say: I was trying to learn something but because I had absolutely no idea what I was after, all the heat and all the blisters and all the flies and all the miles in the world could not teach me. All you ever know is learned by observation, but I thought I was alone and like anything unfinished, how can you ever get it to work if you don't know what it's supposed to be?*

I arrived at the Hyatt hotel in Sydney a week after David. The following morning, I got up early and knocked on his door. He opened it wearing a face pack. He laughed it off, got dressed and sat to attention. I paused, to show my contempt, then launched into the myriad things we had to organise before the start of the walk a week from today. I thought I was motivating David with my stick. Actually this wasn't far from the truth: he was motivated by it, but not to do what I wanted. In the early days, the lashings he took cut him more deeply: it's very easy to hurt someone if they hold you in high regard and I held this position because of what I said and believed I had done and what it implied about my strength. But you only show your strength when you take the strain.

N

Perth, Fremantle
Northam
Kellerberrin
Coolgardie
Norseman
Balladonia
Cocklebiddy
Eucla
Madura
Nullarbor
Penong
Ceduna
Venus Bay
Port Augusta
Crystal Brook
Adelaide
Coonalpyn
Tailem Bend
Ballaraat
Horsham
Albury
Canberra
Sydney

— Australia Walk —
1988

The first day out from Bondi Beach was much the same as the New York charade except that I had more of an idea of what I could pretend to be by copying David's love of sports clothes. The thrill and the fear again and the words 'don't worry Fi, you're just going for a walk' pulled back the anxiety of the job ahead into a more manageable task: all it is, is one step in front of the other. If you keep doing it for long enough, you'll get there.

This time I walked out from the waves and up the beach, to walk across the continent and into the waves at the other side. A good clean walk. The questions and the attention were reassuring in that I'd been there before, I knew this set-up better than anyone else around me, they were all strangers in my territory of experience. But this position of knowledge was a novelty and it made me think I knew more than I did.

David swung up into the cab of the tiny pop-top camper van that had been donated half by Newmans of Australia and half by Scholl. It pulled a small trailer which had been the donation of a whip round by friends of Marian Spencer at National Mutual, whom I'd met in London, and it contained the food and the loaned Yamaha 125 motor-bike for emergencies. David had spent most of the night making a Sport Aid '88 donations banner for the side of the van but even though he was tired, he kept up the banter with members of the local 'Race Walking Group' who had come to walk the first ten miles with me. He drove on up the road, his blond head and his suntanned right arm hanging out of the window, looking back at us shouting, 'Come on, ladies, this ain't a stroll. Work those bodies!'

This was going to be one hell of a walk.

After the press conference and out of downtown Sydney, past the amusement arcade I'd worked in five years before, the entourage hailed a 'break a leg' good-luck wish and left us to it. As the sun set on the first day, I was still walking. The schedule of forty miles a day for the first week, then fifty a day for the next ten weeks dictated everything now; there was no leeway for distractions if I was to make it to Perth on the money I had. I knew I mustn't think about tomorrow, for now I just enjoyed the sense of achievement: from a standing still position nine months before, I'd created this project, worked out how to make it happen and then got this thing on the road and it felt pretty good.

But then came the shock of what I'd actually created.

Instead of droning along behind me as Brian had done in the States, I asked David to wait for me at the end of each ten-mile stretch where I could sit down for half an hour, eat some pasta, drink litres of water and get out again. He did this through town until well after dark, when he pulled up beside me.

'Hey Fi, I've been looking for you.'

'Hullo, what's up?'

'You're going the wrong way.'

I had handed over responsibility for my direction to somebody else.

Back on the right road, I asked him to find a place to sleep for the night. I followed as he pulled off the highway into a residential estate and popped up the roof.

There was just enough room for one person to stand up in there, a slight comedown from the RV in the States, but I didn't knock it. There was a gas stove, a fridge, a pump-action sink, two cupboards for crockery and food and this was all we needed – except for the size of the bed. When we finally got the sofa to pull out and down, we were faced with something not much larger than a single for the both of us. We looked at each other. Even though our banter over the last week had bordered on the flirtatious, this was a bit sudden. We took our places, drew a mental line between us and slept for a few hours.

The road I took to Canberra is one of the fastest in Australia: long-haul trucks in convoy, burning gas and tyre rubber, race the smart business cars trying to get somewhere fast – for them it's not the journey that matters, just the destination. It was the most direct route and I couldn't afford to deviate into the pretty country, but walking against the stinking tailwinds of the semi-trailers was unpleasant and the sight of everything overtaking me formed an optical illusion and I felt like I was actually moving backwards, which added to the frustration of trying to reach those horizons. Horns on road-trains are painful to the unprotected ear, especially when they come up from behind and let off the blast when you're not expecting it. I think I made more progress during those jumps, but I often wondered whether they were doing it to encourage me or to attract my attention, like throwing a stone at a caged animal.

Even though the PR people at the Hyatt in Sydney had organised the press conference, the media coverage between the cities was up to David. I'd hoped this wouldn't happen but in these first few weeks, like the States, we needed to take advantage of the picking grounds before the population petered out in the desert. We needed the coverage, not only to repay my sponsors but to raise money for the charity. But it meant that David was often late in getting out to me and even though I didn't need him for directions now that the road was straight for a few hundred miles, I was dependent on him for food and water. Placing the responsibility of your body's needs onto someone else is frightening, especially when they're not in need themselves.

I guess he felt he couldn't win: I'd send him off to phone the newspapers ahead, scold him for being late, then cover my face in despair when he said a couple of reporters were coming out to chat for half an hour a piece. Even though the first week was walked at a break-in pace of forty miles a day, it took twelve hours at maximum pace with a break every two and a half hours, bringing up the time on the road to fifteen hours. Taking an hour out to give interviews wasn't possible and asking them to walk beside me was, the world over, a non-starter. Trying to time it so they'd reach us at a break only worked out once, so it was a toss-up between my needs and the needs of my sponsor and the charity and it often ended up that all parties suffered: I'd agree to take time out, but be so wound up at the ticking clock, that I wouldn't put my all into the interview.

Had I made a rule about it from the beginning, something concrete to stick to, I would have saved us both the daily anguish and produced good results. Even though I had been through all of this before, in the frantic run-up to getting the project on the road, I had forgotten about the next stage – actually doing it. And that went for keeping to the schedule I'd so easily written in my clean, safe flat in London.

There, I'd forgotten that I'd be conscious every inch of the way, physically propelling the body forward, not so much against the hills, but against the desire to stop. There's a law of physics which felt much the same as the battle going on in my head: every action has an equal and opposite reaction. The harder I whipped myself, the louder the other voice yelled out to stop. The trick is, remove the stick and replace it with a carrot. Then the law changes to one of magnetism, from force to desire.

I noticed this for the first time when David pulled over, got out of the Wombat (which we called the van) and tied something on the back of the trailer. His body was so tanned and so taught and his flirtations so amusing, that I started to walk towards him. It was much like my addiction to nicotine: I'd have one smoke, put the packet in the van, let it drive ahead and then gun it to get another fix. During the hours in between, I could daydream, escaping from the massive challenge ahead of me in the filthy world of diesel, into a world of bougainvillaea flowers and antiseptic white tablecloths and glasses of chilled white wine under the shade of palms on the edge of a beach. For stimulus, I'd invent car chases, in white Mercedes sports cars, dodging police road blocks on a mission to get even.

I found the interruptions hard to take when reporters pulled over on the road, stepped out of their air-conditioned cars and loaded on the joviality. Their first question was always, 'So why are you walking across Australia, Ffyona?'

'To raise funds for Sport Aid '88, a worldwide collection of charities which benefits underprivileged children. If you'd like to make a donation, you can either call the following number or send it to any one of these banks.'

'Don't you think it's a bit excessive? I mean, I can think of more fun things to do than plodding along the highway.' But, just as Shuna took her anorexia very seriously, I could not laugh at my pain because it was self-inflicted. I'd shoot them one of my infamous withering looks, which I figured was the right way to deal with such disrespect. When they left, and I struck out again in the heat and the noise, I'd set them in place, lined up on a wall, and blow their smiling heads off with a pump-action shot gun which I carried in my handbag. If I couldn't put them straight into a daydream, I'd set up a mantra of hate towards those who dared to enter my world with their questions, daring to be jovial at a time like this. I thought they were laughing at me and they probably were, but only once I'd tried to put them down.

I was spending twelve hours alone on the tarmac with these thoughts and they started to drive me crazy. I couldn't seem to get away from this 'why?' question. People in cars pulled over and asked it, kids in playgrounds asked it and even the birds when I heard them over the racket seemed to ask it too. If I pulled on my headphones and tuned in to the local radio, sooner or later I'd hear a recording of '. . . and one of our reporters went out to catch up with her to ask the only question: why?' and I'd be listening with curiosity, wondering if I'd said something which would give me a clue but no, 'because I really like walking' just didn't cut the mustard. I couldn't understand why I was hearing it more now than on the other two walks.

Within the first three days of walking twice as far a day as I was used to, my muscles started to stiffen till I felt like a gnarled old lady, shuffling down the road, trying to reach the Wombat before I completely seized up. David would take me through the paces of stretching before I heaved myself into bed to sleep for six hours before getting up to do it again.

During the fifth day, I could hardly bend my right leg or put any weight on it. If I did, a sharp hot pain shot through my shin from the base to the knee. David found some ice at a break and packed my leg with it over a compression bandage and raised it above my heart level. He had been a fitness instructor in Hong Kong and he guessed correctly that I had a shin splint in there. Caused by the imbalance of one muscle group against another, the weaker muscle starts to tear away from the shin bone.

After an hour, I took off the ice, put on my shoe and sock and got out to carry on as David drove away to wait ten miles ahead. Wound up and in excruciating pain, I tried to get a grip and sing to keep my spirits up but when I heard my voice quivering away over the tears it all sounded so pathetic. I was sick of singing, sick of distracting myself, sick of trying to get somewhere that didn't even matter, sick of being coerced, sick of pretending, but I had no alternative.

A car pulled over then. The driver waited till I was level with his window, which took me a little longer to reach because I was limping. He stretched over and rolled down the window, 'You 'right?'

'Yes, I'm fine thanks.'

'You need a lift somewheres?'

I looked up and looked around, then back at him and his safe seat within inches of my painful world. All it would take to cross between this pathetic push and the pain relief was raising my hand four inches and slipping my fingers through the door handle then moving it down by two inches. Some little imp was shouting, 'Go on, do it, do it, do it, do it', like it does when driving over a bridge and all there is between life and death is the four-inch downward movement of your hand on the steering wheel. My only concern at those times was to shoot the little imp.

'No, thanks. I'm actually on a charity walk.'

'Oh, good on ya. Look, er,' and he shifted some papers off the seat, picked up something and handed it out to me, 'here's ten bucks for the kitty.'

My pride at the restraint took me more easily through the next few miles till, rounding a corner, I saw the blue and white side of the Wombat waiting for me and the greatest joy in the world. But here the emotional pendulum started to swing: I'd been pushing for so many miles just to get there that I'd built it up to be the end. Within an hour, I'd have to get up and get out and the whole business of counting down the kilometres would start all over again. And so I asked myself the same old question: what on earth was I doing? Why didn't I have an answer?

The following day was a killer: the shin splint deteriorated so that I could hardly stand, let alone walk. But I couldn't stop and rest it; we had to be in Canberra that night for a press conference the following morning and I wasn't going to throw away all that I'd been through that week by marking the road and driving in. In order fully to relieve all the tension, I needed the climax of seeing the van parked by the sign for Canberra City limits.

David cut me a good stick to use as a crutch. We were thirty-five miles from the city limits at 12 p.m. and each ten-mile stretch took anything from one to two and a half hours longer than normal. 'Knuckle down and get it done; there is no alternative' was reduced to a good walking mantra of, 'Damn, damn, double damn, two bloody hells and a bugger!' I could manage it, but if a car slid over and a cheery face leaned out and asked me why I was doing it, I snapped out of the trance, stumbled with the pain, waved away the face and collapsed inside once more, whining away for miles till I built up control again.

David came out and walked with me for the last seven or eight miles that night in the rain. He distracted me well by recounting stories from his wild days in Hong Kong and we sang a few songs till finally, after a staggering twenty-one hours on the road that day, we saw the Wombat and the sign for the Canberra City limits. Punching the air and doing a Blues-type shuffle, we got to the van, clambered in, sank down into the seats, feet up on the dashboard and drove to the Hyatt hotel.

There is nothing so beautiful when in pain than to have it suddenly taken away from you and replaced by luxury. It's a very fine hit and it's manufactured by drug companies everywhere.

Into Canberra to a hail of praise from the porter on the door, to the PR girls and the press who arrived the next morning. But I didn't find their praise fulfilling; rather, it filled me with a sense of contempt. I misread their modesty about their own achievements in the face of my own as being an admission that they were weak and inferior to me. In a way this was satisfying as a sense of revenge towards the kids who had rejected me as a child, but unless the whole world lay down at my feet in homage begging forgiveness, it wasn't enough. I took their praise as being an affirmation that what I was doing and the way that I was doing it was very good. It blinded me to any need for change. I might have passed the test of endurance, but I had failed a test which completely eluded me: inner strength is not measured by how far you can walk with the muscles ripping off the bones; it is measured by how you deal with someone who has pulled over to wish you well. This test eluded me because I was being praised by everyone for my willpower. Pass points are cumulative but so are failures, often in ways which are too subtle to notice if you're not aware of what's really going on.

A local chiropractor spent much of the day giving my leg deep-muscle treatment with ultrasound to improve the rate of healing. He had treated other athletes – like Ivan Lendl – with great success when rest was not available. Either I would walk through it and out the other side, or it would deteriorate even further – time would tell.

But I was only in the 'break-in' stage. After this week, I had to up the mileage by another ten miles if I was to hit the average I needed to walk fifty miles per day for the next ten weeks. I was actually pretty scared at this point: scared of pain, scared of finding enough motivation to keep going, scared of egg on my face if I failed. In a way I used this fear of failure as a way to keep going. While 'I don't have an alternative' was a good one-liner in times of despair, it hindered my search for the real reason. I felt the panic rise but I put it in check: 'One step at a time, break down the distance into manageable chunks, next stop Melbourne at the end of the following week.'

No matter how much I lived every single second of the luxury, digging in my heels like the final few hours before being sent back to boarding school, the moment came when we had to check out, drive back to the sign and carry on. By allowing David to announce our departure instead of turning to face it myself, I failed another test.

By the afternoon of the next day, I was delirious: the shin splint had healed and I was fair smoking along the road despite the rain and the arcs of water from speeding cars. I burst into the Wombat and almost hugged David, rubbing my chin furiously to defrost it so that I could proclaim that I knew why I was doing it: I absolutely loved it out there! God knows what David made of it; he didn't know what was going on inside my head during those hours, not yet anyway.

'How're *you* holding up, David?'

'Well, funny you should ask, um, I'm getting a bit bored actually.'

I resented his words and I guess my expression revealed these thoughts because when I got out to my merry world of singing through the puddles, David drove off at high speed, splashing me as he went.

When I saw him again at sundown, I took off my socks and shoes to check on a sore spot. Beneath the soggy white skin I prodded a bulbous lump. Blister. David brought out the medical box, found a syringe and persuaded me that sucking out the fluid was the best way to treat it. He did it for me and dressed the wound.

Unknowingly, he had just given me a shot of an even greater pain: like the chick whose shell was removed by someone else, I was far weaker as I stepped out into the night to carry on. Had I bent down, taken the needle he offered and plunged it into the skin myself, I would have been responsible for my own pain relief.

Relying on someone for your food is one level of dependence, being dependent on them for water is getting critical, but if you are dependent on another person for your pain relief, there is very little chance of ever getting up again. To get up you must have strength, and strength only comes from taking the strain yourself. And, unknown to me because I had never done it, it's never as hard as that first time.

Out there in the dark, limping along, I whined of course, in self-pity. I thought I was being strong by being out there and carrying on, but I had no idea that no matter how far my body deteriorated or how far I kept on walking, I'd still be at the starting block if I couldn't take the real strain on my own shoulders.

When David asked me jovially how I was doing, I'd lash out at him to bugger off. But this is the way of the helpless: we cry for aid, our call is answered out of compassion, but then we punish the helper so that they feel guilty and we can feel stronger.

As I stepped into the van, the blister had spread, forming two chambers now. Again David syringed out the fluid but this time he sent in some Betadine to keep away the infections. There was a split second of fascination as I watched the brown fluid filling out under the yellow skin before the reflex hit and my foot shot out and kicked David in the face. The wound throbbed fantastically while I tried to apologise. I wasn't expecting it to hurt. He gathered himself, brought the foot into position and dressed the wound.

Out again, waving goodbye to David as my pain relief drove me ahead another ten miles, I felt very much alone. If I limped to pro-tect the injury, my other calf took the strain, which might be bear-able for three or four miles up the road, but after about twenty, with thirty left to do that day, I needed balance. I found it was better to ram the heel down on to the road. This hurt like buggery for about ten minutes, then the blisters eased themselves into a comfortable position and didn't bother me too much.

If someone hooted in encouragement, I'd jump, dislodging the blisters and the red hot flare-up sent me into a shuddering firework of obscenities, waving my fist after the car and destroying any equilibrium. There were times when they slowed, like curbcrawlers, taking a long look at me, then speed up and drive on. It made my skin crawl and I'd give them two 'V's. At other times they'd just sit there waiting for me to catch up and if I was thrashing myself along the road with force, I'd immediately suspect them of being up to no good. On the other hand, when I was motivating myself through desire, daydreaming about bonking David on a tropical island, I'd see the good and be polite to those who stopped.

At each break David would go through the ceremony of the syringe again, stabbing and sucking out the new blisters, pumping them with Betadine, dressing them then setting me out on the road, and the more he relieved my pain, the more he gave me fuel for daydreams to get through the lonely hours ahead. But when I'd get to the Wombat, meet the real David, he'd always fall off his pedestal.

Daydreams were a way of avoiding the despair of reality, but I couldn't seem to get the energy I needed to carry on if the daydreams kept deflating. I needed something stronger.

Unaware that I had no real inner strength, I groped for some sort of fuel to keep me going. If I got weepy, I'd start to slow down, but if I got angry then I could charge on. And the one thing which filled me very quickly with anger was hatred. All I had to do to turn this on was to remember the only party I'd ever thrown, which I'd held at the back of my parents' house just before I left. The whole of my year and the one above it turned up in force; it was hailed as the best party in the village since Johnny Summers had got pissed and gone out cutting off chickens' heads. As it degenerated and couples got it together, there was a shortage of blankets and I went into my parents' house to borrow a few. They were asleep (God knows how), so I took them from the airing cupboard and was walking back through the car port when my father opened the door. He stood there very calmly and asked me what I was doing. I said I was borrowing a couple of blankets for folks who were staying over – this being in the middle of nowhere and they weren't sober enough to drive home. He paused, then he walked towards me. He shook his head very slowly, reached out and took the blankets. Still shaking his head he walked back into the house and closed the door behind him without saying a word.

It was a good one; could get a good fifty miles out of that one. And the more I conjured up that shaking head and relived the fury of my helplessness against the power he had over me, the more I could hammer out those miles no matter how many blisters I had on my feet. This deep-seated anger dawned on me that maybe this was the answer I had been looking for because I needed a very strong justification for why I was out there, walking on in such pain.

I built up a picture of my father as the enemy. He was the one forcing me to do this or else I would be worthless. I'll fucking well show him! Yeah, this is why I'm doing it. And the questioning stopped. I had my banner; I knew my mission and I wouldn't stop the push. Like a big brother twisting back my arm and pinning me to the floor, demanding I give in, I wouldn't do it. If a driver pulled over and offered me a lift, even goading me with, 'Oh, come on. We won't tell', I wouldn't even entertain the idea, so strong was my new-found mission.

Around this time, the blisters started to multiply out of control. Around a baker's dozen rose up on each foot, but it was hard to tell since many of them had deeper chambers. Stoically David syringed them, dressed them, suffered my lambasting to pump myself up then drove off leaving me to hobble along, rudely waving off any offers of help till, after twenty hours on the road, I'd get in, strip off the socks and dressings and, lo and behold, find several more blisters, throbbing and ballooning under the skin.

It was a vicious circle: the more blisters I had, the more rude I was to those who only wanted to help me; the more I felt my shame and guilt at waving them off but didn't change my ways, the more blisters I seemed to get.

Over the thousands of miles which followed, David pulled pints of pus out of my feet every week. There were blisters within blisters, over layers of blisters; blisters with staphylococcus infections and blisters deep under callouses, around my heels and between toes. But mostly, they spread out across the soles of my feet. Yet when I passed that test of endurance and wouldn't give up, the hardship changed up a gear.

Out across the Eyre Peninsular and into the desert, the temperatures reached sixty degrees centigrade and shattered the thermometer on the side of the Wombat. My ears thumped and the soles of my shoes stuck to the melting bitumen. My breathing came in short puffs for fear of burning my lungs, but even those puffs caused my nose to bleed. I felt sapped of energy. Birds nodded off in the thrumming heat as everything slowed around me. Discarded snake skins lay drying in the verges like parchment scrolls and the flesh of rotting roos curled away from bones and stank. All around me the scrub, blue bush, sky and sun, merged into a blur. There were mirages and I must have sweated enough to look like one myself to the road trains which thundered past. They moved over for no one, their whiplash tailwinds belched the stench of burning rubber, heating the mirages. But at least they dislodged the flies for a moment. I was overheating quickly, dehydrated and teetering off balance. The Wombat was like an oven when I reached it.

My plan to walk at night to overcome this was probably harder than simply pushing on through the day. Fifty miles takes twenty hours, so I'd take the four hours of rest at midday, getting out again at 4 p.m., walking through the heavy afternoon, the dusk and the night and the dawn and the morning to noon the next day and then try to sleep till I got up to do it again. But those hours at midday, stuck in the sweaty heat of the van without shade, were not conducive to sleep. I had to keep the dressings off my feet because they were beginning to rot but, left open, the flies got in and fed on the wounds. Even wrapping them up in my sheet they were tenacious bastards and would wriggle in under the folds, drawn by the scent of decay. They woke me constantly, having to pull off the sheet to flap them out of the folds, then cover my feet quickly before they shot back in again. If we closed the door we'd suffocate.

David was in charge of my water and I felt trapped between wanting to instil the importance of it in his mind and wanting to protect myself from the misuse he might make of his power over me as Chris and Brian had done. On one hand, I'd be praising him and on the other I'd be telling him that I could easily find a replacement. Instead of nurturing the bond between us by accepting that he was keeping me alive on the road, I kept him there by trapping him. I was aware that I hadn't given him any motive for the worth of all this struggle so, when he drove beside me I allowed the bitterness of those childhood memories to froth up into an acrimonious bile which I vomited all over him. I told him these things in a way so that he would pity me enough not to desert me.

There was no respite from these lashings until one day, hundreds of miles into the desert, we pulled into the desolate gas station of Yalata, on the edge of an Aboriginal reserve. The road was narrow and cut through banks of thick mallee transforming the open plains into a heavy tapestry of blue and green. Oil stains in rainbow circles patched the concrete of the truck stop, wasps hovered over the rusting five-gallon drums and the air lay still, heavy with the stench of old drains. Aboriginal artifacts covered the walls inside, but there was no money for the artists because the road brought no tourists. The word from other truck stops was to keep clear: Yalata was a danger zone. I ordered a Coke and sat in the corner, watching. The bell tinkled over the door followed by a scuttle of two pairs of bare feet on the linoleum, drawing a sigh from the cashier.

The young Aboriginal woman was tall with long thin legs, ankles the width of my wrists and a flash of white on her soles. Heavy breasts protruded through an orange sweatshirt which nudged the band of her pleated burgundy skirt. Her face was knotted and silent. A small naked boy skipped beside her as he confidently surveyed the sweet counter. He dragged a wooden chair from one of the tables set for lunch and launched himself onto it. Small brown fingers delved into the jar and caught a bunch of chocolate drops in a fist that was too big to pull out again.

A few old Aboriginal men in varying states of ill health scuffed through the door and took up their places at a table, slouching against a wall. There was no movement amongst them: they each chose a focal point on the floor or wall and simply observed. Perhaps they too kept going by dreaming. They were neither bushmen nor western men; they lived on the edge, a displaced desert tribe brought to the thick gum land of Yalata. With money every month from the government, the convenience of the truck stop replaced their interest in gathering bush tucker – even if they did know what to look for in land which was not their own.

The precious hours of coolness and evening light were upon us. Time to move on. As David paid the bill I went out and sat on the driveway. Dark Aborigine faces peered out at me from a battered old Holden.

'You the one walking?' one of them asked gently.

'Yes.'

'How good is it?'

'Bloody awful.'

'I'll walk with you to Perth if you like.'

'I'd love some company.'

I was amazed. He hadn't asked me why I was doing it. But then, Aborigines understand the need to make a journey. Some believe their ancestors had walked across this land in lines, singing the world ahead of them into being: the grass, the trees, the gullies and creeks. These features remain in the landscape, each with its own tale of the journey which created it. Some Aborigines inherit his or her own stretch of a 'songline', and he must sing the song as he walks it, healing the land and in turn the land heals him.

I waved goodbye and limped along the road and when David passed me to drive ahead and sleep, the night grew very black. I had a sense that I was being watched but not by anything scary, rather a comforting feeling. I took up the reigns on my hatred and began the nightly lashings to drive me forward but then something very odd happened and I'm not entirely sure whether I simply imagined it because I needed to, or whether it really did happen. I felt someone move up behind me. I didn't see him, but then I didn't look round either. Someone was walking very easily beside me and my limping was completely out of step with his easy footfalls. It's hard to keep the wrong rhythm against the drumming of an even beat and, gradually, I started to walk in time, in balance and relax. And when I felt him leave, I kept up the rhythm all through that night and out the other side.

David was softly sleeping when I reached the Wombat. Instead of tearing the sliding door closed behind me, I left it open so as not to wake him. He murmured a greeting.

'Ssssh, don't get up,' I said. 'I'll make some breakfast.' It was one of the first times I had not demanded that he get up and make me food, the first time I realised how exhausted he must be too. I was careful to be quiet while I made breakfast, dawn was so peaceful in the cool drapes of pale yellow light. He sat up slowly, I placed a bowl of porridge in his hands and when we'd eaten and I got out to walk, I felt a serenity which had eluded me all my life.

You can lament the lack of love till you're blue, but at some point I had to turn – from getting love by receiving it to getting love by giving it.

The miles seemed effortless that day but because I hadn't quite grasped the cause and effect of what I had witnessed, I searched for this sense of peace in my mind instead of with my sacrifice. Though the blisters started to heal then, as callouses of hardened skin over the wells of fluid deep underneath, their symbolism was lost on me.

At the end of 3,200 miles in ninety-five days there were no great revelations, despite the last line of *Feet of Clay* which says, quite mysteriously, ' . . . and, I knew *why*.' I still hadn't a clue.

I think I know the reason now, all these years later, now that I know the world is round. No matter how much I tried to disengage myself from the laws which govern our planet, what goes around comes around is inescapable. When I cheated in America and denied it had happened, at some point I would start to pay for it. I walked across Australia to see if I could really do it and I blamed my father because I could not accept that I had done something wrong. I see my blistered soles as symbols of punishment, but at the time I couldn't bear to admit it. Perhaps my own conscience, buried from view beneath years of pretence and years of twisted isolation, actually did direct my next step because even though I had passed the test of endurance, I had failed at many others. Though I never wanted to walk again after Australia, another voice spoke out to the waiting microphones in Perth and said, 'I'd now like to walk the length of Africa.' For God's sake.

I noticed the girl's spots with more understanding now, now that I'd witnessed her selfish behaviour. And I decided to set her up for a lesson

'I'll tell you what. We can share my smokes,' I said and lit one and handed it over. Back and forth it went until the meal service came round and I tapped out the tiny stub, saving it for later.

David and I drove back to Sydney, spent a riotous Christmas with everyone at the bar of the Hyatt and agreed to go our separate ways. We stood outside the hotel on the morning of 31 December 1988, exchanged the last of our things like hostages, shook hands and said goodbye. At the point where I turned away from him to walk up the hill, I felt an incredible zap of freedom as I'm sure did he too. I was fit and tanned and I had $4,000 in my pocket from my publisher with which to go and write a book. I'd spent so many hours daydreaming about living in a bamboo hut on a tropical beach and now I could put it all into practice.

I figured Queensland would be the place to go looking so I boarded a bus up to Rockhampton and spent New Year's Eve with a bunch of hooligans, swapping tall stories about hoop snakes and drop bears. At two in the morning I got off and lugged my rucksack over to the taxi rank and asked him if there was a youth hostel nearby. Fortunately it was open. I paid for a night's kip and went through into the communal room where a German girl was watching TV. She'd been travelling for a while and we got onto the topic of bamboo huts on beaches.

'I don't think you're going to find much around here. It's pretty expensive, too. But you'll definitely find what you're looking for in Bali.'

'Is that near here?'

'Well, sort of. It's an island in Indonesia.'

'How do I get there?'

'You can fly from Cairns I think.'

Fuck! That's where the bus was going.

I found a bus timetable at the reception desk, saw there was another one leaving in an hour, gathered up all my gear, said goodbye and walked down to the shelter in the dark.

In Cairns I found that I couldn't fly out until the day after next because of the bank holiday and it would be cheaper to fly from Darwin. Back on the bus and across the top of Australia, watching the desert fade into tropical rainforest from the luxury of an air-conditioned seat, I now knew what it felt like to watch from a position without pain. In Darwin, I bought a word processor and a one-way ticket for Bali.

I called the bank in Sydney, which had been receiving donations on our behalf for Sport Aid '88, to make sure they knew what to do with it. The balance came to around $10,000, which was a fair amount. But then I got the bad news. Sport Aid '88 Ltd, the company which organised the fun-run event, had gone bankrupt. I immediately looked round for David to ask what we could do, but I was on my own now. I spoke to one of the trustees, who reassured me that none of the donated money would be used to repay the creditors of the bankrupt company. That's why they had set up two separate entities. The money we'd raised would be sent to Bangladesh to help with the children of the flood victims under the supervision of Care Australia. Satisfied, I boarded a flight for Kuta, Bali.

The morning I landed I left my gear in a hotel room, hired a jeep and drove around the island. Up in the north I only found black beaches and as it was getting late I decided to turn back and carry on the search the next day. There seemed to be a short cut across the island and down to the south coast, but I didn't notice it meant driving over the top of the volcano. Though my jeep looked good on the outside, it wouldn't start and the clutch was worn out. I got a push from some of the villagers and roared away, up into the high volcanic hills. But this route was the favourite of the goods trucks and they move very slowly. I had a terrible time double declutching behind them so as not to stall, or I'd never get started again, and I couldn't pull over. Down the other side and eventually to the beach, I drove to the small village of Candi Dasa. Bright coloured ribbons and pretty flowers adorned carved pillars of pale grey pumice. A vacant sign made me stop. Natia Homestay, it was called and when

I got out of the jeep several brown-bodied kids came over and reached for my hand. They touched my skin, their laughing little faces turned up to me, and with the sea breeze cooling me after the humidity of the forest I figured this might be a good place to stay.

Past the bamboo bar towards the sea, they led me down a little path, bordered by one- and two-room huts which they let to travellers. At the end of it, the path opened up to a wide patio where another bar perched on the edge of the sea. I felt the full force of that breeze and the wide open expanse of ocean the colour of peppermint mouthwash before me with its three little islands sitting out in the bay. Beside the bar, full face to the ocean, was a two-storey bamboo house. I pointed to it. One of the boys went for the key and took me around the back, up the steps and into the top floor. I opened the door and went into a fairly dark, bamboo-walled room. There was a bed on one side and a bamboo sofa on the other and at the back was another door. When I opened this, the whole view of the ocean hurt my eyes after the darkness. It was framed top and bottom with bamboo like a great balcony only with walls at the side and a roof. A palm tree just outside it and a crimson and yellow flag fluttered in the breeze. This was the place and it was more gorgeous than even the most vivid of my daydreams.

I bargained hard for a four-month deal with breakfast, cleaning and laundry, drove back to Kuta for my luggage and went round the markets for various things to make it a good place – some fabrics to cover the seats, a large desk and some paper – then drove back to set up house. This is the time I love most about moving. I settled into a routine, getting up fairly early for a swim then a cold douche in my little bathroom, having breakfast of fruit salad brought in and then I'd write until midday. I'd leave it all, go out for another swim and lie on the beach with the other travellers for a couple of hours till I'd shower again, write until dark then print out my day's work and take it down to one of the little bars on the seashore to correct it.

On Wednesday nights there'd be a Barong dance next door, a full display of dancers who seemed to be double-jointed right down to their fingernails, but after I'd seen it a few times the drums and symbols crashing next to me got a bit irritating. So once a week I'd hire a jeep and drive up over the volcano to the north side of the island and buy a 'special' mushroom omelette, which I'd place on the engine beside my seat to keep warm. Occasionally I'd make the pilgrimage with a few travellers and we'd eat our omelettes back in Candi Dasa then, with bottles of water in hand, we'd walk along the beach, feeling like we were in a movie or something, laughing ourselves silly.

The two lads who took care of my house for the owner were both called Ketut because they were the third-born – there are only five first names and each denotes your position in the family. One of them was infatuated with the western way and he slicked back his hair with coconut grease and loved to lie on my sofa looking at himself in the handheld mirror. The other, a beautifully proportioned young man who was much more shy than his friend, kept his traditions alive. His father had been killed when he fell out of a palm tree but if Ketut had any fear of them, he didn't show it. The two of them dared each other to climb the one outside my house to bring me coconuts, but only the shy Ketut could ever get high enough. From time to time he'd bring me breadfruit, called sukan when it's cooked and sliced very thin and then fried. I was later to try this method in Africa when it was all we had to eat. He taught me how to weave the small baskets they used on special days to steam the rice and he explained the meanings of the flowers which were laid on every doorstep each morning. They are for the spirits, he'd said, out of respect. Like most of the other people in Bali, the Ketuts were Buddhists; they lived every day to the full, explaining to me that the mood they are in at the point when they die will determine the form of their next life. After the dark days in Australia, I felt intoxicated by their laughter.

On occasions we'd go to their village or to a ceremony and one of their sisters would deck me out in traditional Balinese dress, which was mightily tight and uncomfortable. But it didn't matter, I was falling in love with the people around me because it seemed that, despite and perhaps because of the close proximity of death, nothing could get them down.

I, though, was not very good at dealing with disasters. When the rains came in storms day and night, I'd knuckle down to my work but the government electricity surged and I'd keep losing what I'd written. Even if I saved the work after each paragraph, the whole system might shut down and I'd be unable to get back into it. The owner brought me a petrol generator for my computer, which wasn't too loud, but still the power cuts would occur when it ran out of gas.

My lower back began to seize up now that I was sitting down all day and it would take me half an hour to get off the floor in the morning. Ketut took me to see the Chief of Tengannon, a small village of Hindus who had refused to change religion each time Bali was invaded by new ones. The chief had learned acupuncture, so twice a week I'd make my way to his house and he'd stick electrodes all over my back, connect them with wire and then switch on the electrical current. I got quite a kick out of the surges, but it worked.

It was a time of peace and allowed me to open my eyes to what was around me. Not that I had the wisdom to interpret it, but one observation I made, I felt had more significance than I knew. Each morning at sunrise I would see women down on the beach gathering broken coral in baskets. I asked Ketut what they did with the coral and he showed me where they pounded it into powder to make bricks. With these bricks they rebuilt the sea wall where the water had eroded it. These erosions fell into the water, where the sea pulled them back and out to the coral reefs where the polyps used them to make the coral. In time the sea would break the coral (or it would be broken by the fishermen when they used dynamite instead of nets), sending it back to the beach where the women bent and scooped, collecting it to pound into powder to make bricks to rebuild the sea wall.

I felt this was such a contrast to my life on the road, which began at one point and stopped at another, never to return again. I felt their sense of peace had something to do with this but I wasn't quite sure what it was.

After three months I had to leave the country to renew my visa. It was a pig of a journey to Singapore: a ferry to Java, a fifteen-hour bus journey in a seat half my size to Jakarta, getting out into a den of thieves and then looking for a non-existent ferry despite what it said in my traveller's companion. I had to fly to Singapore from there, which completely wiped out my funds so that I had no money for a room for the night. Fortunately I met up with an American who was cycling through Indonesia but was stopping off for a couple of days to pick up his next instalment of money. He got a luxury hotel room, took me out to dinner, then bonked me senseless.

After another month in Bali, the first draft of *Feet of Clay* was finished. It was supposed to be around 70,000 words long but I'd gone a bit over the top with a quarter of a million. I packed up house, said goodbye to the two Ketuts and lugged the manuscript home by way of Singapore. I'd got a staff stand-by seat on British Airways back to England, but there were no seats available. I had to be home within two days or I'd miss Shuna's wedding. My mother's cousin, Digby Collis, worked in Singapore and he had a word with the head of British Airways, who got me on the jump seat.

Back in London, Shuna met me at the airport. We had so much news to swap that we didn't stop blethering for hours. I had met the man she was about to spend the rest of her life with a couple of times before – a rather bumbling but very charming Eton/Oxbridge guy who told her he worked in corporate finance in the City and composed music. I spotted him as a cad from the word go – takes one to know one I suppose. I'd warned my parents of this but they'd brushed me away. I found myself in new territory now: I couldn't let Shuna go ahead with this unless she knew what I knew about him, but when I told her, she sped even faster into his arms, thinking, I suppose, that I was just jealous.

My parents had moved again while I was away, this time down to Devon, where they'd met and where they'd lived when I was born. After thirty-odd house moves in twenty-five years, this one formed the completion of their first circle. Shuna and I drove down without a map and ended up on the wrong side of the river mouth five minutes after the last ferry. We back-tracked to a bridge and traced our way to their house with directions from my mother over the phone.

As we turned the last of the corners and down into a steep little lane, one last check at the directions and, 'That's it, that's the one, just there on the right.'

We looked at the palm trees out the front, then looked at each other, adopted the heavy cockney of our gossip sessions and said in unison, 'Ooooh, very nice.' As soon as I'd turned off the engine, I heard the squeak 'Colin!' And the little mouse threw open the door of her new home, her face alive with delight and hugged us both.

My mother was always at her best in the middle of a crisis. The cause of this one was Shuna's wedding. A month earlier, still living in Scotland, she'd got a call from Shuna saying the Knightsbridge wedding which her fiancé had promised her had been called off. They'd have to find another cheaper venue and decided to hold it in Dartmouth, to where my parents were about to move. But they hadn't bought a house there yet. My father made several trips to look for one and, with this added pressure of organising Shuna's wedding and holding the reception in the garden, they bought the best of a bad bunch, packed up and moved in. That was forty-eight hours before we arrived.

In that time, my mother had not only organised all the furniture, unpacked and arranged all the crockery, the silver and the ornaments, but she'd hung all the curtains, dozens of pictures and was now in full swing with getting the garden ready for the reception of her eldest daughter's wedding the day after tomorrow. My father juggled a clipboard with two sets of actions lists: house and wedding.

He managed the carpet fitters along with the flower arrangers, chimney sweeps with rehearsal times, removers' bills with hotel room deposits for members of both families. Far from being exhausted as they should have been, both were in their element.

On the eve of Shuna's wedding, I wrapped up Big Ted again and I gave it to her. She was surprised, but she didn't remember the incident because she didn't give him back. Then I asked her, if she was in a life boat, who would she give the other life jacket to. She said, 'I'm sorry, Fi, I don't know any more.'

I think that was probably the loneliest moment of my life.

So Shuna married the scumbag but instead of going on honeymoon abroad as her husband had promised, he took her bed and breakfasting in the area. When they got back, the house they'd been promised by her father-in-law wasn't ready so they stayed with my parents. I had to admire my sister for taking all these disappointments so well. I could see she was hurt but she was damn well going to stand by her husband come what may.

It was a full house with me there too and there was a pretty strong sense that we should all be on our way. After being a witness to the closeness of the families in Bali, this attitude made me feel even more lonely. But I doubt I did anything to change this myself: after all, I had just walked across Australia screaming obscenities at a man who now gave me hospitality.

I got a part-time job on the beach as a waitress while I rewrote the second draft, which Michelle Field would edit and send down to me. In order to get the second instalment of my advance so that I could leave, the manuscript had to be quartered.

In the meantime, the scumbag got a job in a local pub, quite a comedown for someone who'd supposedly put together multi-million pound deals. Piece by piece, his lies were exposed. And for my parents, who trusted people until proven otherwise, this was fairly frightening. He'd said he was waiting for an £80,000 deal to come through, a fair chunk of it they'd already spent together. But finally it dawned on my parents that their son-in-law was not who he said he was and he didn't have any money.

Shuna and the scumbag left to move into their new flat in London, which was a miracle, and I stayed, waiting for my advance to come through. Perhaps my father was just sick of hearing about 'deals' because he sat me down one day and said, 'Look, there is no advance. How much d'you want to borrow to get out?'

I was incensed.

Fortunately, the advance came through the very next morning, I packed my bags and left for London where I got a room in a flat and set about making some money. I couldn't go back to working for someone after all this time, so I hired myself out as a freelance researcher for the headhunters. Stupidly, they told me I was the best in the business, so my prices went sky high and I charged around £300 for two hours' work. If I only got one job a week I was happy. Though this lifestyle was a bit depressing after the previous year, I dealt with it by immersing myself in the planning of my next great escape.

Perth, Australia, had marked the halfway point in the journey around the world. Whilst I might have wanted to call it a day then, I simply felt there wasn't a better life waiting for me back in England – or anywhere else for that matter.

England wasn't my home, it was just a place that I knew, a stop-gap between searching for what I needed. I'd always known a life on the road and even though it was hard, it was a place which I made my own. This was my conscious reasoning. I had decided on Africa instead of Asia as the next continent because I couldn't get a visa longer than twenty-four hours to cross Iran, which I would have to overfly, and I wanted to walk from one end of a continent to another. I'm sure I could have found a way around this, but I was more fascinated with the dark continent.

Times had changed since the early explorers of Africa and war zones and bandits, saboteurs, mercenaries and ex-colonialists with chips on their shoulders were the new ordeals. To walk the length of it, I'd need to cross long stretches without food or water and again I turned down my initial desire to go alone by deciding to take back-up. Of all the walks, this was the one which really needed it and with hindsight I made a very wise decision – I wouldn't have got out of there alive if it weren't for the men who were with me.

I wanted to find a charity which worked in the countries on my walk route. Save the Children Fund turned me down, but then I came across Survival International which campaigns for the rights of tribal peoples around the world. It stands for their right to decide their own future and helps them protect their lives, lands and human rights. I remembered the Aborigines, lost in no-man's-land, and the pride of the shy Ketut, trying to defend his way of life against the encroachment of capitalism. No doubt I would come across many more people like them. Survival agreed to receive funds, though I warned them there would be no press conferences in the African bush, just the beginning publicity, any articles I sent out and the finale. I could not act as a fundraiser myself; they would have to do that while I was away.

There was so much to find out about – visas, vaccinations, carnets for the vehicle, types of kit, types of vehicle for spares, routes and resupply, food, diseases and languages – so I went to the Expedition Advisory Service at the Royal Geographical Society and they gave me the name of a guy who hired himself out as back-up on expeditions.

I met Charles Norwood and felt unsure of him straight away. He, on the other hand, saw a pretty blonde who giggled when nervous and who thought that walking across America and Australia was preparation for Africa. He thought I was naive. And he was right. But what he didn't see was that I had a very strong personal motive which meant I could never give up. Having failed in America, it was do or die. I often wondered whether he took the job, the full fee in advance for a year's hire of himself and his Land Rover, half expecting to be back within a month.

During this time I was introduced to Mark Lucas of Peters, Fraser & Dunlop, a literary agent. I'd heard nothing from Heinemann Australia and I wanted *Feet of Clay* published. Mark is a very lovable man, a bit shaggy, a bit overworked, but very even in his dealings with people and he has a good reputation in the market – I know, I checked him out before I walked in the door. He was still in the process of building up his client base and so he took me on – a very good move on my part as it turned out because now, ten years later, Mark is one of the top literary agents in Britain. Which is great if you can get hold of him.

Since Heinemann Australia had broken their contract by not publishing the book within a year of completion, Mark could take back the rights and then sell them on. This he did to Heinemann UK at the staggering advance of £15,000. But there was a huge amount of work to be done on the manuscript and he asked if I wanted to work alongside another writer. I hate the term ghostwriter, because to me that implies someone else writes the book for you. In this case, someone else would heavily edit the manuscript, rearrange paragraphs and try to find the story.

Mark introduced me to Max. And Max Arthur became my second wise man. I found in him, more than in anyone else, a sense that he knew about the dark days and had found a way to come through them and out the other side. A paradox of a man – in his fifties (I think, it's hard to tell), he also taught aerobics in his spare time despite his lack of rhythm. As a teenager he'd been in a car accident and had never regained it. His class were used to this and even though he had used the same piece of music for ten years, he still had to rely on them to keep time. They were as loyal to him as I became, largely because of his ability to make you feel good. No matter how painful it was to re-trawl through the confusion of Australia, he could lift my mood by lapsing into one of his many characters, performing a sequence from his own, bizarre imagination. I don't think our relationship was entirely one-sided though: he had never married and had no kids and I think he needed me to guide as much as I needed him.

Max had written several books on the services, definitive works which were a collection of stories from serving men he'd interviewed. Each time I went to see him in his little basement flat in Hampstead, he would read me one of his latest stories. They were always about courage. Real courage. He never put a fine point on why he was telling me this; I would have to make the connection myself. Max must surely be a man of great restraint because, at the time, he was dealing with a young woman who was riding high on the praise of others for something which was, on the surface, incredibly selfish. At the end of each story, he would tell me what the servicemen had said about the incident and each time it showed great humility. I asked him many times what humility was and patiently he'd tell me, but I can't remember what he said because I didn't understand it. Unless I learned about humility I could not appreciate other people's achievements, and unless I could do that I would, of course, remain friendless.

I didn't feel that I was lonely, though; there were always plenty of guys at parties who, attracted to my energy, chased me for attention. I enjoyed the set-up of dating but I didn't want to be involved with any of them. I wasn't looking for a partner so I'd rotate about five at any one time, seeing them once a week, bonking the hell out of them and then leave. As far as girlfriends were concerned, I had nothing in common with anyone I met: looking for husbands wasn't interesting, nor was the corporate ladder. I didn't share anyone in common, so there was nothing to talk about.

I got a personal trainer to go through a training routine with me, working out in the gym three times a week, but again my lower back and the shin splint injuries began to surface. Through the British

Sports Association I found a miracle worker, Dr Ken Kingsbury, who accompanies our athletes to the Olympics and treats our judo players, pulling their dislocated shoulders back into place and then letting them out on the mat to fight again. He is the leading sports medicine doctor in Britain.

I called him up and he asked me what kind of athlete I was. 'I walk across continents,' I said.

'Well, you'd better come and see me.'

Half expecting to meet some kind of Amazonian woman, he was quite surprised when a petite 5' 5" stepped into his consulting room. Ken has the kind of laughter which comes from the edge; you can't help but feel everything's going to be all right. He massaged my back and manipulated the sacro-iliac joints in the hips which often slipped out of place – something I probably inherited from my father. He put me in touch with Simon Costain, who makes insoles to correct the pronation problem which causes shin splints, and an osteopath to treat me each week. Then he wished me well. His energy and enthusiasm was a refreshing change from the majority of responses to what I was about to do.

The problem with the independent life I led was that coming across teachers was a bit of a hit-and-miss affair because I didn't know I was looking for them. I was, nonetheless, more attracted to them, and probably sifted them out subconsciously.

I was asked by the Expedition Advisory Service at the RGS to come along to an open-day seminar on travel and be on hand to answer questions from anyone proposing to make a journey on foot. There was a series of lectures during the day on anything from expedition photography to planning and sponsorship. But one of the lectures touched a chord with me which had lain dormant for years. A young man took the stage. He was broad and looked tall even from where I was sitting. The lights dimmed and he showed a series of slides set to music. He didn't speak. He didn't need to: the images of the English woodland and its animals merged from spring through summer, into autumn and winter, arousing something very primeval and exciting in me and doubtless many others in the audience.

I left my seat as soon as the lights went up and raced down the aisle to speak to him. He was trying to make his way to the garden in time to set up a demonstration of his work and he simply told me he'd answer any questions I had when he could get out of the hall.

A little later, I found him in the gardens surrounded by jars of dried mushrooms, piles of natural fibre cordage, deer's brains, spears

(above) Botswana. Animal magic.
© *Oli Ryder*

(left) With an armed escort, the Land Rover has to follow me in bandit country. Zambia.
© *Blake Rose*

(below) The day of the Tse-tse fly swarm. © *Bill Preston*

(above) Squeezing jigger's eggs out of Bill's feet. Zaire.
© *Blake Rose*

(right) The villagers are unsure what's protecting me. Zaire.
© *Bill Preston*

(below) Convinced we aren't slave merchants, the men pose for a photo. © *Bill Preston*

(above) What happens when you don't do the washing up. Zaire. © *Blake Rose*

(below) 'Jambo Mama!' Zaire. © *Bill Preston*

(above) Serenity and strength. The Zaire women reveal the nature of womankind. © *Blake Rose*

(right) Alive and well and living deep in the African forest. © *Blake Rose*

(below) The Land Rover presumed lost in the rebellion. We push our cart. © *Raymond Mears*

(above) If we were lucky, they'd put a monkey on for supper. Central African Republic. © *Raymond Mears*

(right) Zaire river. In search of the lost Land Rover. © *Raymond Mears*

(below) The fire plough is lit as Raymond unearths the old ways. Central African Republic © *Raymond Mears*

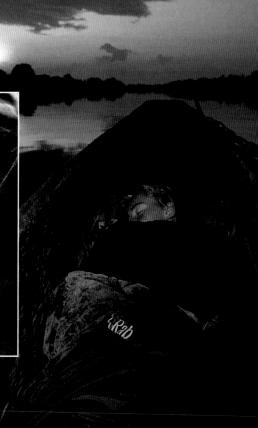

(above) Come and be a missionary in the West. Zaire. © *Raymond Mears*

(left) The only day of primary rain forest. Zaire. © *Raymond Mears*

(below) With the adolescent guide. Zaire. © *Raymond Mears*

(above left) Medicine from the Aka Pygmies. © *Raymond Mears*
(above right) Raymond Mears tests the way of the Pygmies. Central African Republic. © *Ffyona Campbell*
(below) The girls keep trying. Central African Republic. © *Raymond Mears*

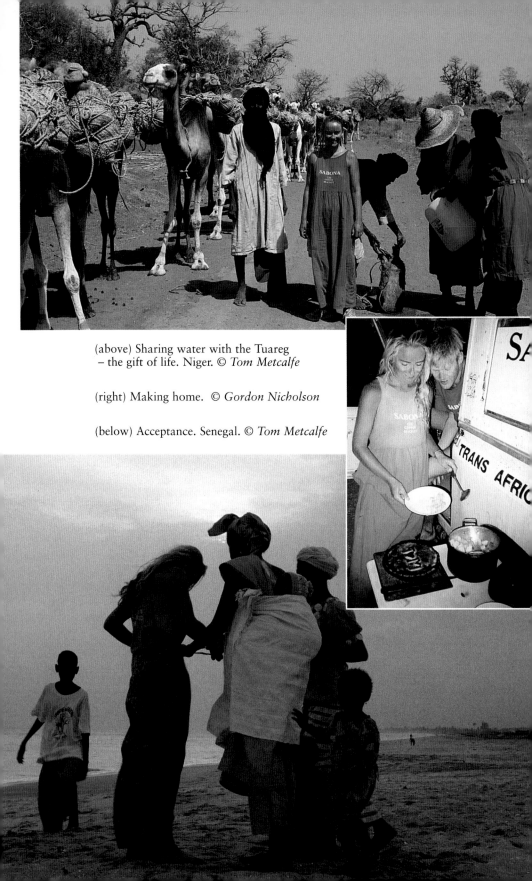

(above) Sharing water with the Tuareg
– the gift of life. Niger. © *Tom Metcalfe*

(right) Making home. © *Gordon Nicholson*

(below) Acceptance. Senegal. © *Tom Metcalfe*

and a crowd of people. I nosed my way through and saw him sitting calmly, showing the audience how to make fire with sticks. He'd taken off his shoes and was sitting on the grass with one foot resting on a flat piece of wood with holes along its centre. Into one of these holes, he'd placed the end of a stick, which he rubbed between his palms, moving them down towards the base. After a while, smoke began to curl from the point where the two pieces met. I expected this to burst into flames but no, he stopped whirling, took out the stick, lifted up the bottom piece of wood and tipped a black powdery but glowing coal into a bundle of tinder shaped like a bird's nest. This he held up to his face, and began to blow very gently and smoothly on the coal. The smoke got thicker out the other end as he moved it around to catch the wind, holding up and blowing, till the flames burst out. There was something so sexually charged to this act that I couldn't walk away from him.

I hogged Raymond Mears for much of the afternoon, accidently putting his girlfriend's nose out of joint and probably those of many other people who wanted to speak to him. I just couldn't get enough of what he was telling me. When I heard he ran week-long courses to teach these skills, I knew I had to do one, not only because of my natural desire to learn them but in preparation for the Africa trip.

The week before his course I'd been kicked out of the room I rented (probably because I am a scruffy animal by nature) and Charles Norwood, who was chasing my affections at the time, offered me a room in his house. It made sense to keep the hub of the walk's organisation in one place, I felt I could withstand his approaches, so we packed up my gear and I moved in. As I unpacked, he and his other flatmate made a show of their territory by keeping up a banter of private jokes. I knew this well and just ignored it.

The search for sponsorship was, by this time, well under way. Charles wanted £25,000 for his services for a year, which included the hire of his vehicle and its fuel, maintenance, carnets, shipping and himself as driver. I'd need another £25,000 on top of that for everything else. He introduced me to an old friend of his, Luly Thompson, who had recently been made redundant from her PR job and had set up on her own. They'd shared a friend in common who had committed suicide and in memory of him they'd organised a journey from Cape North in Norway to Cape Town in a fire engine to raise funds for The Samaritans.

Luly struck me as being straight as a die, intelligent, fun and enthusiastic. Yes, she'd help me out with drumming up sponsorship, writing proposals, identifying targets, sending out press releases. In turn, an impressive expedition would expand her contacts and give her the exposure as a freelancer that she needed.

I took a week off and drove down to Selbourne for Raymond's course. 'Woodlore', as he calls it, is the quintessence of survival. It works from the inside out, changing one's perspective on nature, but not just through confidence with newly acquired practical skills, more through an introduction to all one's dormant instincts. Unfortunately, we can't learn the ways of our own ancestors because their knowledge has been lost forever. Only the native people still living the old ways and those who were studied by explorers hold the clues to living in harmony with the land and it is upon their teachings that Woodlore is based.

In woodland on a private estate near Selbourne in Hampshire, four men and myself arrived on a Sunday evening in late July, far from our western occupations as diverse as a helicopter pilot to a shop salesman. Our experiences of military-style survival courses revealed the same dissatisfactions: we were fed up with roughing it under psychological duress in miserable conditions. We wanted to learn how to live well from the land, taught at a pace which kept in time with nature.

Raymond's foundation course is unique. The techniques are not found on any other course, because rather than learning his skills in the SAS, he is self-taught from years gathering primitive technology from ancient manuscripts and time spent with native American Indians, bringing them to life through application and experimentation.

Stooping under rucksacks piled high with camping kit and the burden of apprehension, we students laughed to drown the noise of the unfamiliar darkness as we pitched our tents in the woods and unpacked our gadgets. When we'd finished, we trooped into a dome-shaped lodge made of branches and tarpaulins and plonked ourselves round the central fire in a circle.

Raymond sat with crossed legs at the head of the ring, waiting patiently for us to settle, surrounded by things he'd made from the woods: flint headed spears, carved ladles, arrows in rabbit skin quivers, hides and cordage and totems. He looked much bigger than I remembered and he exuded that fine mix of strength and gentleness, confident but with no ego to satisfy. Much of his introduction fell on ears deafened by western laws, but we had nothing to fear – this was not a power struggle.

The circle we formed within the lodge was the focal point for our learning, it brought a sense of unity and hierarchy to the group and all skills were demonstrated here. It echoed the ways of the native Americans, who take their adolescents far from the village until they have mastered the skills to join the ranks of men.

Dawn on our first day saw us breakfasting on muesli, gathered from Sainsbury's by James Locke, an African-born expedition leader. Hiawatha might have stalked off in disgust at our reliance on western delicacies, but since we were still as vulnerable as babes in the wood, we kept morale high with food which was easy to catch.

As the only female on the course, I took it upon myself to supplement the diet with my own brand of banana bread which, after two days cooking by the fire, never quite baked. If my skills in the kitchen didn't improve, at least I learned how to make fire.

Raymond demonstrated the use of a bow drill set, then let us loose on the woods to select sycamore sticks, carve them into shape, then practise the friction technique. It worked on the same principle as the hand drill demonstration he'd given at the RGS, only instead of whirling the stick with your hands, you curled a piece of artificial sinew around it attached to a curved 'bow'. With this, you drew it backwards and forwards, spinning the stick into a hole in the 'hearth'.

It took me hours of frustration, exhausted muscles, indignant glances at my trusty Bic lighter, blisters and blood to produce my first glowing coal. Holding it to the sky in a bundle of tinder, I gently blew, careful not to douse the tiny coal with the dampness from my breath, moving it around to catch the wind. The smoke began to billow out through my fingers, but I was completely unprepared for what it felt like when the nest burst into flames – something primeval and very sexual. Fascinated by the flames, almost feeling like they belonged to me because I'd made them, I couldn't put the burning bundle down. Raymond was in stitches.

Now that we were warm in muscle and in morale, we gathered in a ring to learn how to stay that way. We considered what or whom we were sheltering from, what resources were to hand and whether or not to relocate. We agreed to stay where we were since the sticks and leaves of the beech woods provided enough bedding to fill a dozen airing cupboards and though people lived in the valley below, we didn't consider them hostile. Four hours later, we snuggled into our individual lean-tos, exhausted but fulfilled.

By the end of the first day we had laid aside our matches and our tents. Throughout the course we were rewarded by the removal of each piece of equipment, replacing them with the skills required to make our own from natural resources. This mentality is quite the reverse of our western ways, where we strive for devices to reduce our labour, losing the progression to independence and the satisfaction of stamina which Woodlore develops.

During the next day, we replaced our knives by learning the craft which has dominated ninety-five per cent of man's tool-making history: flint napping and bone working. As we tapped away at pieces of flint, I watched Raymond select a large chunk and set it beside him. I asked him what he was going to make. His answer gave me a clue as to how he was able to bring out the best in all of us. He said, 'I don't know yet, I'm waiting for the form inside the flint to reveal itself to me. My job then is simply to help it to come out.'

For the fishing trip that evening, we fashioned bone hooks and made line from stinging nettles, stripped and twisted on the thigh to be incredibly strong. Though our expedition to a nearby pond didn't prove fruitful, we learned the uses of many plants along the way which we could gather to fill our bellies, heal our wounds or fuel our fires.

In the light of the campfire that evening we worked on our skills, spinning nettle yarns and making bowls by burning and scraping the centre from sections of pine. Each of us would have to produce twenty feet of cord and a bowl deep enough to hold a ladle of water for our test on the last day. Though this test hung over us, the pressure represented urgency: if we were ever in a position to have to rely on these techniques, failure would mean much more than the loss of a certificate.

To be truly independent, we needed to find and purify our own water. The next morning we went in search of it where streams run dry and sterilised it without holding it over the fire. The trick was to make a bowl from birch bark, heat some pebbles in a fire then lift the pebbles into the bowl of water where it would boil.

Now that we had fire and shelter and tools and vegetables and water, we needed to find meat.

In order to kill, a hunter must understand the mentality of the animal he hunts and he must be armed with a combination of weapons and senses. We built traps – only those that would kill instantly – and we practised with slings shots, 'throwing sticks' and bolases. Gradually, during that day, our awareness grew keen as we learned how to hear the kiss of a mouse, how to see movement beyond the barriers of hedges and how to combine them both with tracks to locate our prey. And then we practised hunting. One person was blindfolded, the others crept towards him; we played hide 'n' seek; we played tag – games which nobody had to teach us as children, and we remembered just how terrifying but exhilarating it is to be hunted.

Our instincts sharpened by that afternoon, we were poised for something more. Had Raymond not known this and planned an evening of storytelling, our frustration would have festered. We needed to climax.

Following the traditions of the native Americans, we set about building a sweat lodge. Raymond directed us to our individual tasks and even though he was managing men much older than himself, he seemed to bring out the best in them without a hint of ego. A couple cut hazel withes – the young saplings which bend easily – and these would be sharpened at one end to stick in the ground in a circle, then bent over and twisted together to form a dome. Others dragged in dead wood to build a mighty fire beside the lodge, then gathered rocks which would be cooked in the fire then transferred to a pit in the centre of the tarpaulined dome.

Making the pit was my job. I scooped out the earth, then lined it with clay which I gathered from the soggy river-bed. Raymond squatted down on his haunches beside me as I smoothed it out and he whispered to me that I must dedicate the sweat lodge to something by carving out a symbol in the clay. He knew I would understand this. It was the first time there'd been a hint of the spirits which accompanied these skills. I traced a circle into the clay with my finger. Within this circle I laid some leaves: old man's beard for its dried vines which made our tinder bundles, a birch leaf for the wood which burned hot and fast on our cooking fire, hart's tongue fern which would lead us to water, soapwort to crush and cleanse our hands, bramble leaves which flavoured our tea with the taste of blackberry, nettle leaves for our fishing lines, burdock for its nutritious tuber, beech for our bedding and yarrow for its antiseptic quality to heal our wounds.

Then I gathered long bracken stems and laid them on the ground in a ring around the pit, sticking their pointed stem into the side of the clay basin forming a complete fan. I gathered bundles of the stuff and laid them down for us to sit on.

While the fire was built up and our chores had been done, we each found a place somewhere in the shadows and watched the flames and the embers. I sat high up on the edge of a rotten tree root which protruded out above the clearing and I'd never felt more wholly feminine and alert as I did then, amongst men who had hunted. It made me very aware of Raymond's movements.

Stripped to our bathing suits we took our places in a tight circle around the pit under the tiny dome. Raymond and James pulled out the rocks from the fire outside with spades and laid them in the pit. The flap was pulled down and we were in darkness, our senses so heightened we could recognise each other by our individual energy: the shy, the boisterous, the nervous, the strong, the self-conscious, each could be distinguished from the other. As for me, I don't know how they recognised me, I hardly recognised myself – because I wasn't acting.

The first douche of water on the rocks and our lungs restricted against the heat. When we'd calmed down, the next douching took us higher. Fighting it meant you'd have to get out pretty quickly to cool down, but going with it was even better than taking dope on a roller-coaster. Sitting there, I could live the ride without moving, without drugs, with just water on hot rocks. It felt like a holy communion and we were being cleansed.

In time, each person lay out on the grass and steamed, looking up at the stars. Nobody spoke but everyone communicated on a level of understanding which, despite our infatuation with forms of communication back home, we had never reached before. If the best writer is the one who communicates his thoughts in the least amount of words, surely the highest level of communication is understanding without words. And the mind-blowing thing was that this was just the first letter of an alphabet in a language we knew nothing about.

One by one, they left the sweat lodge, but Raymond and I stayed behind.

The measure of the ceremony was felt by all of us while scraping deer hide with flint the following day. We no longer chatted about our lives in the outside world, no longer searching to top the last wisecrack, or to fill the embarrassing silence when nobody could. Instead, we scraped the hide on another ride. In pairs we worked the skin strung up in frames. At first our different speeds were irritating, but then quite by accident or by rousing the dormant instinct, we fell into a one–two rhythm which sustained the labour and turned it into a high. Bonking the hide, the heart beat as the drum.

So much had changed within us since we had stood blind and burdened under the weight of modern advances. Advances towards what, I often wonder. After the test, which we all passed with the highest award, we ate our last meal and packed up our belongings. I looked out over the valley beyond the wood and wanted to pick up the patchwork quilt of fields and shake all the people off it.

We gathered at a watering hole in Selbourne to say our goodbyes and watched the people drinking there. They were on edge, they sat closer together, their voices were louder and more self-conscious, as though they were being filmed, and I think they sensed there was something wild nearby, watching them. And it dawned on me that in severing our link with the land, we had cut off our ability really to be alive. You can be whatever you want in the western world except one thing: you cannot be what you really are; you cannot be animal.

London was a terrible comedown after this. The only way I could deal with it was to get on the phone with more fervour over sponsorship. Charles felt I'd been seduced away by the woods and he finally accepted there would be nothing between us. Around this time he was persuaded by the polar plodder Robert Swan, who was also his boss, not to go to Africa but to send others in his place so he could remain working for him in London. I didn't mind this, except I didn't know the men he'd chosen and who would be my lifeline.

But none of this would happen at all if I didn't get the sponsorship.

My aim now was to get one main sponsor since in Australia each sponsor's PR company had wanted more than their pound of flesh, often calling the same magazines with the story, then fighting over who was due for what, and I'd felt pulled apart by horses. If the contract was watertight so that they couldn't keep threatening to pull out, one sponsor shouldn't be a problem. I've been turned down only once for sponsorship when I've actually got in front of the decision makers, but now nobody wanted to meet me. The recession was biting hard, Saddam Hussein had invaded Kuwait and the charred remains of a British girl, Julie Ward, had just been found in a Kenyan game park – all these years later, her father is still fighting for the men who killed her to be brought to justice. Companies don't like sponsoring individuals at the best of times because of the high chance of failure, and no one wants their logo on a dead body.

Almost in desperation, I went to the British Footwear Fair at Olympia in August 1990, hoping to meet marketing directors. It was the wrong fair: all high heels and slingbacks. Kid's slippers with elephant motifs were about as African as it got. But Hi-Tec was there, standing out like a stubbed toe. I picked up their hiking boots and read the blurb. 'Tested on expeditions around the world,' it said.

So I asked the guy on the stand, 'What expeditions?'

He didn't know. I told him about my walk and said that if he really wanted to test them, he should sponsor me. Luly and I were invited to make a follow-up presentation to him at his office, which we did. But I had some questions of my own: Hi-Tec's niche in the market seemed to be offering lower quality goods at lower prices than the big name brands and I wanted to know why this was. Luly was desperately trying to cover up my question by kicking me under the table, but I was adamant: if I was going to promote their shoes and wear them for 10,000 miles, I wanted to know what I was representing. The meeting went well and they agreed to get back to me within a fortnight.

Three months later Luly got a call to say no. I heard of this on a Friday night, but by Monday morning I'd got them back on the phone. They didn't really want to commit to a journey which would take longer than a year because they felt the media interest would just peter out. I pitched for all I was worth, without realising that this was exactly the position in which the marketing manager wanted me: if he heard any sense of desperation, he could cut a meaner deal. Finally he agreed to be the main sponsor, to have the walk named after Hi-Tec, but he'd only put in half the money. The other half I had to raise before the end of February or no deal. Just £25,000 to find in two months, then.

Raymond and I had got a flat together in Wandsworth after the course. Not quite the woods, but we made it the best we could and his presence at a time like this kept me going. At the end of days spent pitching on the phone, grappling with words to communicate to a world I did not understand, I could arrive home and be greeted by a great bear of a man who knew just what I needed. He'd drain the bath and remove the stinging nettles which were soaking there, run me a hot one then hand me a towel from the airing cupboard under the layers of drying racks for the harvest of our mushroom forays, and make me coffee with milk from a fridge which was stuffed with deer's brains for tanning hides. By Thursdays I'd be so wound up, he'd pack up the tent and pots and bow drills and knives and we'd drive into the woods for the weekend. During the day we stalked the wild mushrooms. Having to be very quiet or else we couldn't see them, we'd catch them and cook 'em up. But Raymond never picked magic mushrooms. He said, quite simply, that life had its own highs and he didn't want to miss even one of them. Instead, he introduced me to the giant Penny Bun (Boletus edulis), the king of mushrooms which would remain crunchy during cooking and add flavour to our soups. The oyster fungus found on fallen trees was delicious cooked in garlic and butter; but my favourite was Chicken of the Woods, a sulphur-yellow bracket fungus which grows on the side of living trees, often frustratingly high up. It has the slightly stringy texture of the finest chicken breast meat. We'd marinade very thin slices with chicken stock and simmer then layer into a pastry case with other mushrooms, put the pastry lid on and bake. We'd serve it up to our friends then show them a picture of what they'd just eaten.

I'd never felt happier than making a place, a good place in the woods and gathering food. You never knew what you'd find and Raymond's knowledge was endless and his manner so gentle. I had never been taught by someone who didn't use criticism as the method and those around me noticed the change -- a mellowing, the edge smoothed off the anger. Perhaps this was what sustained me during the last few months, under pressure to find the remaining sponsorship.

Mark Lucas introduced me to Nick Gordon, the editor of the *Mail on Sunday*'s *You Magazine*, who helped to bridge the gap. Over a round of carpet golf in his office I was very glad that he got straight to the point of buying the story because I can't play golf and it was my throw. He put in £10,000 for the rights to cover the story as a feature from beginning to end. As it turned out this was more hassle than it was worth because in the contract it said *You Magazine* had bought the rights to the feature story so we couldn't give any other interviews and in the next line it said we should get as much publicity for *You Magazine* as possible. When news items came out, Luly had to deal with their lawyers over the following year and Hi-Tec, feeling their restriction, felt they weren't getting the coverage they needed.

Christmas came and with it the first copy, hot off the press, of *Feet of Clay*. I had not told my parents about its forthcoming publication because I found that whenever I mentioned the possibility of a deal coming off, my father questioned me so much I felt like I was lying and went away feeling negative and somehow ashamed. Instead, I shared the daily successes and setbacks with Raymond and Luly. This would be my first Christmas with my parents in seven years and together with Shuna and the scumbag and Raymond, we drove down to Devon.

When all our presents had been opened bar one, I went next door with Raymond and set a tray with champagne. We handed round the glasses, then I proposed a toast 'To Ma, the woman of substance.' And I gave her the last present. She set down her glass, opened it up and stared at the cover, momentarily thinking it was the latest Barbara Taylor Bradford novel because of the toast. Then she squeaked, 'Colin! Do look!'

'Oh, yes,' he said. 'Have you signed it for her?'

When she opened the book, and saw it was dedicated to her, she burst into tears. It was a good Christmas.

Late one night a few weeks later, the phone rang. 'Fi?' It was Shuna. She was calling from a phone box. The next question was hardly necessary. 'Can you come and get me?' I didn't understand the courage it had taken for her finally to leave him and, in a way, I secretly wanted an apology from her for choosing such trash over me, but when I saw her, standing under the street light, I felt just incredibly protective. If I'd seen the scumbag then, God help him. I brought her back with me and made the put-you-up for her in the kitchen. Over a bottle of gin, she told us what had happened.

Over the last eighteen months she'd struggled to live up to the legacy of my grandmother who had been incredibly loyal. She knew of the scumbag's lies but he had reached out to her, saying she was the only one who could help him. She wanted to take care of him, to protect him, never to leave him so that he had the security of knowing she would always be there. But his lies didn't stop. When guys from the corner shop or the local pub rang to ask when they'd be paid for a debt Shuna knew nothing about, she worked hard to cut back so that the money from her job in public relations would cover it. The scumbag's salary was apparently being paid directly to the bank to cover their earlier debt from the money which had never existed. Over the months, they were making headway and had reduced the debt, by his calculations, to a manageable £2,000. But that morning, the bank manager of their shared overdraft account had called Shuna and asked her, 'What are we going to do about this £19,000 debt?' It turned out that the scumbag had put on his suit every morning and gone out, not to work, but to gamble. When she got home and confronted him, he begged her to stay. 'Please don't leave me. I love you. You're the only person who can help me out of this.' She'd felt the tug of protection and loyalty towards him just as strongly as before, but from somewhere she'd found the real inner strength. 'No, the only person who can help you is yourself.' She took her handbag and walked out the door.

I think she cried herself to sleep that night and probably many nights more over the coming months as the scumbag's total debts began to emerge and his voice on the phone was charged with a new helplessness. As his wife, and a joint signatory on the account, Shuna was liable for half the assets and half the liabilities. On a salary of £12,000 a year, she had to pay off the marathon debt of £8,000. And she's just done it.

I knew she'd be OK though, and Raymond said he'd look after her. He, too, was having some troubles over the split with his last girlfriend. She was so distraught when they broke up that her mother went down to take her out and cheer her up. As they window shopped, her mother noticed something which might revitalise her daughter's spirits. She picked it up and said, 'Here, read this book, I'm sure it's just the thing to give you inspiration.' It was a copy of *Feet of Clay*.

I promoted the book around Britain on a tour organised by the publisher's publicity department. It gave me a platform to say what I was doing next and to spread the word on sponsorship. I then left for Sydney in early February to promote it across Australia, crossing my fingers for a miracle to bring me another £15,000 in two weeks.

A sports injury equipment salesman heard me on a radio chat show in Perth while driving home from the office. He called me up with an offer: a free massage in my hotel room. My first reaction was to tell him where to shove his sports injury equipment, but I accepted dinner. That evening I just pitched him for sponsorship. Eventually he said he'd get onto it. I said I'd heard that one before.

I was tannoyed at the airport the next morning. Nicholas Duncan had persuaded his company, Niagara Therapy, to put in 5,000 Australian dollars. In fact, I later found out that he was never reimbursed and paid for it out of his own pocket. With two weeks to go before I headed for Africa, I was still £12,500 short.

When I got back to Charles's office in London, there was a box of shampoo waiting for me, sent by the marketing director of Paul Mitchel systems. 'Because I heard your voice on the radio and thought you must have beautiful hair,' said the accompanying note.

I called him up, thanked him and asked him for money. Four days later we met in Kensington and he agreed to put in £4,000 – two now, two at the end of the walk. They never paid the money at the end of the walk but then, I suppose they didn't get the kinds of photos they wanted of me in the bush with their shampoo. I was still £10,500 short on my original budget. On paper it looked fine because Scholl had put in £10,000 two years before, which I'd spent on training, on treatments for my lower back and on Luly's salary. But the shortfall meant there was nothing left in the pot to pay her for the work ahead. I said I was sorry, but we'd just have to call it a day. Then very gallantly she offered to continue working for me and be paid out of sponsorship for the walk through Europe and in the meantime take the payments for newspaper interviews and foreign sales of the book.

The Land Rover was duly shipped to Cape Town, loaded up with food and supplies for the remoter places, in time for the start date on 2 April 1991. Towards the end, the pages in my work book looked like a wall of graffiti until the scribblings were given a priority number: 1) sew badge on late jacket; 2) get re-shaped insoles from Simon; 3) to bank, get replacement for stolen credit card and T/Cheques; 4) Phone Aunt Rabbit; 5) sign four (six) cheques for Shuna re old parking tickets; 7) put car in bin; 8) take back video; 9) clean flat of perishables; 10) bone for Fraz; 11) PACK!; 12) record answering machine mess – 'Hello, this is Ffyona Campbell. I've gone for a walk . . . '

Raymond and I drove down to Selbourne to spend our last night together. More students would arrive the following morning, but until then we had the woods to ourselves. We made a place, swept away the leaves where the hearth would be, laid out our blankets neatly in the tent, arranged our cooking things and lit the fire. After we'd eaten, Raymond gave me the tooth of a fox we had known. He'd dug up the skeleton and boiled it white then threaded a piece of rawhide through the top to make a necklace. It was to protect me. He'd made one for himself, too, and we put them on each other.

Raymond had also made a sheath and antler-horn handle for the carbon steel neck-knife he had specially commissioned for me from Wilkinson Sword. He had dyed the cord deep red to show that I had earned my spurs in bushcraft skills. Finally, he gave me his moccasins. Then I prepared my medicine bundle. I had brought with me a selection of small totems from my life: some hairs from a pet heifer I'd had at Reivesley, a favourite ring Shuna had solemnly given me when we were little, and so on, and I held each one in my hand. It reminded me of the real gifts I had received and made me feel stronger. I put them in a buckskin pouch and sat for a while thinking about the journey ahead.

I didn't want to leave Raymond, but I felt I had to do this before I could rest.

Though I still had not admitted what I had done, the essence of it was there: I felt if I backed out of a commitment I'd made, I'd always have it hanging over me as something unfinished. Maybe it would have taken more courage at this point to let it go now that I had found what I was looking for, but, who knows, it may have festered even more inside me in the years to come.

Besides, who was I, if I wasn't the one walking?

11

*We have finished eating. Soon she will feel the craving. I won't
offer her a smoke, I'll just watch to see how she tries to get one.*

Somewhere over Africa, I made the change from one who had
made the first step towards peace, to one who had taken two
steps backwards into bitterness.

I arrived in Cape Town on my own; the others would come later.
In some ways those two weeks of promoting Hi-Tec around the Cape
at sports events and doing interviews for the book were both sus-
taining and frightening. I'd never experienced quite such a build-up
before a walk and on one hand it gave me the feeling that I'd already
done the deed and so was worthy of such attention and on the other,
the more people who knew about what I planned to do, the more egg
I'd have on my face if I failed. I found this to be a very strong motive
in itself to keep going. I don't know whether this can be twisted to
reveal some unsightly female ego, or whether this is just self-respect:
I've paraded my pledge, no matter what happens, I'd rather die than
give up.

It was during this time of publicity that the question of motive
came up again and again and again. I wished to God I knew the
answer because the question was really starting to bug me. 'Because
it's there' was Sir Edmund Hillary's reason for climbing Everest. 'To
pay the bills' was how Sir Ranulph Fiennes dealt with it. 'To impress
girls at parties' was the reason Robert Swan gave for walking to the
South Pole. The underlying need for men to seek adventure almost
lets them off the psycho hook, but for women there must be some
darker reason. Since humility was beyond my ken, and humour in
the face of self-inflicted pain was a taboo in my mind, and so too the
admission of the real reasons, I opted for something rather twisted,
but partially true: 'To gain my father's respect.'

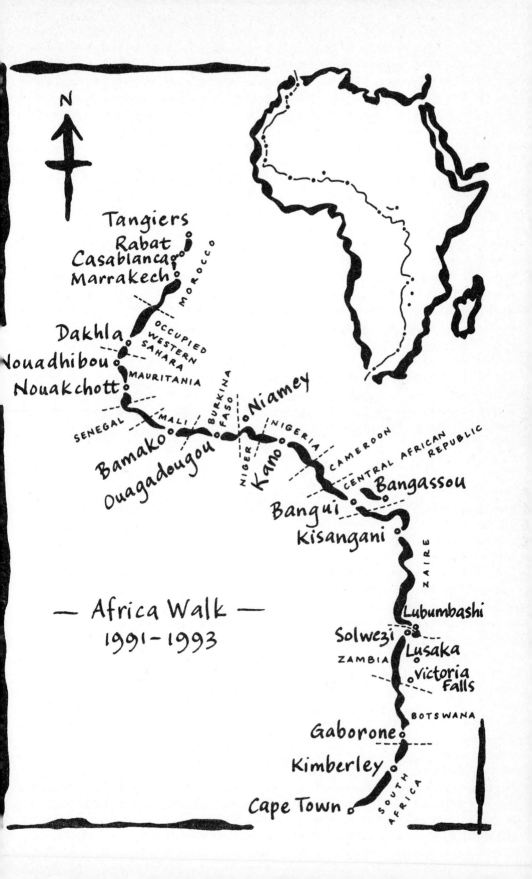

N

Tangiers
Rabat
Casablanca
Marrakech

MOROCCO

Dakhla

OCCUPIED
WESTERN
SAHARA

Nouadhibou
Nouakchott

MAURITANIA

SENEGAL

MALI

Bamako

Ouagadougou

BURKINA
FASO

Niamey

NIGER

Kano

NIGERIA

CAMEROON

CENTRAL AFRICAN REPUBLIC

Bangassou

Bangui

Kisangani

ZAIRE

— Africa Walk —
1991–1993

Lubumbashi

Solwezi

ZAMBIA

Lusaka

Victoria
Falls

BOTSWANA

Gaborone

Kimberley

SOUTH
AFRICA

Cape Town

Whilst I was hailed as a heroine for standing there on the beach in Camps Bay about to walk the length of the dark continent as an affirmation of human potential, positive thinking, faith in myself etc., etc., I was also standing there as a coward with all the contempt that goes with it.

Climbing the pedestal which Hi-Tec and the gathered media had built for me, Brad Lemkus the director introduced me to the waiting crowd: 'Ladies and gentlemen . . . Ffyona Campbell!' Applause. He handed me the microphone. Oh God! Who am I going to be? The pedestal was built for what I said I could do physically, not what I could do verbally. The speech came out exactly as you would expect from someone in my position: a mixture of several different characters I'd seen on TV, including the eye movements of Princess Di.

I got off the pedestal, waved goodbye and started walking down the road, followed by the cameras and the local race walking group. Everyone else thought I was just doing dummy runs for the TV cameras as I'd had to do in and out of the ocean, so they stayed behind eating canapés. Ten minutes later I was crippled by a stitch.

The term 'back-up' is not short for 'at the back, up your arse', though I think Gerry Moffatt and Oli Ryder might still consider it to be so. Charlie had chosen them to support me, waiting up ahead every ten miles, thirty miles a day, but the real challenge they faced had less to do with the great unknown of Africa and more to do with keeping their sanity at close range with the enigma of yours truly.

Gerry had lived on the edge all his life. He was one of the world's top kayakers and, until he met me, I doubt he believed he took shit from anyone. Oli Ryder was too positive to know what was really going on except that he knew a good guy to follow when he saw one.

At the first break, I rounded a street corner and saw the Land Rover pulled over on the verge. They'd set up the table and chairs on the grass and, as I approached, they stood back and gestured for me to take a seat. I was genuinely surprised that they'd taken so much care over laying out the meal; it had been so many years since a back-up driver had thought well enough of me to push the boat out. And I actually thought I deserved this.

The test, of course, was way too subtle for me. They might have forgiven me for being a prima donna in front of the press and had given me another chance to see what I was made of when it was just us. They laid on the 'waiter' bit and I played along. But at the point when we'd all sat down to eat and I held out my glass and asked for a refill, which would mean one of them getting up, Gerry must have got the message. What I really admire about him is that he kept giving me more chances. I guess the belief he has in human nature just wouldn't allow him to accept what was really in front of him.

On the second night out, as Oli was preparing macaroni cheese in camp, I picked up the cheese grater to help. In reality, I don't believe I really wanted to do it, I just enjoyed the rush of attention my offers produced, whisking me away to an empty chair so I could do nothing without feeling guilty. Charlie was with us for the first ten days. He took me aside at this point and said, 'The guys have to find their own working methods, just leave them to do their job.' Quite happily, I took this to mean it was OK to leave them to do all the work.

The years of hard-edged expeditions had produced a safety valve within Gerry himself. When things got tough, he'd party. On the surface, there seemed to be nothing testing about South Africa, where food was plentiful and beer was cold, but this in itself was soul-destroying for a man of such calibre because the greatest decision Gerry had to make each day was whether or not to curry the vegetables. I mistook his sense of fun to mean he was really enjoying himself. It was quite a shock when, three weeks into the walk having spent every evening in drinking games or partying with the farmers through the Karoo, I learned Gerry wanted to leave. And so did Oli. They'd sent a fax back to London suggesting it was better to have a rotation of drivers every three months, their morale was very low, they couldn't stick it for a year to Cairo but they'd stay till Botswana, the next country along. By this time Gerry and I had gone over the top one night during a provocative drinking game and had woken up beside each other feeling very ashamed. We vowed not to do it again, but we did.

I might have got away with this trashing of drivers if it wasn't for Africa herself. She doesn't take shit from anyone, period.

We reached Zambia, having had a few adventures along the way, crossing the world's largest salt pans in the Kalahari and almost losing the Land Rover as it began to sink in the quagmire under the salt crust. The guys dug, I took pictures. Then they cooked the meal, but I did, at least, dress their wounds. We'd spent a week in Victoria Falls. (I later read a quote from one of them saying, 'we were fifty miles from Victoria Falls but Ffyona wouldn't even drive in to see them', which was rather odd.) And we all spoke behind each other's backs to the reporter from *You Magazine* who had flown out to do another story. By the time they'd spent two weeks waiting for me every ten miles through the Zambian bush with swarms of flies crawling all over them, we'd all had enough of each other.

We drove into Lusaka where the new drivers, Bill and Blake, would relieve the exhausted crew. When I saw them walking out from the terminal, I took an immediate dislike to these strangers, coming into my territory. For some strange reason, I actually judged a person's worth by what they looked like – perhaps it was the easiest thing to see. These overweight whities just didn't cut the mustard. So I ignored them, hoping they'd work out pretty quickly that they would have to earn my respect before I gave it.

I didn't know either of them and I wasn't that tame that I'd hand over the end of my lifeline without wanting reassurances. Words wouldn't be enough. Words like Bill Preston had driven trucks through Africa and Asia for years and was one of the most experienced men on the trail. I had no respect for either of them.

In the beginning, Bill used subtlety to try to teach me a lesson. At day's end, when I sat writing my diary while they washed up the meal they'd cooked, Bill would say, hunched over the dishes, 'Don't let me mates hear about this. Me? Doing the washing-up? Fuck off.' Or, ' You know, it never ceases to amaze me how at the end of the day, sitting in the back of the truck, the punters get out and spend the rest of the evening writing their diaries – I mean, what the fuck have they got to write about?' I reassured myself very quickly that this didn't apply to me as I hadn't been sitting in a truck all day. As for Bill doing the washing-up – that was his job.

It is quite fortunate that Bill is a man of tougher stuff. Fortunate, too, that Africa came to our rescue at that point by sending me my first lesson, in the form of a swarm of tse-tse fly. To avoid the bandit-riddled road to Lusaka, we had chosen a 'road' through the Kafue National Park, a game reserve which was once a great hunting ground for the people who live there, then for the white men. But once it failed to produce the game any more, the government lost interest. The road was actually a track which was so overgrown, Bill and Blake were often driving blindly into the foliage hoping to God there wasn't a fallen tree across their path. Bill got bitten, severely bitten, by a fly. It left a great welt on his thigh and he knew it to be tse-tse. From his experience of driving through Africa, he knew they could come in mile-wide swarms to suck your blood. Their proboscis is designed to penetrate hippo hide; human skin is like butter to them. He told me to cover myself completely the next day. 'That means all the gear, mate, the hat, the mozzie net, the trousers tucked into the socks and, if you haven't got any gloves, pull the sleeves over your hands.' I'd been given several double-thickness silk jumpsuits by my clothing sponsors Survival Aids. The salesmen had said they'd been tested in the jungles of Belize and were brilliant against the insects and the humidity. Mine was pale blue and Bill's and Blake's were black. Little did I know, tse-tse are directed by colour and their favourite is pale blue.

The next morning, the tse-tse were on me before sun-up. I thrashed at them with branches, but they grew in number until my dance grew wilder and the attempted bites more frequent. One got under the head net and I tore at it frantically – face to face with a blood sucking tse-tse, there wasn't room in there for the both of us. Another slipped under the ankle grips and started injecting his proboscis into my thigh. I screamed and smacked it hard through the suit, but I couldn't dislodge him. Meanwhile my arm was not protecting my right side so I felt the prick of several more in my neck, lashing them, lashing down to dislodge the one inside till he fell off and was trapped inside my trouser leg, panicking to get out. I tore at the ankle cuff to release him, but as I did so, the material was pulled tight over my bum and I felt the proboscis injections in there too – slapstick stuff. But not as comic as going to the loo. Exposing my privates and fiddling with a Tampax. I couldn't stand around to bury the used one but left it there. As the sun got higher, the tse-tse grew more vicious. The zoot suit was so hot I thought I was going to dehydrate and die all neatly wrapped up in my own designer body bag.

When I reached the Land Rover for breakfast, I found Blake cooking pancakes. He was under attack and should have been inside, but had chosen to make me breakfast. I had never felt a real rush of admiration and humility before this moment. It was a major turning point in my view of Blake and my relationship with both of them. The tse-tse were drawing us together.

The next quarter was the same. For mile after mile, the tse-tse flies were buzzing around me like hurdy-gurdies. I drew the hood cord tight around my neck so that no skin was exposed on my face, but I grew lightheaded trying to breath and my glasses steamed up until I could see no further than the sand at my feet. Even with the netting I was kissing tse-tse as it leant against my face in the God-sent breezes under the first cloud for weeks. My right eye lid was bitten almost closed and it was difficult to see. But the mental torment was indescribable: I could not get away from them and they would not leave me until they'd had their fill.

At lunch the guys darted out to put up a mozzie netting and chair for me and opened tinned veggies and made tea. I sat watching them dance in their suits. They refused to come inside, saying it was better out there. They were right: the tse-tse were coming for me in my blue suit but I had to take a load off. Bill lit a fire on the track to try to smoke them away but they soon went of their own accord as a swarm of dehydrated bees arrived, heading for a leaking jerry can of water behind my head.

Bill's smudge fire was burning the wrong wood and he promptly vomited from the poisonous fumes given off by the burning sap. The bees didn't notice and darkened the sky around us. We packed up quickly and I reassured them I was OK. They drove ahead to day's end, but the tse-tse followed me.

An old man going fishing had told us that a lone male lion had been seen two days earlier. Lone males are often most dangerous because they're usually old, injured and cast out from a pride by younger competitors. With no females to hunt for them, they will attack only the weakest prey.

I looked anxiously about me, knowing that I came high on that list. Through the netting of my hat, my vision was limited and I knew that an attack would come from behind. When the woodland grew thick, I should have been able to use the noise of monkeys and cicadas as warning signals, but the noise of the tse-tse drowned out everything but my cursing. A lion could smell blood over a distance of twenty miles and I was not burying my Tampax deep enough, if at all, leaving a nice neat trail of blood for him to follow.

I kept turning around, shouting like I was many people. My knife hung from its cord around my neck and I imagined what I would do if I saw the lion. I unsheathed it and carried it in my covered hand, waving it around to thrash away the tse-tse. Fat chance of being able to live through an attack, but it made me feel less vulnerable.

The last of the three ordeals that day lay just around the corner: bush fires. Great yellow tongues licked through the dry bush, billowed by the wind across the track, consuming the grass on either side. I had no idea how far this lasted but since Bill and Blake hadn't returned to warn me, I figured it had either begun after they'd driven through or they were stuck on the other side, unable to cross back again. Actually, I was too tired really to give a damn if I didn't make it; anything was better than the torment of the tse-tse. It took several leaps to get into the middle, then several more through the next bank of flames and out the other side. Most of the flies had gone, but I've got to hand it to the others – they were determined little suckers.

I marched down the track, thrashing them off and rounded the bend to see the Land Rover waiting. I had never felt such relief. Blake was looking out for me and saw I was still covered in tse-tse. He ran towards me with a can of insect repellent, spraying me down and tearing off the sodden mozzie net and silk 'body bag'. My face was swollen and right eye completely shut.

'Good onya, cock,' Bill called as we approached. 'There aren't more than four people who live on this stretch because of the flies and you're the first person I know who's ever walked through a tse-tse belt.'

'But the hell ain't over yet,' I called back as I rummaged in the first-aid kit for antihistamines. 'I'm cooking tonight.' They didn't know how bad it could get until they'd tasted my 'one-pan wonder'. They weren't as surprised as I was when I actually gathered the wood, built the fire, cooked supper and washed up afterwards. At last we'd all had something tangible to fight against, instead of each other, and we'd pulled together. We later heard of a man who'd shot himself when attacked by tse-tse. I think we could all believe this.

Setting off for Solwezi, the track was soft sand, sucking my feet down and making me stumble forward when I hit an unexpected hard patch. Around me the bush changed every few hundred yards from autumnal trees with russet leaves and burnt charcoal under-growth from recent bush fires to lush green canopies with an abundance of vibrant undergrowth. After a couple of days, the track turned to tarmac and, a few kilometres after I'd waved to Bill and Blake as they drove to the end of another thirty-mile day to make camp for the night, I walked into a village.

Three plump little girls ambled along chewing sugar cane. Their under-developed breasts bounced beneath white cotton shirts that hung loose above their navy skirts after a day at school. They ran hard to keep up with me, kicking dust with their flat black shoes.

From between the family plots of sorghum, ragged and laughing, the little boys streamed onto the road around me as though I were the pied piper leading them out of town.

A young man about my height with thin lips and a face like a Mutant Ninja Turtle joined me, asking questions. I told him I'd walked from Livingstone. He was astounded and disbelieving. When I looked back the whole road teemed with dancing children, laughing, clapping, shouting questions. I felt self-conscious after three weeks of solitude in the bush. They wanted to look in my pack, so I showed them my water bottle and they seemed satisfied.

'How long are you going to be with me? My husband is up ahead and I know he'd thank you for escorting me.'

'We're just following you,' the young man said. 'Why don't you slow down and let people see your face?'

'My husband is waiting for me; they should run and keep up with us.'

'What political party do you support?'

'Neither. I don't know about them,' I replied.

Neither did he, it seemed. He was wearing a UNIP T-shirt but making multi-party signs with his fist. He slowed me down with his pace, constantly smiling while his eyes furtively looked behind us. Although he asked many questions, I knew he wasn't listening to my answers.

A truck going the opposite direction stopped on the road behind me. A tall, muscled man in shorts jumped from the back, strode towards me, pushing his way through the kids. He grabbed me by the arm and pulled me towards the truck.

'Hang on, what are you doing?' I demanded.

Suddenly the atmosphere changed. The laughing kids were howling like Red Indians, shouting, spitting, shoving me.

A young woman in a headscarf screamed in my face, 'This is Zambia. You can't walk alone in Zambia.' She grabbed my neck knife. 'What's this for?'

'For cutting food . . .' I couldn't think quickly enough.

From behind, somebody grabbed my hair and yanked my head back. Another unsheathed my knife. I felt it pressed into my windpipe. Desperately trying to stay on my feet, I was being dragged sideways with my head held back facing the sky. Suddenly all the advice I'd ever been given about these situations came flooding back along with the repetitive acknowledgement that this actually was a *situation*.

I spoke softly. 'I'm just going for a walk in your beautiful country; my husband is not far away.' Suddenly aware of the appalling smell of their excited bodies, I wanted to vomit.

The woman screamed 'Spy!'

It electrified the crowd. I was almost lifted off my feet and dumped at the truck. The driver hung out of the window, trying to make sense of the commotion. I told him that I needed a lift. He was frightened. He shook his head. I pleaded with him until I heard the military Land Rover pull up. The sight of that uniform frightened me more. In Zambia the militia rape, rob and murder. I'd walked for three weeks through an uninhabited game reserve to avoid them. But now I had no choice but to plead my case.

I shook hands with the officer. 'My husband is not far away. Please take me to him. I've just been for a walk in your beautiful country . . .' My words sounded hollow.

He listened to the crowd. He considered me with the knife held to my throat and looked away. With a slight tilt of his head, he indicated the back of the truck. I took back my knife roughly, and climbed awkwardly over the side on top of a bamboo bundle.

I looked away from the jeering crowd, now out of their reach, and shouted, 'Stupid paranoid idiots!'

We drove for a few miles. All the way I strained to catch sight of the Land Rover parked in the bush for evening camp, frightened that if I missed them I wouldn't be believed.

The guys always made sure they were out of sight of the track in case of trouble but their marker for me wouldn't have been placed yet: they weren't expecting me for another hour.

Luckily they were still on the roadside, but also under arrest. The local chief had seen Bill walk into the bush to find a camp site and sent two men after him. He accused him of planting a surface to air missile to bring down President Kaunda's plane. I think Bill probably planted something else in there.

As I got off the truck, I rushed to 'my husband'. Bill was very calm and explained to the army officer exactly what we were doing. My hands were shaking as I lit a cigarette.

Flatly and with no grounds for discussion, we were ordered to follow them to Solwezi, where our authorisation would be checked at the police station.

The station courtyard was full of rotting Land Cruisers and the little shade was taken by officers in khaki shirts. Inside, the counter was like a kitchen table, except underneath were stacks of cartridges for their multitude of guns.

Slowly we began explaining what we were doing. Although in control, I could see Bill nervously eyeing the guns that were being twiddled absentmindedly around fingers. The last time Bill had seen guns, he'd been shot by one of them. That was in Pakistan and he'd spent three months in intensive care before being fit enough to fly home for scores of operations. Yet his voice did not quaver.

For two days Bill negotiated for our release but grew frustrated because there was no way of knowing exactly who was in charge. It was as if they were just waiting for the whole thing to blow over by itself. Finally we saw the head honcho. He gave us a letter which sanctioned my walk and would hopefully appease any more village chiefs who thought we were spying.

We drove back to the point where we'd all been arrested and then drove another ten miles further back. It was past my point but I couldn't remember it, so better to walk an extra five miles than miss any out. I didn't even see the chief as I walked through the village but the atmosphere was tense: Dr Kaunda had been canvassing for votes and everyone was very confused.

We learned that northern Zambia, where we were heading, was virtually a war zone. Unpaid Zaire military were crossing the border with guns, hijacking cars and taking them back into Zaire to sell. That same day, bandits hijacked a busload of people and took all their clothes and provisions. They arrived naked at the police station in Solwezi, their clothes gone, along with the bags of mealie maize.

The Zambian Government tried to counter the robbers by placing paramilitary along the border, hidden in the bush with orders to shoot bandits on sight. This was a major problem for us because we didn't exactly blend in with the normal traffic and a Land Rover waiting mysteriously in the bush for a couple of hours every ten miles would be a sitting duck either for the robbers or for the paramilitary.

Solwezi was only a day's walk south of the Zaire border but the actual road ran due east, parallel to the border for 115 miles before turning north to cross into Zaire, then looping back again on the other side. Bill and I checked the map closely, wondering if there was some way I could simply walk due north. It would save time and it would avoid the long stretch of bandit country. We spotted a small track on the map which completely cut off the loop and, after finally gaining permission to walk on the path because it was a military zone, we were given an armed escort to ride on the bonnet as the Land Rover now drove beside me. By the end of the day we reached a rusting sign which pointed to Zaire. We couldn't cross there because there was no official border post to stamp our passports, so we built a cairn of stones which we would find again once we'd driven around the loop. A week later, after many adventures along the way, we finally pulled into the village of Mumena, just a few miles north of the cairn. There, we were taken by the military down to the border to start walking again. But the concrete pillar which they took us to was not the same as the one I'd walked to. No, they said, that rusting sign is five miles south of here and if you try to reach it we will shoot you. If we wanted to walk to it, we had to get permission from the military in Lubumbashi to cross the border into Zambia, plus Zambian permission from Lusaka to prevent us getting shot if we did so. This was impossible.

We were out by only five miles. Either we could just leave it be and carry on walking, or we could spend two days driving back to Lubumbashi, cross one of the most difficult borders in Africa through twelve checkpoints – any of which had the right to search the Land Rover – drive another day to Solwezi, battle for two days to get permission and an armed escort and then walk three days through active bandit country before crossing the border again. That paltry five miles in forbidden territory would cost me sixteen days, not to mention the increased risk.

I had laid down the rule of my walk from the start: I will walk every step from the Cape to the Med. Non-negotiable. This five-mile stretch was the first real test.

So, back we went and walked the long way round, through bandit country.

Just as I needed reassurance that they would stand by me, I think they needed reassurance that I wouldn't shy off when things got tough. Because if the girl only walked some of the way, how could they be expected to defend me against what lay around the next corner without trying to reason me out of it.

As it turned out, there were thousands of villages around the next corner. The people in these parts of Zaire have rarely seen a white person and were very scared of us. Believing we were either cannibals or slave merchants, they'd ambush Bill and Blake with their spears poised, demanding to know what they were doing. Blake's true colours began to shine through at these times. He would stand in front of a gathering crowd of angry villagers and somehow he could turn their fear into laughter. He never lost his temper; if he had, they'd have gone for him. His patience was awesome, as awesome as their courage to let him speak.

As for me, alone on the track for ten hours each day, I aroused so much suspicion in the villages because they didn't know what I was up to that the kids would stone me. It is very humiliating to be run out of a village and at first there seemed nothing I could do about it: I couldn't run away and I couldn't stone them back. But, I could use their fear against them. One day I'd had enough of their screaming chants and I spun round, shot out my fingers as claws and growled, 'Ya!' The kids turned and ran like impala changing direction. At a safe distance some would look round, see that I was laughing and then come running back to me and take my hand. They'd all follow, laughing and clapping, parading their tamed monster till I reached the far side of the village.

But there was one sure-fire way of preventing these attacks in the first place: I never once got stoned, or baited or spat on or run out of the village if I had done the washing-up.

I came across this quite by accident at the end of a long thirty-five-mile day – four more than normal. Bill and Blake were up ahead and they'd had a puncture getting water and were an hour late. Normally they'd have set up camp by the time I arrived but this time they pulled off the track, brought down the wheel and started repairing it. It would be dark within an hour, so, I just got on with it: gathered the wood, lit the fire and cooked the supper. Then I put up their tent and pulled out mine, which sat on the top of the Land Rover.

Both of them were too engrossed in the heavy but fernickety task in front of them to notice the coming darkness. I waited till they'd finished the job, then called out, 'Wash hands for supper!' Bill turned round, saw what I'd done and said, 'Oh, cheers cock.'

They were so tired, they didn't speak as they ate. When we'd finished, I got up, took their plates and washed them.

The next day I felt so high that I started to sing and when I saw women walking towards me with their baskets on their heads, I just carried on and they loved it, swaying in time with me in their bare feet, gliding so easily over the stones like Africa was some kind of musical just waiting to happen. Walking into a village, I felt a tremendous climax of affection as I yelled out, 'Jambo Mama!' And they yelled back, 'Jambo sana, abadi?'

'Abadi *missouri* Mama!' – I'm very, very well. And all through the village they waved and laughed with me.

Like I said, I never got stoned by the kids when I'd done the washing-up.

Deep in the forest where there are no horizons, I could tell I was approaching a village by the sounds of the beat. That familiar one–two rhythm of my hide-scraping days could be heard long before the singing: women pounding their cassava, two to a bowl, the beat providing the drum for their songs, getting high on the endorphins and the rhythm, interspersed with laughter when they took the piss out of the men. I'd round the last foliage barrier and watch them before they spotted me: so elegant in their brilliantly coloured pannier wraps; their arms so long and perfectly formed;

firm, defined muscle under shining mahogany skin, and they moved as though they were very aware of their sensuality. Chubby little children ran around gathering more cassava of their own accord, as though they were inspired by watching their mothers turn drudgery into fun, like Bobby and Amy I thought, racing to do the 'California Brushing Song'.

But there were other stretches when I knew a village was coming from the dull, unbreaking beat of an engine. As I approached, I could not hear any singing. Instead, I would find the women sitting in a row beside a milling machine, waiting with their cassava to be milled by a device which saved their labour. They didn't talk to each other; they didn't sing; they didn't call to me as I walked by; they just sat there, slumped over with the flies in their eyes in the oily dust. And the kids looked just as bored. I felt like calling out, 'That's the way girls: get contented, get Radio Rented!' It seemed that when the engine was fired into life, it killed the life around it. I was scared of these people. Doing the washing-up couldn't protect me here.

I could tell how dangerous a man on the track might be by how he treated his knife. If his machete was carried in a woven liana sheath, I knew I was safe because the man walked with pride and would always greet me jovially in Swahili. But if a man carried his machete in a plastic bag, more often than not he would not greet me, he would stare at me from sullen eyes. These men did not seem to walk with pride. And a man without pride is like a lion without pride.

There is always a strong temptation when meeting a snake to poke it, especially if your eyesight has been damaged by malaria prophylactics and you suspect that the black thing lying across your path is really a piece of tyre rubber. Black Mambas did rise up and strike, but only at the passing Land Rover.

Wherever the white man had been with his donations, I braced myself for hostility. But where I trod in virgin land, I couldn't stop the villagers gifts to me. I started to see humanity in its purest forms: life had evolved here through the simple process of doing what worked best, not through any imposed ideal, and it was all displayed right there in front of me. I saw men return from hunting after short sharp bursts of energy, exhausted; I saw women pound cassava for hours, keeping up a steady rhythm, harnessing their different energy and combining it. I saw men competing with each other over everything and women stepping in to calm them. I saw men wandering into the cooking area and women shooing them out, I saw them wave goodbye and walk out of the village with their spears and nets to go hunting but then I'd find them in the bush, sitting in the shade, drinking palm wine. But the women seemed to know this, as though they'd made a secret pact: you can get the credit for the hunt, but I am the one who cooks it for you, who tends your wounds and tells you how wonderful you are so you can go and hunt tomorrow. Forget this at your peril. I saw young boys and girls playing and competing on the way to fill their calabash bowls with water from the river, meeting children from other villages, taking pride in their responsibility. I saw adolescent boys going hunting. I saw adolescent girls driving them crazy; I saw the albinos who couldn't stand the sun, sitting in the shade making baskets; I saw babies on the backs of their mothers, comforted by the rhythm; I saw old people holding council, receiving gifts, giving advice to the young; I saw them all raging through the night, dancing so hard and so high they were talking to the spirits, and I saw them mourn.

But I never once saw any evidence that they wanted to change each other. And I didn't get the impression that they were spending much time wondering why they were there, either.

Walking past their lives, when they called out to me and asked, 'What are you looking for?' I clamped up against a terrible sense of loneliness. My life had been a series of questions even from my own kind. Where do you come from? And later, why are you doing this? Statements, really, confirming that I did not belong. This isolation hurt me as a child but I'd dealt with it by thinking that one day, at the next school or round the next corner, I would come across my people, all I had to do was to keep looking for them. Now that I was surrounded by people I was looking for, it struck me that no matter how far I walked, or how hard I worked or saved or did the washing-up, I could *never* belong as they did.

Even in my own camp, my people did not share the things which affected my days. If I made a joke about morning fly, I had to explain it and with that explanation, all comfort was lost. Instead, the conversation centred around what Bill and Blake had experienced that day. Bill would make an observation and, like a pound coin dropped into a space invader machine, a whole scene appeared on the screen of their minds, a whole scenario which had rules and an objective. He turned to his friend. Take your positions. And they're off: Bill and Blake down the track, bantering away in top gear. I heard this banter develop over the weeks, added to like a series of graffiti on the back of a door. I watched how they knew when they were beaten, when they gave in gracefully, acknowledging the winner with applause. But I didn't notice all of the unspoken banter, though it developed, with whole episodes conjured up and played out between them, in gestures and eye contact relieving their tension. I saw how there was rarely any misunderstanding between them and how they knew, without asking, how the other must be feeling.

I had no encounters to share, or if I did, I discarded them. When you are not expecting to retrace your steps, you don't remember the landmarks. I wanted to throw out an observation and for them to give me the sound bites, the stories to reveal what I knew was there and draw back the curtain for me. This sense of despair at being unable to see or to feel or to be felt was far greater than any hardship, greater than walking with malaria, or under attack from moisture bees or convulsing with diarrhoea while the children watched. Greater because I could not walk through it and out the other side. The further I walked, in fact, the further away I went from finding even the most superficial level of communication. And in a way I felt I'd been betrayed.

If I thought of giving up, I'd ask myself what the alternative was and images of misery in the dark damp days of London were enough to convince me that no matter how bad it got, this was better. I had no home to go back to; my home was here, on the track, in my camp on whatever level of kinship I could make in the few months we had together.

My fear of dependence on my drivers for food and water wasn't so great as on the other walks because they had to find it for themselves too. But they were still taking care of me more than I took care of them and this added to the imbalance between us. Again, Africa came to our rescue, this time in the form of a small worm which buries under the toenails to eat out a hole and lay eggs. Chiggers. Bill and Blake were way too macho to dig them out of each other's feet, so I became bush nurse. In the evening, as Bill kneaded bread by the fire, I'd pick out the worms with a pin and squeeze the white bubbly eggs from Blake's feet. To be honest, there was a little more to this than simply taking care of them: chigger squeezing is like coming across the biggest zit you've ever seen.

When food grew scarce, Bill and Blake cut down on their own portions during the day and gave me more. They said they weren't hungry. But at day's end, we would all work for several hours to produce a meal to sustain us. One evening, we'd found a bag of veggie burger mix amongst the last of the stores. For four hours, we set to our tasks of making bread rolls, slicing and frying cassava chips and onion rings and burgers till we laid it all out on the table, ready to assemble. The table leg broke and it all slid off into the sand. We looked at it and then at each other and just laughed, hysterically at first but then evenly, like the laughter of the villagers, and it bound us together and took the sting out of the blow. Just as the brightest light is found next to the darkest shadow, laughter on the edge was the highest I'd ever been.

But all this was taken away from us when we walked into a war zone, were evacuated by the French Foreign Legion and I woke up in London, in my sister's flat, listening to her making tea and Capital radio giving the traffic report from the Flying Eye.

All gone.

12

Without a cigarette, the girl fidgets. Her fingers go up to her face; she drags the skin on her cheeks as though trying to get something out. Finally she gets up, squeezes past me and goes into the loo. After a while, she comes back again and I see that her collar is wet.

I gorged on food for the first few days; you could find it every-where and so much of it. I could walk down the street without having to coerce kids into not stoning me. I could go to the loo and shut the door without dozens of noses pressed to the window. But like walking into a headwind which suddenly stops and you fall over, I started to collapse. There seemed to be nothing tangible to push against but there was still hardship – like South Africa had been for Gerry, this place was hard because it was so safe and so easy and I felt weakened and incapable. I wanted my walk back but Zaire was now a war zone.

Sick of being ripped off by a corrupt dictator, the Zairois people had burned the buses when they heard the fares had doubled over night. This rebellion spread like wildfire across the country: on ram-pages, with guns, they burned the shops, the cars, the boats; they looted the diesel and the goods and they wrote on the walls a message to their President: 'Hey, Mobutu, thanks for the party.' Did the destruction hurt him, sitting in his houseboat with its solid gold taps on the Zaire river? Possibly, but he'd never show it. Peace at any cost was how he said he justified his embezzlement of his country's gold. And even though the villagers were under his control, they still had their pride; no matter how small they were by comparison, they could still have a go at making a dent in their Goliath. They were more free than he because they had a safety net: if things didn't work out in the town or the city, they could always go back to the bush, they said.

When the Foreign Legion flew into the capital to evacuate the expats, the plane was shot at. If any white soldiers had fired on the Zairois, it might have been seen as whites backing Mobutu. For us, in the third largest town, Kisangani, far out in the rainforest, we'd had no choice but to join the evacuation. The rains had come and washed away the roads out of town so we couldn't drive out to a neighbouring country even if we could find fuel after the looting. We couldn't stay there and wait it out because Bill and Blake had come to the end of their three-month stint and had jobs to go back to. I couldn't stay alone because there were no communications or flights, so Charles could not get new drivers in to me; and I couldn't walk on alone: the villagers were suspicious enough without being in the thick of civil war and I would be seen as a spy.

The word from the Foreign Office was to keep away from Zaire. It could be months or years before it settled down again. I called the *Guinness Book of Records* and asked them what I could do. They said, no problem, the two men who had walked around the world before me had run into war zones and had flown over them, carried on till the country was safe enough to return to and made up the distance. Kisangani was 600 miles south of the border with Central African Republic. I would begin from Bangassou, a town on the border, and walk west from there. I had wanted to walk to Cairo but I knew there was a civil war going on in Sudan which I'd have to cross on the way. If the war hadn't abated, I'd have to walk a longer route, following the path of the overlanders, through Central African Republic, Cameroon, Nigeria, Niger and Algeria. At this point, the war between the Muslims and the Christians had got worse. I would have to take the longer route to the Med.

But, returning to Bangassou meant I wouldn't have a Land Rover. We'd left ours in Kisangani with an overlander, Geoff Roy, who said he would either drive it out to Burundi when the fuel started to come back and the roads had dried out, or he'd leave it in a safe place. But after three weeks, we still hadn't heard from him. There had been more riots since we'd left; we had to assume the worst – that our Land Rover had been taken.

I didn't have enough money to get another one and Charles's insurance didn't cover loss in times of war, so if I wanted to carry on walking, I would have to go unsupported. The thought terrified me but there was no alternative. If I was really committed to doing this, I must have the courage of my convictions. I knew I hadn't a chance in hell of making it alone, but to find someone who could actually

(above) Sahara walking. © *Gordon Nicholson*

(right) My Father joins me in Senegal.
© *Tom Metcalfe*

(below) Fast walking. Got to reach the border
before it closes. Mauritania. © *Gordon Nicholson*

(above left) Pete. © *Ffyona Campbell* (above right) The only shelter from the wind. The Sahara. © *Peter Gray* (below) Peace. Western Sahara. © *Peter Gray*

(above) Hitting Morocco. © *Peter Gray*

(right) It doesn't get much better than this.
© *Desmond Boylan*

(below) With Pete, saying goodbye.
© *Fiona Hanson (PA)*

(above) With Pete, Tom and Shuna. Tangier. © *Detmar Hackman*

(left) With Bonita. Spain. © *Ian Maclagan*

(below) The flies. Spain. © *Ian Maclagan*

(right) With 50lbs on my back. France. © *Ian Maclagan*

(below) Little Anne, magical donkey. © *Joanna Beaty-Batista*

(bottom) The farrier points to where the nails should have been. © *Ffyona Campbell*

(above)Despite the negative press, the kids turn out in force. © *Dennis Jackson*

(left) DIY in Europe. © *Ffyona Campbell*

(below) British walk. The Ceremony of the Syr in camp with Raleigh. © *Dennis Jackson*

(above) The morning of the end. © *Dennis Jackson*

(below) The warehouse desert. © *Ffyona Campbell*

(above) In search of a stone. © *Ffyona Campbell*

walk with me seemed impossible. Except, of course, that the ability to do something isn't based on your physique but on your desire to do it. The one man I knew who wanted to do it, was also the man I had rejected after the first few months of Africa. I had told Raymond not to wait for me. I couldn't deal with such a long walk by straining for the end so that I could be with him. This attachment had felt like I was on the other end of a stretched elastic cord and if I relaxed I would ping back to my starting place. I had to cut it. I needed to be free in order to learn and grow. But it hurt him. However, when I called him on that Sunday morning and asked him if he wanted to go back to Africa with me to walk unsupported, he immediately said yes. But Raymond has too much dignity to be used. He made the rules: we go as a team, we work together, we're partners but we aren't lovers.

Raymond had lectured extensively to teams going off on expedition, but he'd never been in the field himself. If I had any worries about how he would cope then I didn't know him. His professionalism was awesome, right down to decanting the medicines into watertight bottles and relabelling them to get across borders. Within two weeks we'd planned a new expedition and were ready to go.

In early November 1991, Raymond and I tried to pick up our rucksacks at the railway station. Looking much like Neil Armstrong and Buzz Aldrin, we staggered onto the train, an almighty achievement in just those few steps. But during the course of the journey to C.A.R., I grew increasingly nervous about my ability to carry such a weight for thirty miles a day as well as buying and cooking our food, finding our water, making and dismantling our camp and being our only protection. But then I had a brainwave: we'd get a cart! I'd seen them used way down in the south of Zaire, where men pulled their own loads because they'd eaten their donkeys.

I figured we'd get one made, but on our first morning in Bangui we rounded a corner and saw a hundred thousand carts lined up in the market. We bought one, and a padlock, a couple of umbrellas to protect us from the sun, then were driven for twelve hours through the bush on boggy tracks in a car which had been lent to us by a contact of De Beers in Bangui.

Carts are nice ideas. In reality, unless the road is tarmac, you're in for some serious problems. These tracks were not only boggy, but were firm, they were corrugated and the camber was so steep that the cart would career out of control.

The T-shaped handle had to be pushed from a certain angle to get the wheels moving at all, but Raymond is 6' 2" and I am 5' 5". We found it awkward to push together, so we took it in turns, and it didn't take us long to discover that it was the wrong height for both of us. After all these months in Africa, my new-found awkwardness was highly frustrating. Some way out of Bangassou though, we met the first real problem: a small incline. Halfway up it, heaving and pushing and in danger of slipping back down, we also met the solution: a pair of generous black hands got behind the cart and pushed it swiftly up the hill. All right!

Our friend left us at the top of the hill and we pushed alone until we met someone else on the track who said he needed money and would help us. We made quite a bit of distance that first day despite the greenhouse humidity. That night we camped in a gravel pit as I'd done with the Land Rover, preferring the solitude away from the enquiring eyes of the villagers. We were exhausted, having pushed our city-soft bodies a bit too hard, but now we had to figure out the camp set-up. Like the first few days of any new stretch of the walk, getting into the system is hard work. Putting up the tent and the water filter system, getting the fire lit and rummaging around for food made us wearier still. And we felt very vulnerable. This stretch of road was frequented by the Zargena bandits who came down from Chad to steal at gunpoint. Just a week before, a white missionary had been shot dead in the bush.

The next day we set off, legs swollen from insect bites – a small, black, virtually invisible insect, which I called 'Bitey Bitey', gave a nasty little sting and when you scratched it the stinging got worse. Physical effort in such humidity was debilitating. We rested every few hours, as I'd done before, but this wasn't the same walk and I was imposing my rigid schedule without letting it find its own equilibrium.

That afternoon we crossed a long open plain without shade. We hadn't urinated for several days and began to feel the onset of heat exhaustion. Both of us fell silent, unable to speak. We stopped, put up the umbrellas and emptied our water bottles. During the next two and a half miles, we drank ten litres of water between us.

That night was the worst night of any walk or any other time of my life.

Raymond had difficulty in lighting the fire, and as a bushcraft expert this was pretty serious. I went to look for wood but couldn't see any. I forced myself to take a deep breath, relax and look again. I discovered that I was surrounded by the stuff. Working on autopilot I put up the tent, laid out the bedding and fiddled around setting up the water filter. It dripped one small green drop at a time: to filter twenty litres for a day's water would take a week not a few hours overnight as we'd planned. It was only very much later that we discovered they have to be washed to get the colour and dressing out. We used Chloromin T instead and filtered the dirt with our teeth.

Raymond boiled some water and cooked up one of the six dehydrated meals we'd brought. It smelled delicious and comforting, filling my mind with the image of a joey in its mother's pouch.

Raymond's shits continued throughout the night and weakened him. It started to rain. I lay under my sleeping bag with a lump in my throat. I knew beyond all doubt that there was no way I could do this walk. Not even in the first days of walking fifty miles a day across Australia had I felt such a deep and certain knowledge of my inability to go on, not because of the physical hardship, but simply because I had no motive. I was faced with pushing this cart for at least a year to get to the Mediterranean, yet even if I got there I wouldn't be able to say I had walked the length of Africa. The 504-mile stretch I had missed out would forever be a skeleton in my cupboard. I had often hung onto the line: 'I have walked every step from the Cape; I will walk every step to the Med', but now there was no line to grip. I had no will to get up. I couldn't believe that I hadn't anticipated it when planning the restart.

Raymond had pointed out many times since I'd known him that I tended to rush into things with great gusto but without thinking them through. Sure, I'd say, but if I looked before I leaped, I'd probably talk myself into staying on the diving board. This time, however, I had to concede that he was right.

'Raymond,' I said, 'I don't think I can do it.'

Christ, to hear those words!

He didn't understand what the fuss was about.

'What's 504 miles compared with the length of Africa?' he asked.

'504 miles less than the full distance,' I replied.

I couldn't tell him why, but years later when I told him the whole story, he remembered this second night and said, 'I had no idea why this meant so much to you. It all makes sense now.'

I woke the next morning and the despair came rushing back: this is all wrong; what the hell am I doing here? I got up and cooked some peanuts in palm oil and boiled water for Bovril for Raymond, who was suffering somewhere in the bush with his diarrhoea. The act of cooking – of doing something constructive – must have acted as a therapy, because I began to feel more and more hopeful. When Raymond reappeared, I had a flash of inspiration.

'It's OK!' I said. 'We'll be wanderers! We'll just walk from one village to the next, taking it slowly, throw the schedule out the window till we find our own rhythm!'

I felt much better: yes, there was a way to get through. And as usual, I got very excited with the new plan, disregarding the real problem. But what option did I have?

As Raymond was washing in the stream, he met three men walking to Gambo, a small town about thirty miles west along our route. One of them, a slight man with a mouthful of yellow, peg-like teeth, was going to visit his sister who was in hospital. He said he needed the money and agreed to help us push to the next village, three miles away. We decided this would be our destination for the day and we set off under our umbrellas, looking for all the world like a Victorian expedition.

In fact we covered around thirty miles that day. There turned out to be no shortage of pushers. Not everyone needed the money. They weren't rich, but if they didn't have some particular reason to work for payment, they didn't. But for those who did, there were few ways they could make money and we were providing them with employment if they needed it. At each village we were refreshed by offerings of oranges, bowls of water to wash in, and shade. We never had to ask for anything; they could tell we were hot, tired and hungry. We didn't have to explain the journey either; it was just accepted that we were going somewhere because we needed to. It hadn't been the same when I was walking alone: because I didn't have a pack, I had been asked many times what I was doing.

We learned a lot from our pushers. They thought our way of doing things very dirty, and would show us not only which fruit to eat along the way but also how to do it. Pineapple cut up on banana leaves was sensational. Their eyes were much keener than ours: they killed snakes in our path before we'd even seen them. But it was around the fourth or fifth day that Raymond came into his own. We were taken at day's end to the house of the chief, who was a relative of one of our pushers. Raymond struck up conversation with a hunter, swapping tracks in the sand, illuminated at the right angle by an oil lamp.

'In my country we have deer,' he said, pressing his fingers into the sand in a realistic shape of its footprint. Robert, the chief's nephew, immediately caught on and made an impala track. Raymond made a rabbit track; Robert made a hyrax track, and so on. They made the prints in running formation and altered them for male and female.

'What about lion?' I asked.

Robert drew a hand-sized circle with five dots inside. It wasn't a track he had seen, but it was a representation of what to look for. It astonished Raymond because it was exactly the same method he used to teach tracking. It gave all the right information: the overall size and shape and the number of toes with or without retractable claws.

When Raymond asked about their traditional firelighting method, someone produced a box of matches.

'Show him this!' somebody else shouted from the crowd.

The man came forward with a small plant and used a mime which Raymond read to be the hand-drill. The plant was called nsaba, which turned out to be one of those rare and very important plants with many uses: the bark was used for making cord, the leaves were used for loo paper and the inner stem was used for making fire. Some of their uses for plants must have taken years to work out, but the 'loo paper leaf' I worked out myself – it doesn't take long!

He set up a demonstration and the villagers crowded round. Only the elders had done this before; the young ones had never seen it. They all took turns at whirring the stick between their palms down onto the hearth stick. You could almost hear the older ones goading them on with, 'In my day, I could light a fire in thirty seconds!' And they were probably justified in their shock at how matches had lessened the stamina in their young men. Eventually, the blackened powder from the friction began to glow and held together as a burning coal which Raymond tipped into a tinder bundle and blew into flame. When the flames burst out, a great roar of delight went up in the crowd, the young ones looking at their elders with awe. Few people, if any, had been into these villages and swelled their self-respect about who they really are. These people have been told for several generations that there's something wrong with them, with their religion, with the way they do things. Their environment hadn't changed, but their will to live in it must have been damaged by such negativity. Raymond had become a caretaker of some of their traditions and was returning them to their rightful owners; he hadn't come with new ideas developed around the conference tables of aid agencies but he had come with medicine. But Raymond's medicine was not a pill or a potion.

The inner bark of the nsaba plant was dried and made into a yellow powder as a tropical antiseptic. We saw it applied on skin ulcers caused by scratching insect bites. When the villagers saw us, they'd come and ask us for western medicine. Agencies had worked there before we came. They'd worked hardest at getting the villagers to trust in them by showing that western medicine was better than their own. But we said no. We said we are not doctors. Looking back on it now, I see there was medicine in our words. Life everywhere depends on your ability to get up. It requires stamina and strength and a will to live. Our matches had eroded stamina, our milling machines had eroded strength and our medicine is so strong it can make you better without you wanting to live. Cruelty would be to lift off their shells so that we felt momentarily better. Our gift to them was to let them fight for their own life which would keep them strong enough to live well.

In exchange for Raymond's respect, the chief gave us protection and hospitality for the night and lent us two of his sons for the next day's push. This went on from one night to the next in the same way and, as a token of our gratitude, I always gave to the chief's wife a gift of one of the sewing needles I had bought specially for the purpose.

Raymond was happy with this way of life: he was finding his people; but I couldn't relax as he did. Even though we were settling into the rhythm of the cart and enjoying such richness from the villagers, I had to scratch the itch of that missed-out stretch. What lay ahead were months on end of this kind of effort which would amount to nothing, no matter how hard we pushed, if I couldn't get rid of that itch.

Around noon on the tenth day out, something happened which was to change the course of the whole walk. Out of the dust a British overland truck came hurtling towards us. Exodus Expeditions. I waved madly for it to stop; I wanted news of Zaire. But it kept going. The driver later told me he saw two very clean whites under golfing umbrellas pushing a cart and thought, 'Where the hell do these people come from? I ain't gettin' involved!'

I shouted something after them and turned to see a Land Rover following. I waved for him to stop, and he did. It was one of those epic meetings.

'Wild Jack?' he presumed.

'No, I'm Raymond.'

'Hang on,' I said. 'D'you mean Wild Bill?'

'Yeah, that's it!'

It turned out that Kevin had driven through the desert and spent a night with some overlanders in Tamanghasset. The story of Bill had been told around the fire – his shooting accident in Pakistan was legendary and someone mentioned he was now with a woman walking through Africa. Just fifteen minutes before he saw us, Kevin was calculating where we might be.

The Exodus truck had stopped and was reversing back. Johnnie Simpson climbed down from the cab and ambled over. He was driving down to Zaire, across the northern stretch to Burundi and out to Kenya – the first entry from the north by an overland truck since the riots. One had got through from the south within the last few days and had said it was dangerous, but possible. The biggest problem was the armed rebel militia who had taken over the breweries.

We explained why we were walking along with golfing umbrellas pushing a cart and that my support Land Rover was in Kisangani. Johnnie took his passengers aside and put it to them that he'd like to offer us a lift. He needed as much manpower as possible to get through the bogs; instead of the usual twenty passengers, there were only three left and a couple of hitch-hikers. The others had overflown because they felt it was too dangerous. They didn't object.

He turned back to us and said, 'D'you want to come down with us? We'll take you to the river. You'll have to find your own way to Kissie from there.'

Raymond and I looked at each other. No need to discuss it. Yes! I had a chance to get my walk back. We put the cart on the truck and climbed aboard.

During that drive back over country we'd already walked, the villagers looked very different from where we sat on the truck. Instead of standing tall to call out a greeting, taking a break from sweeping their immaculate cooking area, the women slouched and looked like peasants. The kids ran out, but instead of laughing along with us, they screamed, demanding presents and throwing stones, and the men who had shared their knowledge with us simply waved their machetes at us.

It took about a week to drive back to the border, cross it and then down to the great Zaire river. We had no problems, apart from bogs, but when Johnnie left us there, in the town of Bumba, our troubles were just beginning. There were four of us now: Mike, an ex-US Marine with his bicycle and Johann, a Swedish student who spent his holidays travelling. We hired a pirogue (dugout canoe) and together with a crew, we putt-putted for four days up the Zaire river. Ours was the only boat going to Kisangani since the riots and many times we had to fight people off the boat or else it would sink. The skipper warned us that we should leave Zaire, our lives were in danger, but none of us were turning back now.

My greatest fear was that we wouldn't find the Land Rover and would have to push the cart through truck-eating bogs unprotected in a land with people still highly suspicious of strangers. When we finally landed, the ruined town of Kisangani was not as frightening as I'd anticipated: most people had returned to their villages but none of the goods or traders were there and as we walked through the town, Mike pushing his bike and Raymond pushing the cart, there was an air of *High Noon*.

Without the overland trade the Olympia Hotel, where we'd parked the Land Rover, was now a brothel. My Land Rover wasn't there but the manageress said she knew where it was. Unfortunately she was too pissed to tell me and I'd have to wait till she sobered up. It could wait; we had some celebrating to do. I ordered a round of cold beer and we took a table in the shade and toasted each other. We were so excited to be there, so thankful that we'd made it after the tension of the pirogue journey and all the hype. It turned into an all-night session.

Unable to sleep, I paced the grounds of the hotel. The old guard was pacing it too with his bow and arrow. He knew I was pent up so he took both of my hands and held them in front of him, looked at me with his cheeky, shining eyes and started to shuffle his feet. He sang me a song, chirping and chattering like a little bird. I didn't understand the words but the message was unmistakable: 'It's going to be all right.'

Down a dusty track out of town, behind the walls of a Catholic mission, we found our Land Rover where Geoff Roy had hidden it. And it was in perfect condition. We hot wired it and drove back to the Olympia and toasted Geoff all afternoon. Mike and Johann got a lift out of town to carry on to Uganda and we stayed in Kisangani for one more night before driving back to where I had stopped walking. That night we woke up to a loud banging on the door. Both of us tensed. Raymond pulled on his trousers and opened the door. Johann was standing in the darkness, covered in blood.

After he had thrown up and we'd cleaned his wounds and spoken quietly to him, he sat down and told us what had happened. He and Mike had been thrown off the top of the beer truck at sixty miles an hour, along with all the spare tyres and crates and several other passengers. Mike was in the hospital with a broken leg.

Raymond and one of the hospital staff searched the town for looted plaster. They were successful and Mike's leg was set. For the next two days we made them comfortable, shopped for fruit and kept them clean. When we knew they'd be all right, we bought the last of our needs and drove back down the track, 111.5 miles to the start of the walk.

I knew the place, but I had to be sure. When I found, in the corner of the gravel pit where we'd camped on the last night, a Sainsbury's Chicken and Sweetcorn soup packet, I knew this was the place.

With the first step I took from that spot, I had passed the second test. Now, no matter how hard it got, I knew I could go through anything. I had got my walk back, but more importantly I had got back my will to get up again.

By the time we reached Kisangani again, it had taken two and a half months to walk that three and a half day stretch. Mike had decided to wait till his leg was better and then cycle out to Uganda (which he did) but for Johann, there were only two ways out: either get on another truck, or come with us.

Surely the essence of real choice is how much you know about the outcome of each course of action, but when Johann decided to come with us, he had no idea how bad it was going to get – but then, neither did we. The worst of our troubles were the villagers between Buta and Gemena, a month's walk of about 750 miles which was a 'tourist' trail. Before the riots, if you wanted to drive to southern Africa, this was the only route open because Angola was at war and there was a civil war in Sudan. The bottleneck of fast trucks, which ran over chickens, aroused hatred from the villagers. The forest humidity and sores and digging out the truck only to cover a few miles before it bogs again, make the western passengers irritable too. They might be rude to the villagers, buying up all the food or burning masses of wood on their fires or tactlessly displaying pretty goods in camp and they seemed to have the same attitude as I had once: this might be your village, mate, but it's my road. By tripping over their past, in a way I was tripping over my own.

When the kids saw a white walking through the village alone and unprotected, they had a riot. They'd stream down between the houses to the track and set up their hollering: 'Donnez-moi le Bic', or 'Donnez-moi un cadeau' – give me a Bic (pen), or, give me a present. They'd imitate me, bait me, scream in my ears. Then the first stone would scuff the sand in front of me, electrifying the others, and they'd all be at it. I'd try to greet them and wave at the elders but there was little chance of getting them to play any games: they wanted to beat the shit out of a white in retaliation for the last truck.

At all breaks there would be a gathering which wanted to get aggressive. The pressure was on to calm them, but they didn't want to be calmed, not like the ones down south who'd never seen whites. It got so bad for me alone on the track and for Raymond and Johann waiting for me, that we decided to stick together and they drove behind or just ahead of me, keeping me in sight. But the kids attacked the Land Rover too. Climbing on the sides, some tried to slit the rubber around the windows, others got their hands under the roof tarp, little hands darting into the cab to grab something before the drivers could stop them. Raymond would slam the brakes on hard and they'd crash into the back. That was the only way to get them off.

There was no rest at night, either. We slept lightly, not just because of the drums, but because of what they might mean. One night we were woken by the shrill trilling of a bird in distress. We looked out of the tent at several dark figures clad in black feathers, moving around the camp in a dance. They saw us and started imitating animals, jerking their bodies, weaving their limbs, scuffing in the dust. They made noises which sent shivers all over my body. They had come to intimidate us, these boys, out in the bush to test everything they knew before their circumcision into the adult world. But they weren't sure how far they could go with us, not certain if we were the demon they should confront, afraid to turn away from us in case we were, in case we came from behind, in case they failed. How often did they see white men? What if the last time was in bad circumstances, even for just one of them? They left and we didn't sleep any more that night.

My admiration for Raymond and Johann knew no bounds. It wasn't their great mission in life to drive through these villages at six miles per hour. They had the capability to gun it out of there when it got frightening, but they didn't. They could have said this is too dangerous, but they carried on, defending me against men who ran after me with machetes, buying food at lightening speed before they were surrounded by stoning kids, and when Raymond got malaria and lay in the back, he wanted us to carry on at my speed instead of racing as we could have done to get out of the country. But most impressive of all, they kept their sense of humour and as I'd felt so often before, the harder it got the harder we laughed. On days when they trailed behind me, we'd pull off the track and set up camp together without speaking. In that silence, we perfected and synchronised our individual jobs, making camp and sitting down to eat within twenty-five minutes, and in that silence we knew each other's commitment and that's ultimately what got us through Zaire alive. Despite losing eight stone between the three of us and being attacked scores of times every day, I walked every step and we lost none of our kit.

I had seen men laying flowers by the side of a fast-flowing river which they were about to cross. They told us the flowers were for the spirits, but there was a practical side too: it acted like the Green Cross Code, reminding them to stop and look and listen, taking stock of what they were doing. On our last night in Zaire, we paused to remember what we were about to walk into: civilisation after three months of being out of contact with our families back home. I'm glad we took stock of it, relaxed and yet braced ourselves for what we might find because the next day, having crossed the border without any papers for the Land Rover or C.A.R. visas, we called home to unpleasant news. Johann's father was dying of a brain tumour. And we had completely run out of funds.

Johann flew home but we still had a team of sorts because Charles had sent us a new driver. I thought Tim was a woman when I first saw him. But when I got to know him, I knew that was unfair: women stand up for themselves. Even if Raymond had agreed to go on with this guy, we couldn't without funds. It took two months, waiting there in Bangui to get out. Hi-Tec lent me the money then issued press releases in Britain saying how they'd helped me with no mention of their demands for me to pay them back. Johann returned after his father had had an operation and was recovering and we decided on a way north through the multitude of civil wars which had closed every route to the Med. The most recently closed border, between Niger and Algeria, some two months' walk away, might have reopened by the time we got there. But even taking one step outside Bangui we faced the possibility of being attacked by the ever-cocky Zargena bandits. We knew they didn't attack at night for fear of hitting a military vehicle, so we camouflaged the Land Rover in the bush during the day, trying to sleep in the heat and the flies, and walked through the night. It was a terrible time for all of us but I know beyond doubt that I could not have fought all these battles if I had missed out that stretch through Zaire and if Raymond hadn't been as determined as I was.

During the two-month wait in Bangui, when we were at our lowest, we went in search of a tribe of 'Pygmies' who we knew were living quite happily without Michael Jackson T-shirts. The Aka. Stepping into the forest after all the mayhem, we were taken into a world of wisdom and calm which had grown from hardships of a different kind. Instead of feeling like a puppet on a string, pulled by invisible forces on the end of a phone, we felt our women guides held the outcome of their own life in their hands. The rest was in the hands of the gods. If they obeyed the rules, good would come to them. But if they didn't share half their harvest with a neighbouring tribe, for example, the following year there would be a shortage of caterpillars or honey. What goes around comes around was an unquestioned fact: they didn't know what we meant when we asked them about it.

One of the women showed me how to eat a strange fruit, peeling off the skin, sucking at the contents. I mimicked her. Then she dropped the stone in the earth and absentmindedly stood on it to bury it. She had already turned to show us something else; she hadn't thought it necessary to teach me to bury the stone so that it could grow. I guess she'd never met anyone who didn't know that what you take from the land you must give back.

As we walked with them, or rather tried to keep up with them, they seemed to be singing to the forest through their chirping laughter, letting the forest know they were coming, and it seemed to part for them: the snakes moved out of the way, the monkeys kept themselves out of reach and where we saw a wall of dark green, amazingly they stepped through it and we saw there was a passage. They seemed so amused by our curiosity and our ignorance – like showing an alien a light switch or a door knob – but soon they began to tire of it and they left us, running off into the forest, laughing and chirping, vivacious and playful and I wondered, who is it really who doesn't know any better?

There is only one way to say goodbye to a man who has saved your life: you let go. Raymond's job was done and he had to leave us in Cameroon to promote his latest book, the *Complete Outdoor Survival Handbook*. He had done the best he could to pull Tim into line but now I would be on my own with him and Johann. I tried not to think of Raymond over the days which followed but Tim's apathy and general desire to retire from life infected Johann and I felt very vulnerable without the safety net which Raymond's honour and courage had provided. Through Cameroon and into Nigeria we hardly spoke. I could not let their depression infect me and even Raymond, who was so capable of bringing out the best in people and inspiring them, had been unable to lift their spirits. It seemed that somewhere along the line, Tim had fallen down but had not picked himself up again. And now, he didn't care about anything and he couldn't be bothered to feed himself or find anything interesting in the world around him except for his beer, despite the hepatitis he arrived with. I don't think I ever heard him laugh at anything but the strongest, most charismatic of people. I knew where he lived in his head, but I also knew that unless he found his own way out of his shell, he'd be trapped in there for ever.

It was fortunate that Nigeria wasn't dangerous for us. Who could be scared of the Fulani, with their broad-brimmed hats and their tapping sticks, clucking and singing to their goats and shoats and cattle from one water hole to the next? But the mosquito is the biggest killer in Africa and after Tim and Johann had both gone down with malaria, I got it too. Unfortunately, mine came with typhoid. At the very moment when I needed their help to get me to hospital, they were too distracted by their own needs to notice the danger. By the time they'd sorted themselves out, my temperature was over 104 and I was delirious. They finally found a hospital.

It took a week to get over it and back on the road and for the next few weeks, I felt like I wasn't walking to the border with Niger, but swimming.

By the time we reached the border, the unrest had spread to within a few miles of where we stood. The whole of Niger had closed down after the Tuareg nomads had stepped up their fight against the military for an autonomous region. As nomads they didn't have citizenship of any country, yet they were forced to pay taxes and bribes to underpaid soldiers. In an effort to fight back, the Tuareg warriors had to abandon their camels in favour of trucks. These trucks they took at gunpoint from the overlanders crossing the desert. It was said you always knew it was really Tuareg and not a bandit dressed up as one, because the warriors would leave you water and take your driver within a couple of miles of help. The others just shot a few of you and that was it.

There was no chance, even with someone like Raymond on board, that we could cross the desert. The borders had closed too, and even if we struck out off road to sneak round, we'd have to go via the wells, and it's at the wells that the bandits hang out. I'm glad we didn't wait there for it to calm down and the border to reopen because, even four years later, the situation hasn't changed. They let trucks through but only in convoy at seventy miles per hour. If you get picked off at the side, that's your problem.

There were no other routes open and nothing for it but to leave the Land Rover parked up safely and fly home to wait.

I didn't really care for the people who phoned to ask if I'd made it and then turned away from me when I told them about the war zone. Again the headwind had stopped and I ended up in hospital for a while, suffering from more intense stomach cramps which nobody could diagnose. I still get them today but now that I know they come after a confrontation; it's just my reaction to fear. If I don't drink at least two litres of water every day, I writhe around in agony.

I found I could not get up. I tried to start on the book to keep me occupied until a border opened but that went out the window when my computer was stolen with all the discs. I tried to get a job, but nobody wants someone who has lost their vitality. I had nothing to get up for. I felt frightened whenever I ventured out of my rented flat to get some milk and smokes, shuffling back to close the door and lie down in the dark. I tried to sign on in Brixton, but someone recognised me in the queue and said she never expected to see me on the dole. And I let myself go.

After six months, the phone rang. Encounter Overland had just sent a truck north across the desert, this time through Mauritania and into the Occupied Western Sahara. It was an illegal crossing as the border was officially closed, but they had sneaked through. The final test was bound to be the hardest. The war zone which had stopped me stretched about 250 miles north, the detour around it added another 2,500 miles. And there was no guarantee that when I got there I could make the illegal crossing. But, what the hell, anything was better than this!

Once I'd make the decision to get up, I suddenly saw the hands around me offering help. Nicholas Duncan from Niagara Therapy turned up from Australia and got me more sponsorship from his company in return for giving motivation talks to their salesmen. Anthony Willoughby, who'd first suggested I take the Cape Town to Cairo route, turned up from Japan and introduced me over a drink to his former boss, Detmar Hackman of Sabona Copper Bracelets, who offered me full sponsorship right away. And the owner of one of the other Land Rovers which was left in Kano, Nigeria, because they couldn't cross the desert, agreed to let me borrow it free of charge if I would return it to him. I advertised for drivers in the Antipodean travellers' papers in London, hired one of them, a New Zealander by the name of Tom Metcalfe and another, Alasdair Gordon-Gibson, a friend of a friend who worked in Ethiopia for the Red Cross and who spoke Arabic.

In January 1992, Tom and I flew back to Africa. The borrowed Land Rover was in a terrible state – a twenty-seven-year-old wreck which took Harold Blackburn and his team of mechanics at the Nigerian Oil Mills a whole month to get working. And they did it free of charge. Harold and his wife Karen were also the British liaison officers in Kano; their hospitality and willingness to get behind the project seemed to come from a love of adventure and their attitude to problems helped to calm the troubled waters which were developing between Tom and me before Alasdair flew in.

To say we were engaged in a power struggle would be an understatement. We refused to agree on anything, almost out of principle. I felt Tom was ignorant, which he was, and he felt I was authoritarian, which I was. However, we were too up ourselves at the time to see this. The war was so intense that even G, as we called Alasdair, could not pull us together despite his years of surviving the bombings in Beirut.

As we set off once more, heading due west, these conflicts fanned my fear that they would not support me as I needed. But instead of shouting at them when they were half an hour late in forty-five degrees, I found a new way to teach them about the importance of being in the right place, and how valuable their job was to me. I simply asked them to walk a ten-mile stretch.

The first to have a go was Tom. He started out with great strides, bouncing up and down, leaving me behind as though he felt he could carry on like this for hours and what was the big deal. I broke into it slowly, biding my time, walking efficiently and drinking little. After about half an hour he was red faced and sweaty, gulping down his water. But then, striking out again, he began to slow and overheat at the same time. I told him if he wanted more water, he'd have to hurry up now. He got irritable and then fell into silence, and when I heard him pant, I showed him how to climb into a bush to find shade, then, taking a little water in the palm of my hand, I rubbed his skin with it, pushing him around to catch any breeze to cool him. Heat exhaustion comes quickly, builds up with thumping ears and dizziness. Out on the track, two hours from your vehicle, you'd be dead before then if you didn't learn to control it.

Within another hour, he had started to limp a little with a sore spot rubbing somewhere, then he looked at his watch and saw that we were only just halfway.

I told him at which kilometre marker we'd find the Land Rover and towards the end, as he strained for anything which might be it in the swimming, blurring heat, he silently counted down the markers while I chatted about things along the path. When he knew there was just one more to go I felt him relax with relief beside me, just ten minutes more. Rounding the corner to find no Land Rover, I said quite nonchalantly, 'Oh, he must have forgotten which one to stop at, or maybe he's at the market, having a chat.' I didn't know where G was, but it was a lucky mix-up because Tom now knew the fury and the worry. As it turned out, G was a kilometre further away. When G walked with me, Tom did the same to him by two kilometres.

Funny how they were always, bar some epic adventure, in the right place at the right time after that.

It is not only water which is the source of life, but the way it is given and received. As travellers we were accepting gifts but we were very rarely in a position to give anything back. It had been a source of imbalance all my life which I wasn't really aware of until I met the Tuareg nomads one day in the hot desert sun and I had run out of water. I sat in the shade of a tree, waiting for the Land Rover to catch me up. I fell asleep. When I woke, I saw a camel caravan of about fifteen animals, the drivers all dressed in Tuareg blue with heavy headgear. The camels plodded along obediently, their loads packed in woven mats tied round with traditional sisal cordage which squeaked as it strained.

I joined the last camel and walked in its shade. They didn't mind me walking along beside them, nor did they ask me what I was doing there. Theirs is a matriarchal society and women are respected as equals. I moved on up the line and walked in the shadow of the lead camel. After some time, I offered the driver my water bottle. There was only a small amount of liquid at the bottom, my psychological safety net – but I reckoned that if I was thirsty, then so, probably, was he. The man took the bottle and looked inside. Then he signalled back to one of the others who unlashed a guerba, a water-bag made from a goat's stomach, and without stopping the caravan, poured the contents into a wooden bowl. The water was green and opaque but I didn't care. Thanking them would be rude, implying that I didn't expect them to give me water. I just accepted the gift and carried on until we came to a village, where the camelier indicated to me that he was leaving the track and waved goodbye. The Tuareg are not allowed to ride through villages because they can see the women over the walls of the homesteads. If they do, they are stoned.

At the end of the village, the Land Rover arrived. I drank my fill and we carried on for a few miles to find a place out of the village to have lunch. As we were sitting there, skirmishing and drinking tea, the camel caravan slowly approached down the track. Here was my chance.

I pulled out a thirty-litre water jerry, called out a greeting and motioned for them to refill their guerbas. Very slowly they came to a standstill, climbed off their camels, smiling at me as they unleashed their guerbas. As they filled them, one at a time forming a human chain, I noticed they were filling all the guerbas they had. The Tuareg had given me the last of their water.

I felt as though this was part of a chain of gifts, linking me back through time to that very first act. The chain could only be broken if someone refused to give the last of their water and therefore they died. But if they gave the last of their water and still died, the chain would not be broken, only strengthened. It would be a death of the highest honour and the highest bravery. For the Tuareg, proud warriors, it must have been their wish to die well. Why this should matter I don't really know, but one thing I do know is that nothing else seems to matter more.

Even the smallest child seemed to know these laws. Where the tourists had been and they came rushing down to ask for Bic pens, I was taken aback one day when I replied to a little boy, 'I'll give you my pen if you give me your shirt.' It was probably his only shirt, but he actually started taking it off. How did he learn this? From books? From TV? From missionaries? In that one small gesture I felt the moral cornerstone his world is built on, a world away from the building blocks of my own.

I feel incapable when I sit down: my whole body posture changes and I feel depressed. What would happen to these courageous, intrepid, confident, communicating little sparkles of life if they sat down? These children would soon be educated, ushered in, made to sit down in the classroom to be taught the laws of the universe in numbers and equations. If they could become ignorant for a moment and grasp our primitive attempts at figuring out the workings of the planet, the most they could expect would be to end up as fulfilled as Einstein. We bring them schools, to prepare them for the terrible inevitable – that they will be forced to enter our world. The good people go in advance, maybe out of guilt at their privileged life. 'Look,' said the French missionary, 'I don't know any more what's right and what's wrong. All I know is that it's coming and they have to be prepared.' The scissor men! Coming to cut off their little dreams!

Dealing with the 2,500-mile detour as a detour I found to be depressing, but when I began to see the sandy track as our home, I felt more of the serenity which had eluded me for so many years. As my men took care of me, I took care of them by developing my skills with the fire. Though I was tired after thirty miles in the sub-Saharan summer, I felt a sense of grace when I crouched down on my haunches to sweep the hearth and select my sticks. I took care over them, choosing the right ones for the heat and burning time depending on what I was cooking. My sticks were also the source of warmth and light and the focus of the three of us as we ate in the evenings. There were many memorable camps and, like the bushmen, we called them by the names of what we found there: the place of the bees, the place of the man who gave us eggs, the place of the washing rocks, the place where the lion peed on the tent. And the different trees and insects we came across we called by what they did: the spitting tree, the racing spider, the crochet hook bush.

Over the weeks, as this sense of peace grew stronger, Tom and I began to sort out the hierarchy between us and he came to walk beside me on my path for ten miles every day before breakfast. I loved him because we could share more than the chores. As we walked, we shared the observations, starting conversations in the middle of a sentence until they were pared down to one word which was understood. He was the kind of guy you could ask whether centripetal force is a circle or a spiral. And, even though he didn't know how to spell Maori, he'd know that stuff. No one, bar Raymond, had ever visited my world and he came to it willingly.

But Tom had his own demons. The 'conspiracy of small objects' was one of them. Things seemed to gang up on him and he couldn't control his irritation. I sent him away once for a few days to clear his head after he'd smashed up some equipment and G and I carried on through the lion country of Burkina Faso. When he returned, he seemed refreshed with new commitment to our journey, saying he would cross the desert with me even if he had to carry the water himself. But that was another problem: he tried to take all the responsibility on himself as though anything less would be failure. He could not share much with G because G was not a mechanic.

After two months, G left and Shuna, who was taking care of the support for me back home, flew in with a new driver, Gordon Nicholson, a good mechanic.

Now Tom's position was threatened, he needed reassurance that I could not give him. If he was to be the back-up leader, he had to prove he was the better of the two. In some ways he did this by taking me as his partner. Protective of me, even in the midst of a fever, he woke up and said I'd be coming soon and sure enough when Gordon looked, I had just appeared around the corner. Gordon simply got on with the job of keeping the Land Rover going. One day, after Tom had lost his temper, I gave my reassurance to Gordon that unless Tom gained control of himself, we would not cross the desert with him. Gordon told me later that those words kept him with me.

As for Shuna's arrival for a week, I felt I didn't really know her. She, too, found me different. She had known me only with the emptiness I carried when I stepped into her territory in London. But now that I was in my own place, in some ways I was the older sister again. As for real courage, though, my sister is innocent of who she really is.

One night we bathed under the bright desert stars in a river which flows slowly to Timbuktu. A dark shape loomed near us. I knew it was a pirogue but I told her it was a crocodile and we must be very quiet and move slowly out of the water. She was nearest the shore and turned ahead of me. I shouted, 'Shuna, run! The croc's coming!' She pelted as fast as she could, clambering out on the bank as I screamed again, 'Shuna! Help me! Tom's in trouble!' At that point, I was staggered: Shuna actually pivoted and came rushing back into the water.

I'm not sure if I could have done that.

Through Mali, on tracks which haven't seen vehicles for forty years, Gordon, Tom and I found ourselves in the real bush of Africa, a tiny patch of it left, a hint of what Africa had once been. There the animals weren't afraid of us down at the waterhole by the falls. In the state of grace which had developed in me through the sharing in our camp, I felt more receptive to the song around me. The baboons came first and then the smaller creatures and then the birds swooped down to sip. And lying there on the rocks I neither felt bigger nor smaller than anything around me. I had a feeling of completion and belonging which made the questions of why am I here and where did I come from seem primitive, as though they came from a lower intelligence.

My father was the next to come and visit us. We walked together in the cool of the mornings and we started to speak for the first time. He was in my place now and when he left, and I waved goodbye to him for the first time from my own doorstep, I saw that all I ever needed was a home and now that I had one, I could let go of the pain he had caused me by thinking I didn't need one.

Tom left soon afterwards in Mauritania at the foot of the Sahara desert. All of us felt it was for the best but our new driver, Peter Gray, could not reach us until we had crossed the desert because he was refused a visa.

We endured a ten-day epic crossing of the dunes, during which the camber was so steep I damaged my knee and walked for most of it on morphine. Three miles up a beach and it's barely noticeable, but 150 miles up with 600 to go and the imbalance spreads through your body. After 2,500 miles walking due west with barely an inch of progress north, we reached the border between Mauritania and the Occupied Western Sahara. It was closed and we could not cross.

There was a 400-mile wide minefield preventing anyone from trying to skirt around the military checkpoints. But I wasn't going back without completing my walk and Gordon refused to leave me to cross the minefield on my own. Through our contact at Encounter Overland, we found a man who knew a way through. With some Dutch people who had crossed the desert with us, I walked out of sight of the military and turned north into the minefield as they overtook me to race out of sight of the high land. Halfway across, our guide wanted the rest of his money. He wouldn't go any further, but he pointed to the black, flat topped mountain in the distance and said we must keep going straight towards it. The Moroccan military would be waiting there. I walked in front, not through any bravery because these were anti-tank mines and I wouldn't be heavy enough to set one off, but so that I could scout the ground before the Land Rover came. The track was clear. It wasn't such an easy crossing for everyone: a few years later an overland truck hit a mine, blowing the floor through the roof, fortunately just missing the legs of the front passenger.

Tom and my father had both worked hard back in England to alert that Moroccan military post so they wouldn't shoot us. Word must have got through because they greeted us as though we'd just crossed the Berlin wall and offered us fresh melons and welcomed us to their country.

We enjoyed their warmth but we knew this was not their country. Morocco had taken the Western Sahara after it was split between Mauritania and Morocco by the Spanish when they left. Mauritania couldn't afford to fight over it and gave it up. But the people of the Western Sahara are still fighting to get their country back. They formed a group called the Polisario who, despite their numbers, have held their own against their oppressor for over seventeen years.

One man fighting for his country is worth ten hired thugs, as they say.

For another ten days we were accompanied by a guide to make sure we didn't hit a mine. We finally reached tarmac in the small, military town of Dakhla, where Peter Gray was waiting for us.

I felt Pete's presence as a cool breeze in the heat of the desert, a cheeky little spirit who wanted to play. But Gordon desperately needed a comrade. He tried to put me down, asking how much I'd paid for the market shopping then sniggering that I'd been ripped off when he didn't even know what I'd bought. But Pete didn't want to stand by Gordon and put me down. Pete just wanted to have fun. He has fallen many times but each time has worked his way back up again. His would be a truly inspirational book, but I won't take the wind out of his sails; I'll let him tell it himself one day.

When Gordon finally got the message that Pete would not chum with him, he left and flew back to England. He had been unbelievably capable and hard working, but I think the isolation had taken its toll.

Now that he was gone, Pete and I had the desert all to ourselves, a desert where ancient sandstone amphitheatres have been revealed by the wind, where we made a place for the night, lying out side by side on our camp-beds under the great dome filled with shooting stars. Though we had very little, our days were filled with laughter as we moved north on the final 1,700-mile leg, meeting each other every ten miles, three times a day.

At day's end we worked for hours making a good place for the night, taking care to set the Land Rover at just the right angle to enjoy the full feel of the desert in a kind of fung chouey ritual. We knew when it wasn't quite perfect, and if there's a wrong there must be a right, so we would pack up the whole lot and turn it a few feet in another direction so that we could relax. We did not feel small; we did not feel big; we felt just right, a great sense of relief that we didn't have to fight to conquer anymore.

It was during this stretch with Pete that I became aware of how my own centre had shifted. Instead of crying out to someone else for comfort and for pity, I felt as though I was taking the hand of my own child and showing her how to get up. I felt so close now that maybe just around the next corner or over that dune, I might come across the valley of my people.

It came as more of a shock, therefore, when the people in the next valley opened their robes instead of their arms, pulled out their cocks and toasted me with spunk. Even with my kaffiyeh scarf and my long dresses, the men showed me their erections.

Half of me didn't want to know how much danger I was in, but the other half wanted to know all of it, to feel the fear and go through it and out the other side. Especially when there'd be two of them or even a carload, breaking, U-turning, coming back to have a maul at this unprotected girl who looked like she did not belong to anyone. I'd hold it in, wait for it, wait till they were all out of the car, pulling open their gowns, forming a screen between me and the road. Then I'd quickly stoop down, clasp a stone in each hand, stand up and laugh as I watched them running away.

When I told Pete of the day's encounters he didn't respond with his own stories of being stoned that day, but by wanting to protect me from it. Had I stopped to feel how Pete must be thinking, I might have seen that he was genuinely concerned and felt useless sitting ten miles away. 'What's the point of having support if you won't let me protect you?' he demanded. I tried to reassure him I didn't want him trailing along behind me because it would be unpleasant for both of us and anyway, they seemed like cowards underneath. But what was the point of trying to reassure him if I kept telling him the latest encounter? It was virtually impossible to conjure up that much inner strength to keep the near misses and the skills all to myself when all I wanted to do was to share them, laugh at them and disperse the tension.

I knew the Moroccan's attitude to me was simply a result of a convergence of two ways of life and how it resulted in turmoil – it had been the same everywhere I'd walked on the tourist trail in Africa. But I would not be what my sponsor's PR female had in mind: an advertisement for the Moroccan Tourist Board, encouraging more of it.

This woman arrived too soon for us, though I doubt we would ever have been ready. She screeched in, war-painted with slashes of red across her face, her body contorted on stiletto heels, demanding my attention.

But we just laughed at her, shook our heads and went back to the bush. Went back to the bush where nobody could see us.

On our last rest day Pete lost his boomerang in a ravine and set off in search of it, letting me make a place where I could sweep. I tied my kaffiyeh around my waist over my dress so that it protected my bones from the banging of my water bottle. When my clothes were just right, pressing certain parts of my skin, I felt the sense of grace which let me select my sticks, wholly absorbed yet still aware of what was directly behind me. These sticks I laid in the palm of my hand until they reached the point on the base of my thumb where I knew I could not close it to meet my fingers. For the handle, I broke a dried stem with the other hand just enough to leave the threads of the outer bark intact with the plant. I whipped it straight down to the base then snapped it to me so the string bark flapped loose below my outstretched arm. Placing the base of the stick across the end of my sticks, under my thumb, I pulled the thread down behind the bundle then up and over and down again till I tucked in the end, broke off my stick and made my way back to my place. Now I could sweep. And I thought, as I brushed out the small sharp stones and the flighty wings of insects and the stray bits of weed straw, this is my last home.

The bush was my last home.

I knew we would have to leave but somehow I had forgotten, or maybe I never knew, what it really meant to leave a place for another. I didn't dwell on it: I couldn't imagine what it would be like at the other end of the journey.

Pete had been gone for an hour and I hadn't heard him for just too long. I called his name, he looked up, saw his boomerang high up in a tree branch and climbed back out of the ravine.

After lunch, he set about outsmarting the rat in the Land Rover which had a penchant for sinking his teeth into virgin tomato skin, taking one bite then moving on to the next one. Pete had to think like the rat in order to catch him. So he sat down and thought like a rat. And as the size and shapes around him grew up and his fingers became sensitive feelers and they twitched with adrenaline, he began to feel like the rat.

I must have disturbed him then because he broke concentration and did not catch his prey. But the rat was never seen again. Perhaps he sensed he was being hunted by something which was now capable of catching him. He had stayed for the food and maybe for the buzz of outsmarting such a large carnivore but I think he decided to quit while he was ahead so that he could pass on what he knew. Why this should matter I don't really know, but one thing I do know is that nothing else seems to matter more.

I had found my valley and I thought this would be enough to take with me forever but when the first of my race came I did a double take like the albinos, thinking they were like me. But when their questions were as primitive as those I had asked the 'Pygmies', I could not feel them and I knew they could not feel me. Reluctantly, I brought out an old character to put on in their presence. It was at the bottom of my baggage and was by now a little fermented, a little tatty around the edges and way too big for me.

It must have come as a shock to Pete when the cameras started to follow us, to come into our place and sit in our shade and film me slurping juice from the bowl when I'd always used a spoon. But dear Pete, how could he ever know that I cannot be myself where I am reminded that I am a stranger by my own kind? If only he knew how precious those weeks with him had been. All those days he let me shine were far more than I thought possible, only ever having felt myself in brief glimpses over the years.

It frustrated me that when I tried to speak what I felt it came out as garbage. But maybe that's just the way it works and that's the difference between a world infatuated with forms of communication and a world where you communicate by feeling. Perhaps that's Africa's greatest secret, but its greatest disadvantage too.

We held on very tightly to what we knew when the intruders weren't around but when, four days from the end, I found out that not all Moroccans are cowards and was nearly raped, Pete refused to leave me. He swung up into his seat and trundled along behind me. I felt as though I was being paraded through the streets as a bad woman, especially when the gendarmes followed behind him and it made me feel self-conscious again. But the Moroccan Tourist Board could not stand another attack on me and I could not stand the possibility that they might prevent me from walking any further. Sod had followed me on and off during the trip, but at least for every setback he won, there was another law which had evened out the score. Like a pigeon walking: 'Give a little, take a little,' he says with his head, 'it'll help you get along.'

The scar from the fight has stayed, but as a dimple – the measure of how much I'd fought, which wasn't much. I was surprised at how little my life meant to me, how little I was prepared to struggle. But then maybe I had no strength left, spending it all as I was, changing between outfits.

I hadn't asked myself who I was going to be for so many months that it sickened me to hear that little voice again. I fought against it to the very end. We were to be on the beach at 10 a.m.; it was 9.30 when we reached the bottom of the hill. Pete parked the Land Rover and we went into a café to kill time. We had a Coke. Pete started to cry, and I held his hands in mine.

'Love you, Pete.'

The PR female came in at that moment. Somehow, she'd found us. God knows what she was saying, it was just a noise. She left.

Pete and I looked at each other. It was coming and we must be prepared. We took a deep breath then.

'You wanna go for a swim?'

'You bet,' he said.

I walked out of the café and Pete got into the Land Rover and drove behind me. The gendarmes gathered around and set up their sirens. I walked to the end of the road and turned left along the main road to a gate in the beach wall where a funnel of people were directing me. Someone gave me a bunch of flowers.

I saw the sand and started to cry.

I was hyperventilating, letting out ridiculous sobs, my face all screwed up and I tried to get a grip. I couldn't see where I was going for the tears, but I was aware of people running beside me. Onto the deep sand, sucking me down, I switched into my own four-wheel drive like the desert. They were calling out to me to walk diagonally across the sand.

I scanned the shore for a sign of my people and made out a dense group. Then I realised it was going to be over and I stopped and waited for Pete to catch up. He gunned the Land Rover across the sand till he was beside me. I held out my hand to take his through the window and walked with him for a while till we squeezed the last and I said, 'Goodbye, Pete.'

I turned back to the walk and silently thanked each of my drivers, Gerry and Oli, Bill and Blake, Raymond and Johann and even Tim, Tom and G and Gordon and then I whispered, 'Quarter's end, day's end, week's end, country's end, walk's end.'

I saw the water coming very quickly towards me but I couldn't wait for it. I started to run and as soon as my feet hit the water of the Mediterranean I screamed that I'd made it. I spun round searching for Tom. Through all the shouting press people, I saw him running towards me. Then he was hugging me, spinning me round and round in the water. I hugged Shuna and Max and Vanessa and Pete and then I walked back into the water, turned away from all of it and looked out across the sea for a moment and said: 'Thank you.'

I took the small flask of sand I'd gathered from the beach in Cape Town and filled it with sand from the beach in Tangier. Then Pete and I took down the wood we'd gathered that morning and lit the last in a chain of fires which stretched 10,500 miles all the way back to Cape Town.

When the fire had burned itself out, our home was gone.

The day of arrival was filled with catching up with news from my loved ones but towards the end, Pete and I just felt it was a nice day and we'd be in the bush again tomorrow. Instead, every step we took, took us further away.

I felt the first measure of this on the flight back from Gibraltar when the morning papers from England came round. The PR woman got hold of them first. She started to squawk, bouncing up and down in her seat, which I suppose is the public relations equivalent of an orgasm.

'Look Ffyona! Look! You're all over the front pages,' she squealed. 'Isn't it wonderful? I've made all your dreams come true.'

13

The girl's mind is now directed by her nicotine addiction. She sweetly asks me what I'm doing on the flight. I just smile and continue to smoke my penultimate cigarette.

Cartwheels for the press at Gatwick airport and I felt utterly sickened with myself. But what I felt inside had no voice, had no mannerisms or gait on carpets or linoleum. With all the flashes and all the questions, they were stealing my soul and even the character I wore could not shield me from it. I wasn't prepared for this. I was used to being stared at, but not by my own kind.

Yet some of them were trying to make it easier for me. At the underground, when I was faced with a wall of buttons to get my ticket, a lady showed me what to do and said kindly, 'Things have changed while you've been away.' They certainly had. When I left, Communism was still intact, John McCarthy, Brian Keenan and Terry Waite were hostages and David Ike was a sports commentator.

The first few days were like a party: everyone knew my name and they started conversations in the middle, asking after my feet; drinks piled up in front of me in the pub and taxi drivers refused money for my rides. If they asked me how I was dealing with coming back, I simply told them I wouldn't even have made it across London were it not for their support.

Yet the constant round of interviews to pay back my sponsors and to promote Survival International started to pare away at me. I felt like a mermaid out of water for too long and my body started to lose its shine. I couldn't remember my way back out of studios once I'd gone in; I couldn't distinguish between faces; I couldn't remember all the arrangements for things which were intangible; I couldn't remember pin numbers or phone numbers or room numbers and I felt sick on all the fat in the food.

The end of the walk came after the bath and the long sleep. I woke up in a hotel room but instead of looking out at a panorama of an African landscape, I was staring at a wall. I could feel my core just slipping away and it frightened me. I tried to hold onto it, closing my eyes and remembering the last camp with Pete, but the sound of the phone or the loo flushing or the smell of the painted room reminded me that I had no home to go back to. Without this core of inner strength, the day's questioning from welcoming or hostile people in my own language reminded me that I was a stranger again. I couldn't bear to feel this amount of pain so I sought sanctuary in the home of a daydream.

For thousands of miles I had carried a picture of Tom with me in my mind. Whenever the morphine wore off in the desert, I would conjure up an image of his face and imagine the little cottage where we'd live after the walk. I'd remember him telling me how he'd tried to run away as a small child, dodging into his parents' room to pull out the little suitcase, but it wouldn't budge. And how his mother had come in and asked him what he was doing. 'I'm running away!' he'd shouted, still tugging at the suitcase. 'What?' asked his mother, 'with the sewing machine?' The story reminded me of everything I loved about him: the feistiness and the humour, and had sent me laughing over the pain and the dunes.

Tom and I threw our energy into finding a place to rent together. We ended up in a little cottage in Stoke Newington. I unpacked, fed the stray cats and made a place. But when I saw the birds swooping down on the cats, just out of reach, baiting them, mocking them, daring them, knowing how high the stakes were if they were caught, I began to fall apart. I wanted to feel alive but there was no chance of death; I wanted to fight but everything was handed to me on a plate; and, unless I found some kind of edge, I could not laugh.

Pete was falling apart too. He'd call me in despair: his nightmares of being unable to defend me came back to haunt him; but Tom grew jealous. I'd have to choose between my friend and my lover.

But I did not want Pete's protection. I felt I needed to be frightened to stay alive. I was scared of Tom for his temper. If I wound him up, he would come after me in a rage then the adrenaline would flow and I could use all my skills to dodge him, wrong foot him and escape out the door. Once, I couldn't turn over the engine fast enough and he flung open the door, saw his chance and leaped on the bonnet. I floored the accelerator, sped down the road, trying to shake him off. But he clung on, ripped back the convertible roof and plunged his arm into the car. I thought he'd go for my neck but he reached for the keys too fast for me to stop him, and turned off the engine. He vaulted down, pulled open the door, but I slipped out the other side. Now he had the car and its keys, but he didn't have the house keys: I had them. I ran down the road. He drove after me and mounted the pavement; another car pulled across in front of him, preventing him from reaching me. He got out, grabbed my bag, but I slipped past him into the car. Now I had the car and its keys but he had the house keys.

I guess the real battle for Tom was how hard he tried not to enjoy being animal. Had he understood what was going on, he might not have been in such torment. But his years of conditioning had told him there is something wrong with fear, that the highest achievement of the day is to even out its inconveniences into a line of least resistance. He had been tamed, he liked turning on the tap for a glass of water without the possibility of something leaping out to bite off his face.

But what was left of his animal self, though, made for a fine adversary. Tom would not give up and neither would I. If our chases didn't end in sex, we were like two warriors wounded in the sand. When neither of us would admit defeat, the fighting below the belt began. I'd stand in the kitchen and let him pummel the shit out of me, screaming in my face that I was no good. I took it because, deep down, I knew that he was right.

When Tom ended up having stitches in casualty, I left, as much for his sake as for my own.

I had not been productive while living with Tom. It's very hard to find a computer more attractive than a man standing behind you with a knife in his hand wanting to play. But my publishers wanted a finished manuscript on the African journey within four months before I left to walk to the end of the world. After clearing out my gear one day while Tom was at work, I moved into a flat of a friend. I moved out after a week when he wouldn't accept that I wasn't fair game for what he had in mind, and into another owned by a friend of the guy who had the terrible job of being on the end of a modem to edit what I wrote. We didn't speak much because, after two months of being in the tamed world without my adversary to keep me alive, I started to lose my head, big time.

I couldn't remember what was happening to me. I couldn't stand back and say, hey, this is normal, you've been walking into a headwind for years, now it's stopped and you've fallen over, get yourself up again. There were no markings around me to remind me of what I'd experienced with Pete in Africa and with my tendency to erase the blocks behind me, I couldn't get any kind of grip on what I was doing. I reached for dope then, not alcohol, it's too depressing.

There were two news items on the TV which sent me thinking into the night. The first was about a zookeeper who had been feeding his animals for years. But one day he'd made a mistake and they'd eaten him. I wanted to understand why they'd done this and it struck me that the lions or tigers or whatever they were, had all that they could ask for in the zoo: food so they didn't have to hunt, water so they didn't have to walk, a mate so they didn't have to fight for supremacy, shade without flies so they didn't have to twitch. Yet, when I went to the zoo to see some, they did not look better off. They didn't look much like lions at all. Maybe they saw the man who fed them as being responsible for their captivity and if they ate him, all of this would go away and they could live again.

The other news report was about the increased use of drugs and crime by young people. These reports merged together and I wondered whether the lions, had they been offered drugs, might take them. Born in captivity, they might have sensed there was something missing but they weren't quite sure what it was. One hit and they might have found a substitute. As for crime, what a buzz: almost as good as hunting but with slightly lower stakes.

A young man on the radio said of his criminal teenage years, 'I can't explain it, it was just something I had to get out of my system.'

It struck me that whilst our minds have evolved, our bodies haven't devolved by the same amount. We are still animal. I remembered the torment of my own teenage years, robbed of any activity, any purpose, any guides or anything to fight for and defend, robbed of everything by one man standing in front of me telling me to get in line and do nothing. I did not understand my frustration at the time, I felt I was abnormal and there must be something wrong with me. My parents, the only people I knew, had blamed me for my behaviour and I had felt ashamed.

I wondered why, deep in the virgin bush of Africa, I had not seen the young in such torment. There seemed to be a very different attitude to the needs of the adolescents. They were not just left alone to become adults simply by virtue of their changing bodies. The young boys were given the chance to expend their energy, to be pumped full of adrenaline and to keep their heads and go through the fear in full control, kill well and come out of it the other side into the ranks of men.

I could not see what happened to the young girls, but I knew in other cultures they are taken out of the village every month at their time, to sit on sphagnum moss with the other women and there they would learn the secrets of womankind. They could not win fights with fisticuffs; they won with their intellect. They carried the life of the future inside them, there they learned how to nurture it, to guide it and take care of it.

During the time I wrote, I thought about what was coming – my last walk. What did I want to say with it? Who was it relevant to? I knew of an organisation which understood the need for young people to be challenged, developing them through community and conservation work on expeditions at home and abroad. Raleigh International. Giving young people a chance at their own rite of passage was the closest I could get in trying to make sense of my journey and to give it some worth to others. In turn, perhaps these young people would experience satisfaction and fulfilment from things other than materialism. Perhaps they could stop the encroachment of our demand for raw materials on the lands of our real teachers. Because if the tribal people become extinct, who will teach us the laws of the universe then? The scientists?

Raleigh came on board with a bang, clear-headed, confident, unconfused people who believed in what they did and were at ease with others. Though they were the same age as me at twenty-six, I felt somehow very old and yet very empty at the same time. We decided to concentrate our efforts on the final stage of my walk. Once I reached the shores of Britain, I would walk to John O'Groats and Raleigh would use it as a massive promotional vehicle hopefully to inspire young people to 'get on their feet and make a world of difference'.

But for the stretch from Algeciras in Spain, directly opposite Tangier, up to Calais, I wanted to walk on my own. I had never walked without back-up and I wanted to know if I could really do it. I had never stood on the top of a hill with my fire and my tent and known that I was here and fed because I had taken care of it myself. I had often imagined walking with a donkey, as they did in Africa, and because my lower back was again in trouble, I decided to find a donkey to carry my load. As for corporate sponsorship, I just looked at myself one day going down the road I'd gone before and thought fuck it, I have some money now from the book, I'll fund it myself.

Janet Street Porter had come to us wanting to make a series on European walks. She was leaving the BBC and it seemed she had a career move invested in this series. I said find, she said fine, and I promptly forgot about it until six weeks before I was due to leave for Algeciras, they called up again. It was all on. But I told them my walk had changed. Instead of walking around Europe as I'd suggested before, I would only be walking through Spain and France and into Britain. Somehow, they didn't mind. The focus of their interest was beginning to shift, from Janet on country walks, to a dissection of myself.

Steven Scott, a freelance executive director hired by Janet for the series, got on the trail and started sniffing around at where I'd been. It seemed that he wanted to find something slightly putrid which would arouse and excite the waiting pack. And it scared the hell out of me. Suddenly it all came back to me, the secret I carried which I had never admitted to anyone, least of all myself. And now, for the first time in the journey, I would be standing up and saying I was the first woman to walk around the world. Though I had paid for my failure in blisters and thousands of more miles so as never to make the same mistake again, I had not yet paid the full price in shame.

I felt unbelievably alone. There seemed absolutely nobody to turn to with advice on what to do. Though Max had been my closest guide, sitting on a hill, where I could go to him with my troubles, I could not take this one to him. He was a man of honour. So, too, was Raymond. The more the researchers called me, wanting names and numbers of all the drivers, and the more Scott laughed at old photos he had unearthed or demanded to know what had gone on with my father, the more the progress I had made towards peace started to collapse.

I made an attempt to run away from it by stopping the series as I had not signed a contract. But somehow they talked me back into it, pushing all the right buttons by saying they were on my side, that this achievement should not go unrecorded, that it would help to promote Raleigh and the book. I talked myself into it so easily. It was almost as if I wanted to be found out.

In utter despair, with my answering machine full of researchers' messages interspersed with the enthusiasm of the Raleigh organisers, I had to call someone. At those times, it seems there is only one person: Mother. Thank God for Mother. I pulled the phone out of the window onto the balcony, laid out my smokes and lighter and ashtray and sat down, almost crouching in the corner. I dialled her number with tears streaming down my face. She answered and when I couldn't say anything but hello, she knew something was terribly wrong. I had the words in my head but I just couldn't get them to come out. When I tried to form them into a sentence, the thought of actually saying them and being unable to pull them back made me clam up. I must have smoked the whole packet before her reassuring words finally seeped through.

'Ma?' I said for the hundredth time.

'Yes, lovey.'

'Ma?'

'It's all right my love. Whatever it is, we can go through it together.'

Silence. Another cigarette.

'Ma?'

'I'm here for you, no matter what.'

'I cheated when I walked across America.'

I regretted it as soon as I'd said it. Now it was real. Now it was out and I couldn't deny it any longer.

'How much did you cheat?'

'I don't know. I can't remember. I don't know if it was one day or one week or one month.'

'But you've made up for it? By walking 2,500 miles around that war zone, you made up the distance, didn't you?'

'It's not the same. It doesn't matter whether I walked all the way around the world again, backwards, on my hands, I can't make it go away. And now they're going to find out.'

'Let me think about this for a while. You've got enough on your plate. You just get on and finish your book, go out to Europe and walk with your donkey. Don't let them get to you my love, we'll find a way through this. OK?'

'OK.'

'D'you feel better now?'

'No.'

At the very point where I faced the dilemma of my life, I had called on my inner strength to find it was only as strong as the victim I had played. All the times I had failed the underlying tests had accumulated, just as successes would have done, and now I could not push out of my own shell. I did not have the courage to face my shame alone.

The phone rang as soon as I'd put it down. It was Sara Parfitt from Raleigh. She wanted to know if I would give a talk to their members who would be walking with me. 'They're so excited about it, Fi. Oh, and could you come for a photo shoot to promote our new T-shirts and our newsletter editor would love to interview you about rites of passage for a front-cover story. It's all happening here. It's such a terrific opportunity for us.'

Oh God, what have I done?

I drove out to Gloucestershire to collect the saddle and pannier which Nell O'Connor had promised to lend me. In return I asked her to take care of my medicine bundle. I felt unworthy of carrying it with me. Nell put it in her special place on the high land above the valley of her farm. She told me she would visit it every morning at sunrise.

Then I cut off my hair and turned to face what was coming.

14

There is only one other person smoking now: the man this girl beside me would not sit next to. I watch her asking him for a cigarette. By the colour of her face, I see that he didn't give her one. She goes into the loo and washes her face again. I take out my last, light it in front of her, pick up another scotch and close my eyes again.

At dawn on 30 April 1994 I stood on a filthy patch of sand between the oily dockland cranes of Algeciras. The lapping waves deposited more garbage at my feet. Five people buzzed around me, setting up their equipment and their questions for a fly-on-the-wall documentary.

As the sky lightened and the deep red tip of the sun emerged above the horizon, I saw the clean line of Africa's shores where I had once stood in peace. Eight months of questioning had elapsed, but I had only just started to question myself. Ahead of me lay five months of solitude, away from the muck, in which to reflect. At least, that was my agenda.

The flies, though, had other ideas.

Janet Street Porter told me she was the President of the Ramblers' Association. I wasn't quite sure what this had to do with me but I tolerated her constant questions because that's what people do to me. I assumed she wanted to point out the canyons between her world and mine as everyone else had done; I didn't think for a moment that she was actually trying to find a bridge. I certainly wasn't. I'd forgotten they existed, which must have been fairly frustrating for her because now there was only one game to play: we compete for miles. After all, isn't that the only thing which earns respect?

The executive director, though, had a different agenda: to turn a

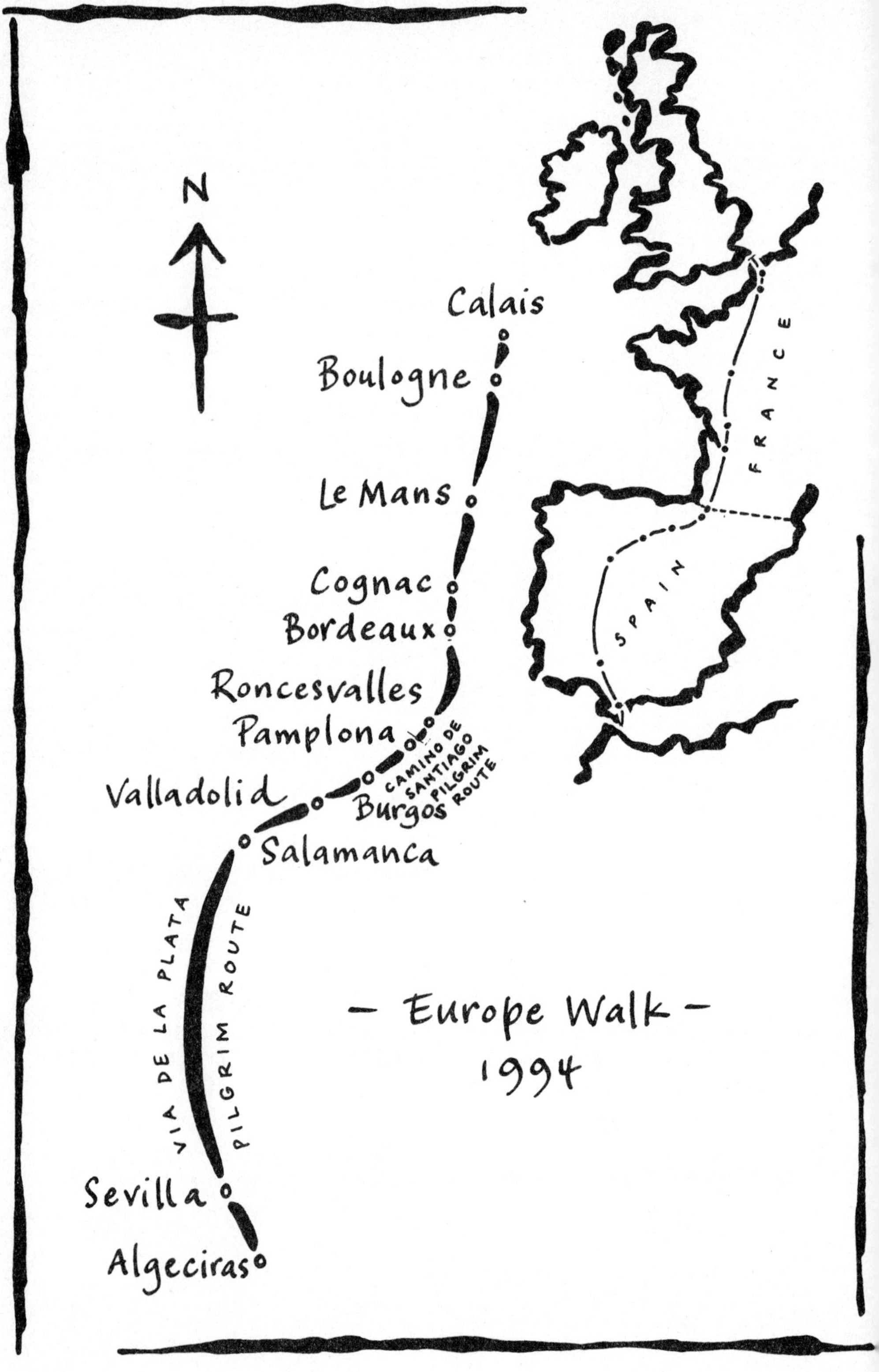

N

Calais
Boulogne

Le Mans

Cognac
Bordeaux

Roncesvalles
Pamplona
Valladolid
Burgos
Salamanca

CAMINO DE SANTIAGO PILGRIM ROUTE

VIA DE LA PLATA

PILGRIM ROUTE

FRANCE

SPAIN

— Europe Walk —
1994

Sevilla
Algeciras

six-part series about walking into something exciting during which he would solve the mystery of the enigma while being aware that he didn't know all the facts.

Bonita my mule had her agenda too: to throw off her pack animal status and be the horse she was born to be. Walking beside me with her load, she actually ignored the greetings from donkeys, preferring to answer only the calls of horses. She would not deign to sleep outside like the other mules; she was a horse and she wanted a stable. I tried to remind her that her dad was a donkey, but she would have none of it. 'I am Bonita the horse,' she seemed to say. 'Forget it at your peril.' After a couple of weeks, I traded her in for an animal who had no identity problems.

I called my donkey Anne after Annie Chapman at the Donkey Sanctuary who had taught me how to take care of donkeys. The crew filmed the exchange, then left for a few weeks.

Though little Anne was white and old and had been roughly treated, she had a great dignity about her. When I offered her water, instead of throwing back her head like Bonita and saying, 'I'm not drinking from that, I'd rather piss in it,' she simply nodded her head as if to say, 'Oh how lovely, thank you, I am a bit parched.'

On our first morning together, I found she had not touched her food while I'd been packing up. As I approached her, she tried to whinny at me but no sound came out. I patted her neck and she immediately put her head in her food and started to eat. At first she shied away if ever I reached for her head, but after a time, she let me touch her until I found the place she liked to be rubbed – just under her ears and on her temples – and she'd reach out to me as I came towards her, offering me the side of her head. At night she would not settle unless she could curl up directly beside my tent and it seemed that what we both needed most in strange places with strange noises was simply reassurance.

As we followed the pilgrim route of the Via de la Plata north towards Santiago de Compostela, we spent several days far away from the traffic, on grassy lanes and tracks where her favourite wild oats grew on the edge of the fields. Perhaps the EEC didn't know about this corner of Spain, because they hadn't felled the homesteads here and swept them aside into miles of unsightly rubble to shave the landscape and plant crops. Instead, we walked past working farms where great black boar hams hung from rafters, and sausage and bread and beer were given to me before the farmers would even consider answering my questions for directions. I knew more words in

Swahili than I did in Spanish, but where the tourists hadn't been, I found the Spaniards to be quite happy to watch me mime what I needed, laughing with such merriment when we'd finally made ourselves understood.

Anne and I covered around ten miles a day. My schedule required an average of fifteen, but it didn't matter in the least because I knew I could make it up in France on my own. When it didn't rain, we plodded on quite happily and I learned to coax her up the hills by filling my knapsack with Nipero fruit, which she loved as much as I do. I'd hold the bag just out of reach in front of her, letting her sniff it until we hit the summit where I would take out one for her and one for me as a reward. I learned the rhythm of her hooves as a guide to the position of her load, adjusting it until the patter was just right; but one morning, after two weeks on the trail, the rhythm changed.

There were two farmers leaning over a fence watching us walking towards them. I stopped to say hello and asked for their advice on her limp. They did as I had done and lifted each of her feet, but could find nothing wrong. They shrugged, I thanked them and we walked on. Within a few hours, though, little Anne was very definitely in distress. I had to get her some medical attention and fortunately, not much further on, we came to the edge of a village. There a farmer allowed me to let her graze in his field and directed me to the house of the vet. The vet, a young man having his lunch, didn't seem quite so prepared to watch my mimes but when I wouldn't go away, he took his jacket and bag and came to have a look. Again he picked up each foot and looked at it. He asked where I'd had the shoes made and I told him back in Gerena by a farrier. They seemed fine, he said, shrugged and gave his diagnosis. I asked him to point it out in the dictionary. He found the page, put his finger on the word and passed it back – cancer. Cancer of the feet, he seemed to be saying.

I asked him about painkillers and he shrugged again, gave her an injection, but wouldn't take any payment. Then left. The farmer seemed to be suggesting that we be on our way too. On our way to where, though? My donkey could hardly walk! I packed her up and led her out of the field. She was walking so slowly it took half an hour to reach the village. I didn't know where we were going to or what I was going to do with her. She couldn't walk much further at all.

An angel came in the form of Juan. He pulled over and asked if I needed some help. Fortunately he spoke French, said he had a small farm not far away and we could rest there for as long as we liked.

He waited for us at each junction as we made our way, inching forward now, to his house. I wanted to tell Anne that it wasn't far now, but, of course, she couldn't understand.

Finally, we walked down the path into Juan's farm, where his dogs set up their hollering. I got her into the shade, took off her load and gave her some water. She lay down then, tired and obviously in pain. My first thought was that I had pushed her too far, I had caused this and now this very beautiful animal had gone lame. I was so unused to feeling emotional pain that it started to get out of control as a monumental panic. She looked as though she was about to die on me. Could I really be the monster I'd been accused of? Was this it? Instead of a burned out back-up driver, here was a half-dead donkey?

Anne was making a terrible sound as she lay on her side. I ran up to the village of Calzadilla de Los Barros and called Steven Scott. I'd given my word that I would call him if anything happened. Something told me that if the donkey died and I had not called him, it would be worse for me. I was in a terrible state when I got him on the phone, almost on my knees, begging that he be sympathetic. My donkey had gone lame and, through the squawking tears, I said I thought I'd done it to her. But I had forgotten that Scott enjoyed the sight of the inside of my head so that he could sell it, not reassure it (and I thought I had the market on that one). He told me to stay where I was, the crew would be out in two days.

I called my mother, bawled down the phone at her too. It had been the final straw in the mounting tensions over the last months in a country where I couldn't speak the language, where I didn't know about mules and donkeys and everyone seemed to be an expert on contradicting everyone else, where I was being scrutinised by the film crew when they were there and was tormented by the fear that they might find out at any moment my darkest secret. But then the tensions seemed to stretch back further. All the hell of the last eight months in Britain, a freak, a stranger, a screamed-at tormented stranger, and then before that, the unreleased tension of being stoned through Morocco, the fear through all of Africa and before that the terrible pain of Australia in such confusion over my motives for driving myself and before that to the shame of America and on and on, reeling back the slippery film of my life trying to find a place to hold on to and stop the tape from running out.

At times like this it's such a pig being emotionally unstable.

The sound of my mother's voice must have been what jolted me out of it, a sound I immediately honed in on and understood. I not only saw the problem, I also saw what I could do about it. I called the Donkey Sanctuary in Devon and asked to speak to a vet. I explained calmly what her symptoms were and what the Spanish vet had said.

'Cancer of the feet?' asked the vet on the end of the phone. 'Never heard of it. They don't give a hoot about old donkeys in Spain. I suggest you find a farrier and get her shoes taken off. You never know, there might be something trapped underneath. Or, it might be something like laminitis, restriction of the blood to the hoof wall.'

'What can I do about it? Will she get better?'

'If it is laminitis, you'll need some phenylbutazone powder, one gram twice a day put in her feed. Take her off hard feed and limit her grazing. You'll need some cotton wool pads and bandages to tie around her feet so that the dirt doesn't get in. Give us a call back if you need any more advice.'

I hitched five miles back to the last village, where I'd been told there was a farrier. I spent an infuriating time trying to find his house. Each time I walked up the street without seeing anything like the word for farrier, I'd ask a pedestrian and they would send me back down it again. Up and down, till finally I narrowed it down to two houses and knocked on the door.

A very wizened old man stood in the doorway. I asked him if he was the farrier. He couldn't understand me but eventually I gathered that he was the farrier. I tried to explain that my donkey was lame and in the village of Calzadilla de Los Barros and would he come with me. 'Bring her here,' he motioned.

'I can't. She can't walk and I don't have any transport for her.'

He shrugged and shut the door. I knocked on it again. A woman answered. She told me to go away. I tried again to explain through mime and a few words that my donkey could not stand, let alone walk five miles. She just shook her head and shut the door. I started to feel the red hot heat of anger, wanting to open that door and smash her shaking head against the wall. Instead, I set off for the house of the vet again.

He also found me irritating – this dumb stranger behaving like a mime artist on speed – and just shrugged and closed the door. I turned away, trying to get myself under control and just thought, well, it obviously doesn't matter. Maybe I should just leave her there. Something in me was incensed at that. I turned back and knocked on his door again. I asked him for phenylbutazone powder. He stopped, midway from closing the door, realising that I wasn't as stupid as he took me to be. He got his bag and his coat and we drove down to his surgery. There he gathered the powder and some antibiotics. But I told him it would be no good unless we got the farrier and the farrier had said no.

We drove to the farrier's house and the young vet knocked on his door. The farrier shook his head, motioning again that my donkey be brought to him. After a very long time, during which the vet made eye contact with the farrier only a few times, preferring to talk to the ground out of respect, the farrier finally agreed and the three of us got in the vet's car and drove to see my donkey. With twenty words of Spanish, I had got this far.

Anne hadn't moved from where I'd left her. The farrier got her on her feet and I held her head rope while he lifted her front right foot and prised off the shoe against her kicking. What he saw underneath brought tears to his eyes. He showed us her foot. The shoes were too big for her and the nails had been hammered into the sensitive rim between the outer and inner hoof. He was visibly shaken and so was the vet. One by one they took off her shoes. Three of them were in the same condition. God knows how she had been able to walk at all. The vet administered the drugs and gave me a supply of powder and antibiotics. He said he would be back again in three days to see how she was doing. It would take time, they said, before she was better. Maybe days, maybe weeks; she was an old donkey.

Juan returned just as they were leaving. The vet was able to speak of the finer points of her convalescence which Juan translated for me into French. I wanted to move her into a paddock by the shade of the trees because the field she was in had no shade and far too many stones. But Juan said he didn't want her to eat his vegetables. I felt such a sense of powerlessness then, I wanted to scream at him that this was Anne and she was far more important than his plants. He just shook his head and shrugged apologetically. How on earth am I going to get you to care about her?

I asked him if he'd ever had a donkey of his own. He said he had and fondly remembered it. After a while, he got up and without saying anything he led Anne into the paddock under the shade. She sank down and I put her water bucket close to her. Juan smiled and he spoke again about his own donkey and how he missed having one. After a while, I asked him if he would like to take care of Anne for me. Yes, he said, he would be delighted and his grandchildren could come and play with her when she got better.

Juan lived in a village; this farm was just his hobby for the afternoons after he had tended to his grape crop. When he left that afternoon to go back to his family, I felt the darkness set in again. The damage had been done, the blinds taken off my eyes and I had glimpsed the mess of my life. I had found no point of stability or truth as a core to hold fast to. Though I had not caused Anne to go lame, the possibility that I could have done was too great. If that's what my walk was all about, I didn't want to do it any more. I packed up my bags, left instructions for Juan on Anne's feed and hitched 150 miles to Seville, from where I intended to fly to Australia and disappear.

I was dropped on the outskirts of the city where I could get a bus to the airport. I saw a sign for Coke and went inside a little café in the cold, ordered one and sat down to try to straighten out my mind. The panic-stricken side of me kept blowing everything out of perspective; I had to find something, just one tiny thing in the whole of my reasoning which I knew to be absolutely true, something, anything which I had done absolutely right. I instinctively knew that if I didn't, I would lose my mind altogether. The voice of detachment was so quiet, I had a hard time hearing it over the raging till it popped a question into my mind which was so strange, I didn't have an answer for it. 'Just what do you think your children will think of you if you run away like this?' I don't know why this should matter so much; all I know is that nothing else seemed to matter more.

I hitched back to my donkey in the dark. It was a pretty scary trip, especially since I was exuding the energy of a victim which, no matter where you go in the world, seems to bring out the bully in people. Anne got up when she saw me and came plodding towards me, letting out her funny little whinny as if she couldn't believe I had deserted her for so long. It set off the raging voice again and I spent the night before the crew arrived fighting for my sanity. They were coming under the assumption that I had ruined my donkey and it delighted them.

The flies swarmed in as I sat in the field, waiting with Anne. I asked Scott if I could speak to him alone before the filming began. He refused and ordered the camera to be turned on. He saw that I was in some torment but keeping my cool, so he started to wind me up. 'That's a very old donkey, Ffyona. Look, she's got white hair. I mean, even I know that donkeys with white hair are very old.' It stung but I kept calm.

'My donkey has gone lame because the farrier put on shoes which were too big for her. I've had the local farrier take them off and she's on medication, which is why she is so dopey. She's going to make a full recovery and Juan has offered to take care of her. I am going to stay here until I know she's well on the mend.'

At that point Anne rolled on to her side with her head on the ground and made such a sound I thought she was going to die. The cameraman got a close-up, the sound man looked distressed and disgusted. Half of me knew perfectly well that this sound was normal, but I had no qualification for saying so. Scott went on with his goading. He didn't want to hear the voice of reason; he wanted me to snap. 'We asked a farmer how much he would give for that donkey. He said it wasn't worth a penny. You got ripped off with that donkey, Ffyona. She's completely worthless.' He went too far. I screamed.

'You'd like to think that I did this? Well, I didn't. The fucking farrier who put on her shoes did this. I'd like to get hold of that guy and hammer nails in his feet and make him walk for two weeks!' And then something quite bizarre happened: I actually changed character within the rage. I felt it and I couldn't get rid of it. I started to blubber; I started to act. Tony, the cameraman, noticed this too. But Scott must have assumed that this was the Ffyona Campbell temper tantrum. Why would he think anything else?

He goaded me some more, until I had destroyed any hope of being able to speak with any authority. Like I was tugging at his sleeve, saying, I didn't do this, I'll find someone to show you I didn't do this. It sounded so pathetic to me after what I had done to make sure she would be OK.

They had what they needed and started to pack up to leave. I had to make amends with them somehow. I could not have them leave believing that I had hurt my donkey. Yet the more it concerned me the more I felt my conscience was getting at me and the whole palaver started again. Even though I knew deep down that I was innocent, I could not find a tone of voice which had a ring of sincerity, no matter which way I said it. My words simply would not fit into a comfortable place with my conscience. Then Scott said, 'I think this is the least of your worries.'

We went up to the little bar by the side of the road and ordered a round. Juan was there. He looked confused as he had witnessed the whole thing in the field. Scott noticed a pornographic video on a rack which showed a picture of a woman having sex with a donkey. He pointed it out to Juan. I felt like smashing his face in. Then he leant forward and whispered in my ear, 'I know your secret.'

Perfect timing, really. He knew damn well how vulnerable I was and he went for the kill. I don't know what my eyes revealed at that time or how much he read in the sudden calm of my voice.

'What secret?'

'The secret in America.' He was inches from my face and he was having the time of his life.

'What secret?'

'It begins with an A.'

I couldn't think of how cheating can begin with an A so I said, 'I don't know what you're talking about.'

'I know about the abortion.'

'How do you know that?'

'Oh, well,' he leaned back in his chair, 'it's common knowledge. But don't worry, I won't tell anyone.'

Then he started laughing at someone else's joke and came back with an equally perverted one of his own. He reminded me of the people in the little ventas up on the sierras who lived by such strict Catholicism yet the inside of their houses were covered with centre-folds.

This was the man who was in control of how my life was portrayed.

I called Mark Lucas, the intermediary between us. I did not want to continue with this series. Mark was in Australia but I got a message back from him saying I was just being paranoid and to get on with the show. If I didn't, Scott would leave it that I had ruined my donkey and had been too ashamed to carry on. Scott didn't want to speak to the farrier or the vet for confirmation of what I'd said. He went off to film some sheep.

I asked Juan to make sure that Anne was not on her own. Donkeys need friends; she needed another donkey or one of the horses which grazed in the fields nearby. He said he would bring her a horse from time to time but he couldn't promise anything full time. This wasn't good enough. I could not leave my donkey without a companion or I felt she would just give up hope. I called Johanna Beattie Batista then. I had met Johanna the day after I'd got Anne in the town of Gerena. She had driven past me and invited me to her corthigo for coffee. We'd plodded up there and found the cleanest stables I had ever seen in Spain. Johanna was English and taught dressage and I asked her advice on the health of my donkey and she'd looked her over and said she was just fine. Johanna had called her farrier and it was he who had put on Anne's shoes. When Anne had started to limp earlier, Johanna came out to check her over and showed me what oils to rub on her muscles as she might be a little stiff.

Now I called to ask if she could drive 100 miles with a horsebox to take my donkey and look after her for the rest of her life. Johanna is a trooper. She said she'd be delighted and she'd be there in a few hours. I called Scott and told him that something very interesting was happening here and I suggested he come down. But Scott thought I was trying to manipulate him and decided to carry on filming his sheep. Had he come, he would have the vital evidence I needed to prove that I had not been responsible for the damage to my donkey. Here was a well-respected horsewoman who could point out the holes in Anne's feet and tell Scott with conviction what had caused them.

Scott said he didn't care whether I'd hurt her or not, what interested him was that I thought I might have done. He didn't make that up; he was just a fly on the wall.

Johanna arrived with her young daughter Natalie and Carmen Rosia, her stable hand. More importantly, Johanna arrived with her inner calm and her humour and within seconds she had reassured me that all would be well.

I walked Anne into the horsebox and she stayed close to me as Johanna and Carmen Rosia fastened two head ropes to keep her stable. They drove her up the road and parked the horsebox outside the little bar. As I walked past it, Anne seemed to sense that I was there because I could see her ears prick up behind the wooden slats and follow my movements like antennae as she let out her little whinny. I reached up to reassure her.

When our meal arrived, ten-year-old Natalie asked me if I would like to try some of hers. When she lifted a huge portion of food onto my plate, I knew without doubt that Anne would be in very good hands. Just before they drove away, I petted Anne as she whinnied and it reached a place inside me which had so rarely been touched. I loved this little donkey.

Natalie hugged me then shoved something in my hand. As they drove away I looked at it – her friendship bracelet. Something for a new medicine bundle to carry with me.

Anne made a full recovery and is the mascot of the corthigo. She has a stable all to herself and continues to amuse everyone with her Houdini-like ability to get out of her stable though the bolt is too far down the door on the outside for her to reach with her mouth.

Now I was alone again. I kept myself together during the following day by cleaning my tack in preparation for sending it back to Nell. Whenever it got too much for me and a little voice said, 'Don't worry about this bit, they won't notice', I thought of the trust that Nell had given me and it made me work more thoroughly. I thought about Anne while I cleaned the tack of her hair. After all these years of pushing on, she was the first to make me stop the grind and feel. Nobody knows how she gets out of her stable. Perhaps she is a magical donkey. I'd like to think so. When I finished polishing, I tucked some of her hairs into my rucksack, then I buried her shoes.

I packed up my kit and took a room in the bar for the night. I needed to have a wash and some privacy while I sorted out what I would have to give away and what to carry in my pack. Perhaps it wasn't the best place to be that night, because I was in the territory of those who had overheard my sobbing sessions on the phone and they made sure I knew they were laughing at me.

I felt robbed and battered. And when I heard the old voice saying, 'Come on, one last ditch effort', I just sniggered. What was the point?

Max's words must have guided me then because at some time during the night, I saw that to give up now would be the most selfish act of all. I had a responsibility to other people to finish this journey, not only to those who had helped me along the way, but to Raleigh International. They were depending on me. It was easier to hold on to this motive as a crutch than to try to untangle the mess of my life.

The first day out with the pack, I walked forty miles. My shoulders were numb when I took it off, my back stank from the sweat and the skin was sore where the pack had rubbed on wet material. I crawled into my tent and slept until 4 a.m. when my judges woke me to begin the trial. I packed up and walked another thirty-five miles, hanging on to any thought during the minutes in the hours of consciousness to keep the battering at bay. I did this every day for a week, thinking my pack weighed about 20lbs. I'd never have done it if I'd known the truth: it actually weighed 50. By the end of it, Janet Street Porter and the flies were due in for another session.

I made a place in the woods by a stream where I swept out the hearth and lit my fire. I dragged stone plinths from the river to make a surface for preparing my food, and baked a batch of hash cookies. I could not face the flies without help. I ate one and waited for the crew. Nothing happened, so I had another. By the time they arrived, a couple of hours late, I'd eaten all of them and the woods had been transformed into my place.

I welcomed Janet and the others with great enthusiasm. When she'd put down her bags, I showed her the 'spare room' where I had put some flowers but, because I couldn't decide which fabric to hang on the tree branch as her wallpaper, I would put her in the yellow paddock. Then I showed her the 'bathroom', where she could wash, excusing my laundry which was churning nicely in an eddy, but as I took her to the kitchen, something caught my eye. I looked up to see a man standing in the bushes with shades on. I totally lost it at this point as it hit me that this was Steven Scott and this was his job.

I finally gained control of the giggles and made Janet comfortable by the fire. Tony the cameraman and Ian on sound, who had both been amused, now crouched close to us while Janet opened her pack and brought out several gifts of food, which was very thoughtful as I didn't have anything but pasta for our supper. Then the questions began. She asked me about my donkey.

Even though I had made it right and had thrashed myself for the last week, I was still unable to answer questions from a point of stability. The dope had mixed with the judges inside my head and I admitted to the worst case scenario even though it wasn't true. I had been telling myself for so long that I was no good, that I thought this was honesty. There was a quiet in the woods at the moment of confession. A silence afterwards and then the words, 'Got it.' Janet turned around to someone and I suddenly realised, as the cameraman and sound man started to pack up their kit, that this wasn't a friend in my house, but a bunch of bloodsucking flies. Yet nobody had betrayed me but myself.

I wanted Janet to spend a night in the woods and then get up and walk a full day with me tomorrow. She agreed to do this, even though we didn't walk a full day and when the crew left and it grew dark, we started to speak freely in the safety of the darkness at the edge of the fire. She began to relax as the clamour of the city faded and she could hear the timpany of the woods at night. Gradually, she told me how things were going with her and how she had lost several friends within the last few months to Aids. She didn't tell me how her life was without them now; she simply started to recall the fun she'd had while they were alive, and by the way she spoke, almost as if I wasn't there and well into the small hours of the morning, it was as though she'd needed some time with them to say goodbye.

I felt incredibly protective of her, especially as I'd heard so many harsh words said behind her back. I wanted to guard her from more pain and so I warned her of a rumour I thought she needed to know. But Janet must have misunderstood my motives, because months later she turned on me and said I had intimidated her. I can only imagine that she was referring to this moment. Instead of seeing a hand offered in help, she saw a sword thrust in when she was most vulnerable.

Amazing really, in a world so infatuated with forms of communication, that there are so many misunderstandings.

I gradually pared down the contents of the pack to a reasonable 30lbs including tent, sleeping bag, clothes, wash kit, Dictaphone, food and water. But my feet couldn't take the extra pounding and they started to blister. I used up my supply of dressings within a few days and went in search of some more. I found a sports equipment shop, selling knee bandages and even though I didn't know the word for blister, I reckoned I could get over the problem with my improvisations, which were much more entertaining than fumbling with the dictionary.

I drew a bare foot with a big bulbous lump on the heel with dashes all around it indicating pain and showed it to the shopkeeper. He'd been looking a little confused but when he studied the drawing the penny dropped and he shouted, 'Si!' and went out back to look. I wished the crew was here; they'd finally see that I was perfectly capable of getting by without any Spanish.

The man returned with a large box. Terrific, I thought, he's obviously got a lot in there and there might be a selection of brands.

He removed the lid and brought out the contents: a pair of black leather trainers with a red flashing light bulb on the heel.

Through most of Spain in the dry heat of the summer, I was too much of an oddity to be able to observe anyone else. Applause in a Spanish bar depends on the skills of the matador on the television. But no matter how well they were performing, it stopped as soon as I crashed in, quivering and sweaty, plonking my bulk down on a chair. All eyes following me as I unclipped my rucksack, stood up without it and wove like a stinking vagrant towards the bar. Even without uttering a single mispronounced word I was aware of ending conversations, creating an atmosphere of tension, and I became an irritation to them, sitting there cooling off in the corner. Why doesn't she piss off to wherever she comes from? said the silence. It felt like the ritual of the eleventh hour of the eleventh day of the eleventh month. I wanted to shout after the moment was supposed to pass, 'What are you commemorating? Did somebody die or something?' But I knew the answer would be, 'No, you just walked in and you are odd and out of place and we want to look at you.' Why doesn't she speak any more Spanish?

Perhaps it was by some divine intervention again, that when I needed to experience the height of my inner turmoil and punishment, I was in a country where for the first time on my walk around the world, I did not speak the national language.

There is something rather seductive about pain, keeping me conscious every single moment of the day. And then there is the orgasm of relief when I went into the loo and sucked out the blisters. In a purely masochistic way, I enjoyed the fear of looking for a place to duck into the woods and sleep for the night, knowing that if I was spotted, I might be in for a confrontation. I pumped myself with visions of what might happen in the woods and this paranoia mixed with the torturing of the judges, allowing me no calm to find a bedrock of anything to stand on, to keep myself together. I was often so pumped with confusion that I actually wanted to meet a real live attacker just to have something tangible to fight and have the chance of winning. As it was, the unspent adrenaline festered, adding physical irritation to the contorted mess of psychological confusion. And perhaps this is what caused the spasms in my muscles.

One morning I crawled out of my tent to find the spasms in my lower back were so strong that I could not even stand up. My lower spine was so contorted I couldn't kneel without putting one hand on the ground and this position made it impossible to stuff a sleeping bag into its sack. I held the end of it in my hand and wriggled on my belly towards a tree, then gripped the bark as I moved one knee underneath me, inch by inch, until I was finally upright with the sleeping bag in my hand. But I had forgotten to pick up the stuff sack. It was lying on the ground a very long way down. With the ingenuity of the disabled I finally got everything into my rucksack, but the worst of it was that now I could not reach my feet to syringe the blisters. I used a stick and a wall to put on my shoes and socks and once dressed felt a fair sense of accomplishment. But then I looked at the rucksack. However, once I'd got it on and started to inch my way out of the field, I reassured myself that it would soon settle down. About a mile down the road it struck me. What the fuck do you think you're doing? This is not going to go away. Get some treatment.

I crossed to the other side of the road and got a lift back into the town of Valladolid. The driver got pretty impatient with me when I took so long to get out. By the time I reached a hotel, I was almost in tears with the pain. I finally got a room and lay down on the floor but no matter which way I lay, I couldn't relieve the trapped nerves. At times like this, there is only one guy who can help: Dr Ken Kingsbury.

Ken was enjoying the first break he'd had in months, stripped to the waist in the garden, making a patio when the telephone rang. Within an hour he had laid a plastic sheet over his patio, packed his kettle and some sachets of soup and set off for the airport with his massage bed and his bag of needles. In the meantime, he instructed me to find a doctor to inject an anaesthetic into my spine. With the help of the hotel staff, I found one and made my way there with the concierge for translation. But the doctor must have misunderstood because he injected it into my gluteus maximus muscle.

By the time Ken arrived, I was in so much pain I felt I had given up hope. The first thing he said was, 'Be still, be tranquil.' Two days in a hotel room with Ken's humour and reassurance as he injected anaesthetics and hours of massage, gave me what had been slipping away for months – a great dose of hope. He put things into perspective when he drew the distinction between what I was doing and the athletes he treated. 'They have internationally recognised targets, recognised rules, people to train them and get them there on time and pep them up. And nobody sends a film crew after them at £1,000 per day to find out what dark secrets drive them to it.'

When he told me that other athletes get depressed, my ears pricked up that I might not be such a freak. When he heard me on the phone, having to deal with keeping the BBC away and trying to help Raleigh find a sponsor, he pointed out that I was trying to deal with too much, that maybe I needed someone in my camp to take this additional pressure off me. But simply by being there and reassuring me, Ken was doing exactly that.

I told him that being different, three things happen: some people knock you constantly, you feel you don't have anything in common with anyone and you don't know what's normal. Like going mad, but I knew that was normal because I'd heard of three people who'd done it. One of them sailed around the world and set fire to his boat in the doldrums. Fortunately, when he came to his senses, there was plenty of water around to put it out. Another tried to walk across the Sahara but unfortunately he had a loaded gun on him and shot himself. And another tried to walk from Tiera Del Fuego to Alaska but ended up in a small town gaol in Central America – he'd locked himself in.

By the end of the first day, I was standing on my own; by the end of the second day, I could walk down to the little restaurant near the hotel and sit for a while as we ate and talked of other things. The following morning, Ken's work was done and he watched me pick up my load and walk down the road to cover a marathon that day and every day for the next 2,500 miles. The only reason I could do it was because Ken knew I could. And it struck me that in all the years of walking, I had rarely met a person who had said, 'Yes you can.'

But within the first day, the judges started to question his words. One side of me enjoyed the sympathy, the other drilled out the words like rotten fillings. You're filth; you don't deserve a man like that. Who do you think you are to believe someone thinks you're OK? But when I tried to fight them with what he'd said, they simply pulled the words apart and threw them back at me, especially the line, 'What you're doing with Raleigh is terrific. There's no better inspiration you can be to young people than to show how you never gave up.'

The BBC would be coming out to film me crossing the Pyrenees in three weeks' time for another episode of: why are you doing this? Isn't it pointless? Why don't you speak Spanish? What a failure you are. But the anxiety of their arrival came to greet me long before I reached the mountains. Because I had destroyed the central pivot of what was right and wrong when I cheated in America, I could not sort out the voices in my head and find which one was right and which were paranoid. At four in the morning, Ken's words were beaten down by the raging voices that I was no good. Ken didn't know that I had cheated once, and my fear that Scott would find out sent me whirlpooling into despair. What lay ahead of me was a sham. I would not be the first woman to walk around the world. I decided to carry on because I knew I would have to be punished. My lot was to be torn apart in public, and I visualised it happening. It got so bad that at one point I went into a loo in a bar, laid down my rucksack and placed the nozzle of a can of whipped cream in my mouth with my finger firmly on the trigger.

Perhaps it was Ken's sense of peace which opened my mind to a solution. One day, I vowed, I would go back and walk across America again! I called my mother. She had been willing me to call because she had thought of the same thing too. Something of the burden was lifted then, until I got real and saw that when this journey was over, I never wanted to do this again.

Max came out for two days on the beach of Bilbao. I couldn't tell him why I was in so much despair; he must have assumed that the

BBC were getting me down. We strolled around the seaside village. I didn't speak much at all, but Max gave me a full performance of his imagination and actually made me laugh. He left me with the words that I must take it one step at a time and look for the joy around me because it's always there right next to the darkest shadow. I think Max was very brave to come out. Someone else's black hole produces a lot of energy, sucking energy.

I now headed northeast through Burgos towards the town of Pamplona, along the much-used Camino de Santiago pilgrim route. The irony wasn't lost on me that though I was surrounded by people making journeys on foot, I was going in the opposite direction. This track had seen many troubled people, searching for a way, for absolution from their sins. The hardship of the journey isn't just pushing on against the pain of the body but, more importantly, against the pain of the sin. The concept of the need for making a journey isn't dead, it's just questioned by those who would rather hide their fear of meeting themselves by laughing at others who are prepared to.

I joined the trail at the point where the pilgrims were two weeks into their journey. Most of them were singing and chatting away and they greeted me like a lost sister. By going in the opposite direction, I could distinguish those who were most in pain. As soon as they saw me the insecure amongst them would visibly panic, trying to remember the last arrow, whipping themselves with the thought that all these miles had been wasted and they were going the wrong way.

But as I walked up the path, closer to the beginning of the pilgrim trail, I met people in various stages of physical pain. A week into their journey and the blisters were easing off; further on, a few days in, and they stank of dressings and eucalyptus oil and were clamped in the trance of pain where I knew they couldn't even see me, let alone hear my shouts of encouragement. Watching those people, from the comfort of a car, you would not be able to understand why they didn't return your wave or why they walked straight past a wall plaque of some historic importance. In fact, if you didn't know any better, you might think they were egocentric and arrogant.

A week before I reached Pamplona, I called the BBC to let them know I would be getting there a week early. I had made up time and I didn't want to lose it by waiting for them to come out to film me crossing the Pyrenees. I also wanted Janet to walk a full day with me so that she could see what this was all about. They said they would meet me in the town but they didn't think they could get a film crew out, nor could they get Janet to walk for a day despite being the President of the Ramblers' Association. This made me very angry. She was coming to judge me again. I would have to meet them in their territory in a town, where I was filthy and they were clean. I would have to succumb to their wishes to wait another week for their schedule or I would have to suffer another onslaught of how uncooperative I was. Why couldn't I stand up for myself? Why did I always let other people walk all over me? All I could think of was Steven Scott sitting there smugly thinking, 'No! She can wait!' and controlling me from a distance.

It was a bizarre act of timing that I walked into Pamplona on the very first day of the San Furman festival – the running of the bulls. Even ten miles out, people walked with their white shirts and red kerchiefs and they got thicker the further in I got till I reached the middle amongst the chaos of Australian travellers drunk on champagne. The director, Nicky, and one of the researchers met me in the town centre. They told me they couldn't get a film crew out for another week; I would have to wait. I wouldn't take this. She seemed to be goading me on by shaking her head till I blew up in her face and told her that I had made up time despite wrecking my back; I needed this time as a cushion against it happening again and I wasn't going to put the rest of the walk in jeopardy by pandering to their petty whims. When she told me Janet wouldn't agree to walk for a day because she had a bad back, I told them she had no business being a judge of what I did.

Nicky said she'd try as hard as she could to get a film crew out. She said I was being obstinate and unpleasant and causing a lot of people a lot of trouble and it would not go unnoticed.

It was months later that I found out the irony of those words and why Nicky had baited me: she'd come wired to that meeting and there was a British camera crew standing on the far side of the square, secretly filming everything I did – a code of conduct that the BBC does not sanction.

I camped in the park that night, where the firework stands had been set up on top of the old Roman walls. They would not be lit yet, but against the sky, the black plastic bags with the cords around their necks looked like hangmen. During the night, several young Spaniards, who resented so many travellers, took out their anger on me. I heard them outside my tent and looked through the crack at the bottom of my zip to see two guys walking towards me with batons in their hands. But they didn't veer off and suddenly the top of the tent caved in. They were beating the tent in. I screamed at them to bugger off as I unzipped and sprang out, but they ran away. After a while I thought I heard more noises and listened again. A few seconds later my whole tent was heaved up, ripping the ground sheet.

I woke early, packed up and went to watch the running of the bulls. At 9 a.m. I called Nicky in her hotel to see if she had made any progress in finding a film crew. She laid it on pretty thick, telling me how Claire, the production assistant whom she knew I liked, had been up all night trying to get a crew out for me and she'd found one. What a crock. We'd meet again that day to follow me into the Pyrenees.

Before I met them, I walked through the festival and checked out the photos put up of that morning's run. I thought it was rather amusing that the photos of male bravery were displayed in an underwear shop, right next to a mannequin modelling a pair of bright red briefs.

Then something really caught my attention. A street artist, who had covered himself in white cement and a white toga, was standing perfectly still on a pedestal like a Greek statue with his arm raised and his eyes closed. In front of him was an empty bag of cement for collecting coins. I was amazed by his composure in all this drunken chaos. He was invisible to those who believed him. To those who saw he was real, he commanded a wide space in front of him out of respect; the wider the space, the more the respect. To drop in a coin, you had to expose yourself, feel small and awkward in the might of his presence.

The circle narrowed and widened around him as the people changed. I could see him feel their presence, because when someone got too close, looking up his nose, he swallowed. They tried to intimidate him. But even when the band crashed into the square, he did not move.

Gradually he dripped bits of cement and from time to time he changed arms as one was lowered with that wonderful rush of warmth, he raised the other and opened his eyes. They were blue and the whites looked yellow against the white of his face. I don't think he focused on anything. I wondered what his skin was like underneath all that cement. Was that why he covered it up and wanted to be stared at? I wondered what he could feel. Perhaps the breezes moving the toga? I wondered about the insects when he felt them crawling on his body and he didn't twitch. How did that make him feel? Dead?

I asked another street artist about him. She'd seen him for years in all the fiestas around Spain, but he never spoke, never spoke to anyone. I went back to him and watched differently, knowing this, wondering whether he was somehow mocking us. Then I saw the joke. And I started to laugh. Whenever I got really down in the months to come, I remembered this sight and I couldn't take anything too seriously. I had noticed for the first time what this god was holding in his hand, raised in a gesture of triumph above the faces turned to him in awe: a blue-handled kitchen spatula.

Now that the white shirts were covered in red stains from the wine not the bull, it was time to be moving on.

Nicky had instructions to make this episode about endurance. But it was a load of crap because she wasn't in the least bit interested, nor was anyone else, in having a go herself. Nicky was frightened of my camp: she didn't know what to do with bits of wood or fire; she was used to directing pop videos with swirly camera actions and, for that reason, they filmed only half the day. At the point where I walked to the end of my thirty miles, up over the high mountains to look for a place to set up for the night, they packed up and went off to their hotel. When I descended into the humidity of France down the other side of the Pyrenees, they all went to sleep at midday as I carried on. And yet they were responsible for portraying endurance.

When Janet finally came out and wanked on that she could walk thirty miles in one day but she couldn't at the moment because she had a bad back, I just thought it was pitiful. Then she told me I'd been an absolute cow. What for? Making up time despite collapsing with my own back problems? And then, she had the audacity to say, 'So Ffyona, you've been alone all this time and you've seen that you can't cope.' What? 'What do you mean I can't cope? I'm a week ahead of schedule.' When she tried another way to have a dig at me and brought up the fact that I didn't speak Spanish, I turned round and asked her, 'Hey, when you were trekking in Nepal, did you speak Nepalese?' She came back with some feeble response that she had an English guide and the funny thing was he didn't speak very good English, so she and her friend were trying to teach him. It wasn't very funny at all.

We met up again a few days later when I reached a beach on the Atlantic shore, by which time the humidity had infected one of my blisters and it was incredibly painful to walk on. But ol' Janet wouldn't understand that; she'd probably never had an infected blister in her walking life. It was decided then that one of the researchers wanted to walk a day with me. Ian, the South African, was really excited about it and the cameraman, Tony, said he'd do it too, said he couldn't see what all the fuss was about.

I took two days off on the beach to let the blisters have a chance to heal and I found, after all the thousands of miles, the best way to treat them. You slit them open and fill them with sand. This was the first time I had been on a beach on the Atlantic ocean since the time with Pete in the Sahara. I walked along the sand, northwards as I had done then, and saw the scudding of the breezes directly across my path. I felt so far away from the home we'd had then, just the two of us, respecting each other. But Pete was no longer with me and I must not have been worthy now of wearing the silver African pendant he had given me the night before I'd finished the walk, because I lost it in the shower unit of the camp ground. Whatever strides I made to stand up for myself went down the drain with that symbol. I hadn't yet suffered the humiliation that I deserved.

I walked very quickly through France. The gullies, through the trees, around the streams were just dripping with vines and leaves, my legs were a furry down of mosquitoes and I felt a panic from the days of Zaire, as though I was utterly trapped. I rarely stopped for anything, especially when walking through the young corn fields with their sprouts of hair like Cindy dolls – only they looked like they'd gone wrong in the factory because they were plumb coloured and not the golden colour of other corn. They looked rather gross: they looked like scalps hanging up.

Sometimes I would keep going for twenty-four hours without eating or sleeping because I couldn't find a place to get out of the wet. I wanted to camp up high, as I did in Spain sometimes, climbing mountains at the end of the day so that I could sit on top and be protected by the height and get a buzz the next morning when I looked out of my tent at the dawn on the valley below. But this land was flat and I couldn't get out of it.

Ian's day was amusing. He carried a tape recorder and lied about when it was switched on. He got his comeuppance, though, when he began to deteriorate nicely. He complained about his knee and I just turned to him and said, 'This is it, pal, this is endurance. Not walking up pretty mountains, but when it's raining, you're cold and in pain and you just knuckle down and carry on.' When he whinged some more, I simply told him he had a choice to make: give up and hitch back or carry on and shut up about it. I was quite impressed when he did shut up and carried on to the end, by which time we were in the midst of a thunder storm. He was about to go into hypothermia, but I got him out of his wet clothes in a bar and gave him the last of my dry sweatshirts. I made him drink plenty of water and rehydration salts which I carried, I bought him brandy and ordered a cab for him to get back to his car. But he didn't even think of where I was about to sleep that night.

Tony was the most enjoyable. He made me feel ashamed early in the day when I walked straight past a plaque commemorating Joan of Arc. But, by the end of the day, he was in the groove, completely shutting out everything around him, charging on down the road. He said afterwards that he had no idea how fit I am nor what it took to do even one day. Great, I thought, you've all been making a film for four months about my failings as a rambler and only now, after you've trashed me, do you find out that I'm not a rambler at all.

Halfway up France, I stopped off at a post office to collect a package which had been sent down by Orion – the first copy of my book, *On Foot Through Africa*. I didn't open it, but made my way into the woods where I ritually made my fire and set up everything as I like it. Then I recalled the first time I had thought about writing the book – the second day out from Cape Town, when I was struggling and wished it were all over and one day I would be sitting somewhere holding the copy of my book in my hands. I carefully undid the wrapper, thinking about the journey and what it had taken to write it and I thanked everyone who had worked on it. When I brought it out, it was more gorgeous than I'd ever imagined.

I had to make a choice between carrying this book with me to give it to my father when I met him in Dover and carrying my pair of 501s. I still find it hard to believe that I actually left my jeans behind.

Like the first tree you come across in the Sahara as an indication that you're coming to the end of it, I heard English voices in a café, talking of how far they'd driven during the night. Standing on a hill just outside Boulogne, I saw the white cliffs of England for the first time. I felt a little empty, a little sad that there wasn't someone to share it with, or any of it really. When I called Shuna to tell her I was in Boulogne, she said, 'Oh, have you gone there for a bit of sun?' She didn't know where it was. She didn't know it was forty-two miles south of Calais. She said, 'Oh, I thought you were supposed to be in Calais by now.' But then, I didn't know where she was at all; I didn't even know who she worked for.

Just as I had found my island place by visualising it in my mind, now I had a vision of a bunker on the beach where I would make a place and rest for two weeks before making the crossing as planned from the beginning on 1 September. I had pushed for this rest time; I needed some time to gather myself before facing the final lap of humiliation which I knew was coming. But worse than that, I had been motivating myself for so long with a stick, I knew I must change somehow or it would not be a good influence on the young people who were coming to walk through Britain with me.

I looked in every bunker along the beach for about twenty miles. It took me two days, stopping, putting my pack down, looking inside but finding only sea discharge and turds. But I knew it was there, I just had to find the shortest distance between where I was standing and where it was waiting. When I was within sight of Wissant and could see I only had about a mile at most left of beach, I did not desert my vision, I knew implicitly that it was here somewhere. Doubts cloud your vision, actually making things disappear so that they don't exist for you. But I imagined the position, the view from it, the way I would duck to enter it and how I would sweep the sand straight out onto the beach. And this is why I found it when everyone else who came looking for me could not.

When I saw it, I felt a rush of calm. There you are.

One of the BBC researchers was in Wissant at the time. She seemed much more fun when she was on her own and she came out to help me remove the junk in the bunker and then gave me a lift to a supermarket where I could buy a few things for it, like mugs and bowls and mats for my guests who would be coming soon. When she left, I stopped. Stopped. Looked around me, heard the sea for the first time now that the sermons inside my head were turned off for a moment, smelt the salt, felt the sand on my feet and in my hair. I missed my hair about my face but that would be for another time. Then I spent a delicious day, fully engrossed in what I was doing, making a place.

But the best was yet to come, as I walked along the beach, looking for treasures. I wasn't used to putting down my house and bringing things to it and my mind had been starved of what it enjoyed most – improvisation. With old bricks and boards I made a two-tiered sideboard and a low table in the middle of the bunker. I laid the grass mats around the table to sit on.

Then I went out again and selected my sticks. I have never known a place where they were so special, sticking up out of the sand, worn smooth by the sea, dried by the wind and bleached by the sun. And they were perfectly straight. These I gathered and laid them out in the entrance to my place and set about lighting my first fire there. I smoothed out a circle until the sand was perfectly flat and clean of bits, then I laid four leaves for the four corners of the earth and the four elements which also acted as a good place to lay my tinder bundle in case the sand was damp.

My fire lit with one match and I arranged three stones into the fire on which to set my pan of water. Between these stones, I laid more sticks so that I could push them further in as they burned down. I made a cup of tea and remembered, just before I drank, to say thank you.

Thank you to the people who had offered me help when I was in need. Like the day I walked into a village after forty-eight hours without food to find a sign for a bar and when I opened the door and found two ladies standing there in dressing gowns and had asked them if they were open, they'd said, 'No, we closed fifteen years ago, but would you like to join us for breakfast?' And the time I had showered in a camp ground, during the worst of my inner torment at how selfish I had been, and heard the woman next to me stuck in her cubicle, panicking and was able to help her by crawling under the door. But then I'd panicked that I didn't know the Spanish for, 'Are you decent?' I thanked the elements for not blowing me off the 300-foot high cliff when I'd camped up there and a lightning and wind storm had reduced me to clinging on to the rocks through the ground sheet as the tent lifted up underneath me, inching me towards the edge. And I thanked my lucky stars that when I was cornered by a man out on a lonely highway, I had thought to pull out my Dictaphone, press the button and shout, 'Alpha Bravo? This is Bravo Two Zero, the suspect's licence plate number is . . .' And he'd got back in his car and drove away at high speed never to return.

It was a fine cup of tea.

I had been concerned that this series would not only humiliate me but Raleigh International, because they were about to be associated with me. But I had no editorial or previewing rights. I had tried, through my agent, to persuade Steven Scott that Raleigh should see the films before they were aired so that they could have the choice of continuing with me or not. Though Sara Parfitt brushed this off as ridiculous, saying they knew about the Beeb, they'd had a film crew out on an expedition who had ended up showing an hour of two people talking garbage, I still wanted her to see them. Scott agreed, then broke his promise. I wanted to see them then. My agent couldn't help, but after a time Scott agreed, but only if he could film me watching them.

The flies came to the bunker and set up their equipment inside. Janet was there and before it began I asked her if she'd had any editorial say in what I was about to see. She said no. She told me I could point out what was wrong and she assured me that if there were factual errors these would be put right. As it turned out she did not keep this promise, possibly because it ruined one of the films: the narrator said my daily schedule whilst walking with the donkey was twenty-five miles. Had it said fifteen miles, which I reduced to ten, the sting would have been taken out of the programme.

They showed me three out of six. I was amazed. I had to hand it to them: they'd done one hell of an editing job to get such rubbish. One of the crew told me in confidence that they were so disgusted when they saw the series they wanted to leave the BBC. At the end of it, there was only one thing I should have said by looking straight into the camera lens: 'Hey, Steven. Sitting in the edit suite, now I know what you meant when you told me the last guy you'd made a documentary about committed suicide.'

Instead, I uttered some garbage, they hung around filming me for a while, sweeping out the bunker after they'd taken their equipment out, waiting for me to crack up and break down. But then I just asked them to excuse me now and I went into the bunker and started to get into my tent, which I had put up in there against the rats. I turned round and saw that Tony had actually followed me in and was filming me. Christ, was there nowhere I could go to get some privacy? Just because I was on my own, they'd got away with a lot of shit because I had nobody else to defend me. Did they really think this was allowed?

He came back in again, without the camera, after I had got inside and he asked me if I was OK. I said I was. When I knew they'd gone, I took out the large pot of sleeping pills which I carried for my back pain and quietly, without any fuss, placed it beside my water bottle. I had just seen the disgrace of my life and I knew it wasn't even a scratch on the real story. I finished a letter, tucked my dirty laundry into a bag and lay on my stomach. The lid of the bottle was adult proof, I had to think like a child to get it off.

And then something very strange happened: Sara Parfitt from Raleigh International put her head into the bunker.

'Fi! There you are. We've been looking for you for two days!' When she saw I was in my tent, she said, 'Oh, we're not disturbing anything, are we?'

The bunker was filled now with Sara and with Susannah Cohen who was in charge of the back-up and Bijan Navabi who had come out to answer my questions about Raleigh's overseas projects. Filled with their enthusiasm and their laughter, I wasn't sure what to make of it and when I tried to join in, I couldn't seem to communicate. But I was too tired to wonder just who I was going to be. I knew what I was.

That night, I explained to Suz the rules I wanted the young people to abide by: they would state how far they would walk that day – ten miles, twenty miles or thirty miles. If they wanted to do more, that was fine, but they couldn't give up between breaks and they couldn't do less than they'd said. I wanted to give them the chance to stand at the end of the day and say they'd done double the distance they thought they were capable of, not half. In turn, she told me all the things they had set up, the scouts, the schools, the Raleigh walkers, the vans from various places including Mitsubishi whom I'd persuaded to help them. The tents were donated from, ironically, Bill Preston at Encounter Overland. And I got a slight feeling that this was not my journey at all. Though I wanted to share it, I wasn't really prepared for what it meant to have another woman in charge of my camp.

But then we noticed that Sara had been missing for longer than a pee break. We went out onto the beach in the moonlight and called her. We finally found her, walking along the shore. Suz was very encouraging and finally Sara told us what was upsetting her: she had been working on this project for a year now and she felt that it was all being taken away from her.

I couldn't believe these words. I wasn't a freak. I wasn't a selfish cow. These feelings were perfectly normal but how they could spin out of control, especially in isolation when your whole identity and view of yourself swings out of proportion.

We laughed so hard then and we laid out our sleeping bags, side by side, just the three of us, looking out towards the dark line of England to fight the battle together.

If Sara had not had to work from the London office and we three had made the journey together, I think things would have turned out differently.

They left the following day and so began a series of visitors who each brought me a special gift. I was due to meet Nick McDowell of Orion at 10 p.m. in Wissant and bring him back to the bunker. When I arrived, I found him fairly tired. He'd been waiting for five hours: we were supposed to meet at 5 p.m. I couldn't apologise enough. I'd forgotten how hard it is to make the change now, from one way of life to another, remembering things I could not see. The next morning he came back to the bunker and, by telling me a little of his own story, I felt, as I had done with Sara, much less alone.

Max came too, with a huge hug. The crew filmed it. I didn't want them there but they insisted, saying some garbage about trying to redress the balance of how awfully they had portrayed me. When they left, he too shared things with me and it struck me that each of these people were coming from their world on the other side of the Channel, to show me that I wasn't a stranger to them. They were welcoming me home.

George Meegan came too, by way of a letter from Japan. George was the first man to walk from the most southerly tip of South America to Alaska. A journey of four years. I'd heard his voice on the radio on the last day when he was asked how he felt. His voice had such a ring of despair when he said, 'I feel like I've just lost my best friend.' Now George prepared me for the end. He told me how the media would rip me apart, without caring how vulnerable I was. He reminded me that the people I met along the way were not of the same mould as the media; he reminded me to hold eye contact with them a little longer because there the strength would be given and received. He also told me how rudely the BBC had treated him, calling him to come over for this series, letting him cancel plans, then calling again that it was all off without a word of apology. I laughed at this, laughed my head off with relief that it wasn't just me they had treated badly.

Yet I could not escape the feeling that I was betraying each person who brought me their gifts. The more they comforted me and confided in me, the more I felt a fraud. I was not about to complete the circle: there was a gaping hole in it and it had grown and grown till I couldn't even remember having walked a single step at all, anywhere.

It was in this state that I sat with Nick and Sara and Raymond in Calais and tried to thrash out an answer to why I had made the journey and how relevant it was to the message of Raleigh. The three of them spoke; I couldn't believe I had nothing to say. It wasn't how the film portrayed it, as being pulled apart by horses; I had just blocked out eleven years of my life and they were trying to help me find it again.

That night, Raymond and I made our way onto the headland in the dark and the rain, with the film crew following in their car, blaming me for taking so long at the meeting because now it was too dark for them to film me with Raymond. I was so completely unable to see anything objectively that I couldn't work out whether to apologise and feel guilty for being so selfish or whether to just say, 'Oh, didums.'

We put up our tents and lit our fire when they'd gone. Raymond was the only person who had ever walked full days with me and our time with the cart had shown him what I went through. He said he was so sorry that I had seen the worst of the BBC; he now had a series too and had found them to be very professional. As the fire grew dim and I knew the hour was coming when I would have to face the beginning of the real thrashing, I felt a parting from him. I could not carry his words of strength with me: I didn't deserve them.

But the spirits do have a sense of humour. We had walked down to the dock the following morning, where we met a group of Raleigh cyclists who were finishing a journey around Europe. We would be crossing together on the ferry which sat in the harbour containing a press room packed with waiting reporters and photographers. But somehow we got separated from them and we suddenly realised they'd all gone and we were alone. The ship let out a blast on the horn. We were going to miss it!

We ran outside, where a dock supervisor got on the radio and summoned a car to take us to it. Raymond shouted, 'Come on, get in, we'll miss the boat!' I flung my rucksack in as the ship let out another blast on the horn. But then: 'No! I can't do this! I can't miss out any steps!'

I ran beside the car across the loading bays and parking lot and onto the ship. Straight into a Sunday morning press gang.

They might have thought I was crying with tears of relief, but I wasn't. They might have thought I was crying for sympathy, but I wasn't. I choked up during my spiel because I realised that I would never know how this boat journey back to England was supposed to feel.

When they crowded around me, pushing and shoving as I walked down the plank with Sara and Annabel James from Raleigh, I suddenly smelt myself and felt disgusted. Some people find they twitch when they feel threatened, other people feel a restricting of their throat muscles and they have to cough, but when I feel threatened, I fart like a skunk.

I knew my mother and father and sister would be waiting for me up at Dover castle; this throng was an irritation. I had a journey to make. And as I walked up the steep hill, making sure the Raleigh cyclists were not missed, I brought out the book I had carried for my father and wrapped in brown paper. I saw them outside the castle. The last few steps were so slow and then I was hugging my mother. She felt so tiny but she smelt so good and comforting. I hugged my sister, who always turned on the buckets, and then I hugged my father. I took him away from the cameras, around the corner and gave him my brown package. He didn't know what it was but his face changed from one of suspicion to one of understanding when he opened the cover and saw it was dedicated to him, I think I actually saw tears in his eyes before he hugged me again. The end of a chapter in our relationship, the beginning of another. But then he ruffled my hair and I felt like screaming!

My mother had made a conscious decision not to think of what I hadn't done. She told me later it would have shown in her face and besides, she felt I had made up the mileage. She scanned the articles every day quickly to make sure my secret had not been found out and then she could relax and read the story slowly. Each time a damning article came out that I saw with headlines like 'Super Bitch!' or 'Stupid Twit's Silly Walk' I felt it was nothing compared to what I really deserved. I remembered George's words especially when the articles hurt, because there were so many people who were genuinely welcoming. In true British fashion, they'd come running out of their houses with a mug of tea or just a wave, shouting, 'Don't let the bastards grind you down!' Many stopped for longer and would say, 'Remember no matter what the press write about you, you know you did it. They can't take that away from you.' And, of course, I felt even worse.

I felt uneasy around so many people, especially the young ones. I was in a black hole and I didn't want them to be contaminated by such negativity. I walked ahead of them, fearful that I would disappoint, but they just thought I was being arrogant. When I slowed down, though, I started to see some very interesting things. As I had done on previous walks, the back-up vehicle waited ahead every ten miles. The walkers knew the distance and on the very rare occasion when it wasn't in the right place because there was nowhere to pull over, they actually got irritable! And for all these years I'd thought, and had been told, that this behaviour was just me. I also saw how they had been longing to see the van which would mark the end of the day, how they built it up in their minds as being a palace, and when they arrived, it was no big deal and there was a sense of anti-

John O'Groats
Lybster
Lothbeg Point
Inverness
Kingussie
Crief
Edinburgh
Kielder
Stanley
Thirsk
York
Selby
Hatfield

Second
— British Walk —
1994

N

Nottingham
Leicester

Oxford
Maidenhead
London
Sevenoaks
Tunbridge Wells
Dover

climax. When frightened, out on the track in Africa, I had often found this anticlimax of arriving, with a casual hello, to be crushing. Though the walkers must have felt this too, they didn't react as I had done sometimes and got cross; they kept it inside and just relaxed. I suppose I shouldn't always believe what I'm told by those who have never been in the same situation.

Along with Suz, who was in charge, there was John Fallis, who was very resourceful – he once locked us out of a scout hut by accident but instead of freaking out, he simply slipped in his credit card and opened the door. There was Caitlan from Australia, who was in charge of buying the food and cooking. Cait was a scamp: she could get anything at a discount and loved to haggle, even in the super-market. Anna Beinssen was Australian too. She was the nurse and would massage you into your grave given half the chance. And Dennis Jackson from South Africa, who had an uncanny knack of taking photos when you least expected someone to be there.

I wanted so much to be part of them, but the attacks on me in the press kept me at a distance. The TV series was aired every week for the six weeks I walked through Britain and Suz had decided she would not watch it. She didn't want her opinion of me clouded by what she saw through the eyes of media scum. But I felt I was bring-ing shame to this group and when I tried to include them whenever the press were around, in some ways I think they didn't want to be included. This may have been paranoia, because Jamie Robertson-McLeod, who was the Chief Executive of Raleigh, and Sara and Bruce Henderson, who was taking care of logistics back in London, always told me that I was giving them a terrific boost.

Bruce was a character; he didn't take shit from anyone. When a journalist called him to find out where we were to do an interview, he explained that we were on a particular road and from the last phone call he'd got, we were taking a break in some bushes just off the edge of a particular park. She called him back some time later and demanded to speak to his superior because she couldn't find us. Again he told her roughly where we were, but he was in an office and we were on an expedition and she'd have to use her nouse. Again she called back, now in a fuming rage and Bruce said, 'Hey, lady, just keep going south, if you smell salt and your feet get wet you've gone too far.' The reporter was Annabel Hestletine.

She finally found us where we were having lunch with Raymond and his parents who'd driven out to see us. She seemed nervous. She interviewed everyone and we left, leaving her to chat privately with Raymond. Hestletine wrote the most damning article I'd ever read, but perhaps it was hardly surprising that she couldn't find anything good to say about something she didn't understand. What concerned me, though, was that she quoted Brian Noel from the America walk as though she'd spoken to him. I wish I'd known at the time that this wasn't the case. Brian had never even heard of her.

Was it irony or something else which directed the happenings on the day her article appeared in the *Sunday Times*? A couple of schoolgirls in a group walking with us cheated. I learned of this as a rumour while I signed their sponsorship forms at the end of the day. I asked each one of them to look me in the eye and tell me how many miles they had walked. None of them in the group admitted to it and I would not let them leave without telling me who it was. I handled it extremely badly because I was so angry. When they were finally pushed forward, I simply said I was ashamed of them. Their teacher had in fact encouraged them to do it. She was concerned for their safety, lagging behind, and she'd picked them up, moved them on and dropped them down again. That was one thing; lying about it was another. They all turned on me then and said I had ruined their day and they stormed off to their van. I felt terrible when they drove away. But, by the hand of the spirits, I got a second chance when they returned five minutes later to collect a forgotten item.

During those five minutes I had spoken to Phil, one of our walkers who worked with young people, and he'd told me what I should have said. One girl stormed past me to collect her coat but I went up to their teacher and asked her if I could have a word with the two girls. She agreed. They got out and I took them round the side out of earshot and apologised for being an arsehole: Hestletine's article had come out that day and I'd been a bit wound up. Then I said quite quietly that everyone makes mistakes and that's human and that's OK because that's how we learn. I told them I would not have minded if they'd come to me and said they'd fallen behind and had to take a ride to catch up. But lying about it only festers. People aren't stupid; they all knew who'd done it. And it takes more courage to be honest but in the end it always makes you stronger. Then they gave me a hug!

We went back to the van. I opened the back door to a crowd of belligerent faces and just said, 'Hey, I'm sorry for being an arsehole back there . . .' and they just cheered and gave the three of us a round of applause. 'Well, I guess we all learned a lot more today than we expected to.' And they drove off waving and laughing. Oh boy, if only they knew.

Looking back on it, I found the hardest on me were often the women reporters. We are just as territorial as men I think, but we don't have such a means of expressing it with humour. There were many women, though, who wrote about how I would not have been treated like this if I were a man, and in some ways I agreed with this. It brought home to me how confusing it is to have been encouraged as women to go after our own ambitions and yet be damned for them as being selfish acts when we return, triumphant. And yet when I said what I wanted to do next was to have a family and a home, I was snubbed: is that all you want, they said, what a waste. It reminded me of the loggers I met in Zaire who had finally got their systems sorted out to meet the demands of the west but now were faced with people coming and saying, 'Hey, why are you chopping down your forest?'

It must be mighty confusing for young people, too, who are put down on one hand for lacking motivation and yet when someone accomplishes something, they see her being put down too. Perhaps it was because I wasn't motivated by what their elders had in mind.

This is progress, but progress towards what I really don't know. It seemed to me that the women I'd met in Africa had a position of respect and here, in my own land of equality, there was nothing but confusion. Where I was celebrated it was because I was a woman as though my journey was amazing because women must be less capable of physical achievement than men. And yet women are designed for endurance: to pound the cassava for hours. I wanted so much to stand up and speak of these things, but I couldn't, my guilt and my shame were too great and perhaps this was the worst part of it all: when I had a platform and something I wanted to say, I couldn't do it.

Joanna Coles from the *Guardian* actually made some valid points: why should we celebrate someone who has made no sacrifice or contribution for the greater good? All I can say to that is I totally agree with her. But perhaps she needed to be reminded that many celebrated athletes do their stuff for their own personal achievement. Others benefit by being inspired to achieve things themselves.

I could understand the betrayal people seemed to feel when they heard me speak: it seemed like they were all pumped up to receive the words of a guide, but I had nothing to tell them. Good guides are hard to find these days, especially since we are in the process of killing them off.

We invited reporters into our home at the end of the long days. We gave them hospitality and we were pleasant to them, but it didn't matter because they'd trash me anyway. I had no place to go and shut the door because, in order to promote Raleigh, I had to be accessible. It was particularly hard on Suz, who not only had worked with such enthusiasm on the project but who had her own reasons for despising the hacks. She had just come out of the Navy where she'd been pulled apart by them at each port, making her feel cheap as they muttered filthy questions about relationships on board. Yet she remained utterly professional and, in the end, neither of us actually strangled anyone.

We took a break from it for a day when we reached London. As it turned out, it was one of the most bizarre and revealing days of my life. Nick had set up a book signing at Harrods which we walked to and then split up, to meet again the next morning in Richmond at the scout hut. Some of the walkers wanted to come in with me, but they were turned away at the door because of the dress code. But they let me in. There was a large desk piled high with the Africa book and I took my place, feeling very small behind it. A line of people formed to my right, waiting to have a book signed. I remembered George's words and spent some time with each person, making sure I held eye contact as I gave them their book. But I started to hear dissent in the ranks. People were actually coughing when I waited till the person I was with to finish his or her story. They actually sighed and I heard them puff and grumble and saw them look at their watches.

Later that evening, I found myself again at the front of a queue, a pile of forms in my hand. I was with Crisis, the charity for the homeless. I asked each person what clothes they needed. If I chatted with one, I heard the others relaxing. If someone was having trouble being understood, a perfect stranger stepped forward to explain to me that this Irish gentleman was not saying 'shorts' but 'shirts' and we had a laugh about that too. One man took me aside to say he'd noticed a new girl on the streets who was only seventeen and pregnant. I made eye contact again. In that eye contact was the gift. I felt it went back and forth, from me to him, from him to me. That was the gift. *I know you.*

It struck me that this was the difference between the two worlds: those who believe they have everything and yet find themselves empty and searching for more, and those who have nothing, but each other. Perhaps Dick Whittington was looking in the wrong place.

Later that night, I stayed with Shuna and we watched the Proms on TV. I saw the people in the audience. Some were dressed up in their finery, others were in jeans, yet they came to feel the same things. How much would they have given to feel this? If they had to make a choice between a gold watch and a feeling of belonging, which one would they choose? But, as Ran Fiennes said to me, Jesus tried to ask people the same question and look how far he got.

James Harvey was our first success story. He started out as a wimp and he ended up as 'Blistie – walker extraordinaire'. I watched him change over the week he was with us, how he began as a very amenable young lad who had pledged to walk thirty miles a day for a whole week in order to raise money to go on his expedition with Raleigh. He seemed quite nonchalant about it, not in any arrogant way, but perhaps because he had never felt real pain before. 'I'll be sensible,' he said to himself when the first blister popped up. 'I'll rest it and then carry on tomorrow.' So he started to fail, falling behind everyone else and then taking the rest of the day off. I would not get him up, though, or the whole exercise would be pointless. I just ignored him. But on the third day, having only walked thirty miles in total, he suddenly saw what he had to do – push on through it. When I saw him do this, he started to laugh like a mad thing. The bigger the blister, the more he laughed. The laughter of the edge and it was music to my ears. I helped him then, syringing his blisters at the breaks, and in turn he was helping me, showing me the worth of the journey. He said of it later that it was an extraordinary experience which he could not get out of his mind. He'd had a chance to push through something painful himself and out the other side and now he felt much stronger for it. A rite of passage. A right of every young person. Yet it doesn't come as standard in our 'civilised society' any more.

There were many who came and walked and were amazed at their ability to push through pain they would have shied away from. Like eighteen-year-old Sally Webster. And this is what she wrote of her time with us which I think explains the whole ethos of Raleigh International.

'When I got home I wanted to write about my time walking with Ffyona and the Raleigh team. I have never had much self-confidence and I never thought I was capable of much worthwhile but being with people who expected a lot of me and with Ffyona who has such a strong belief in people and what they were capable of, my attitude about myself began to change. Instead of wallowing in self-pity, I saw that if I applied myself, I could be useful and not just a waste of space.

'I had come in the first place mainly to see this person who could walk around the world. I didn't realise how hard it was to walk thirty miles or what it really was to push yourself. To be honest Ffyona seemed a bit distant and my shyness meant I couldn't really approach her. However, over the week, her praise meant so much to me. On the first day, I decided I'd just walk ten miles but I soon learned that I could push myself much harder than that and if I'd knocked off then, I would have been letting myself down. After twenty miles, I didn't really want to walk the last ten, but because my friend Francis persuaded me to, I began to realise that I could dig deeper. I felt so proud when I completed a whole day, the pain in my legs didn't matter. I felt totally exhilarated. I felt I could achieve anything.'

Sally continued to walk with us, despite an injury in her knee. Anna massaged her legs three times a day, but no matter how much pain she was in, Sally never wallowed in it, preferring to ask others about their lives and to smile as she felt 'the whole world will smile back at me', and we did. There were times when she rested her legs for a day (after a fair amount of persuasion from Suz and Anna) but instead of kicking back, she mucked in, lending a hand and became part of the support team. She had so much determination, making a promise to herself each morning of how far she would walk and there was no way she'd let herself down. 'I just wanted people to accept me,' she wrote. 'If I could push myself then there must be something in me worthwhile. At the end of it, Chris and Gordon, who had been walking with me, had a really illuminating talk. We all felt we had benefited a lot from this opportunity and we could now do what we wanted with our lives if we just put our minds to it. We could push ourselves to extremes, and I really enjoyed doing that. Having just walked a tiny fraction of Ffyona's walk, we could start to appreciate and be totally amazed at what she had done. But at the same time she looks around her and pays attention to other people's lives. She has a great big warm heart. The support team and their dedication was also a great thing to see. They were concerned right down to the little things to make life easier for the walkers, even down to having water boil at the moment a walker came in, and how often the van should be seen. I learned so much in that week and I only wish other people with little faith in themselves could do something similar and begin to realise that there is strength in everybody. The walk has motivated me to think seriously about the possibility of doing something to challenge myself and learn to grow a bit more.'

It was pretty hard to receive a letter like that after reading articles written by hacks who condemned the walk as a selfish waste of time but who wouldn't take up our offer and have a go for one day themselves.

Andy Smart, though, was a different case altogether. A nut case. He'd been, and still is, an adrenaline junkie but he had pushed himself rather too far over the edge rather too often and had come back from it without much strength in his legs. He still beat me, though, over ten miles, not to mention the fraction of a second it took him to swing over a stile like some kind of ballerina. He'd wait, patiently, for me to figure out where to put my feet, trying to keep my balance. Then he'd be off again with that rhythm in his sticks I tried so hard to keep up with. Then there was the guy's sense of humour, which was devious and hilarious – and I don't know how he kept upright with a laugh like that. For Andy, giving up was not an option either.

If only the media knew, knew what was really going on here on this journey. We saw so much change in the people who walked with us, even during one day, and yet the media were intent on trashing me and the whole inspiration we were witnessing right in front of us was going unnoticed. The only solution we could think of was to get a reporter to walk for a whole day. It never ceased to amuse us how the critics went quiet as soon as the offer was made. Janet Street Porter finally said she would walk for a day but she said unfortunately her train back meant she couldn't. So we told her we'd all get up an hour early so that she could. For the twenty people with us, getting up at 4 a.m. instead of 5 was a huge sacrifice. But they did it. Janet turned up at 10 a.m. That's when I let rip on her. I wanted her to apologise to everyone concerned, but she made up some feeble excuse.

We noticed an article written by a reporter who had walked a day with Ian Botham. Annabel James, who was running the Raleigh press desk, convinced him to join us, not really to make a comparison between the two styles, but simply to get a reporter out on the road. After eleven years, with only four days of the walk left, a reporter finally agreed to walk for one single day.

The reporter, whom I'll call Jim, swung into camp and I wondered how he was going to manage walking thirty-three miles the next day carrying such a big head. There was something unsettling in his eyes, perhaps a loss of opportunity which he tried to cover up for in his arrogance. But I sensed there was fair play in the man.

As so often with new members, he set out with great strides the next morning, high as a kite in rhythm, wondering what the fuss was all about. He told me he had always wanted to be a cricketer, but perhaps he hadn't got what it took he said, because he'd never reached his full potential and was now a reporter on the game. Towards the end of the first ten miles, he was straining for sight of the van. After half an hour's break, he got to his feet with the enthusiasm of the tired and by the end of twenty miles, he didn't want to go on at all. Normally, I would have said nothing and let the lack of fulfilment set in, but he was only here for one day so I walked past him and whispered 'wimp'. He got to his feet and carried on with me. Backwards.

By the end of thirty miles, his arrogance had gone and his true strength was growing with every footstep. I felt his change and the clear, calm confidence which began to radiate from him very quietly. When he turned to say goodbye there was something very different in his eyes – a kind of peace.

On the day before the end, I watched the people on the road ahead of me, walking in pairs or in groups or on their own, simply walking to the beat of their own drum. I knew each of them by the personal burden they carried, and I began to see that everyone has their worlds to walk around, their Everests to climb, and I was not the freak or the strange one at all.

Their gifts to me had been to let me watch how they all overcame the weight of their burdens through their humour and their fight against all the things around them which seemed to say, 'No you can't.' By walking as they did for as long as they did despite their blisters and their toenails coming off, they were simply saying, 'Yes we can!'

I wished this message could go around the world, especially to the next generation who have to fight a battle the likes of which mankind has never known. These young people didn't want the labour-saving device of the car. In fact, they didn't want to use the energy of the earth at all; it drained them. They wanted to use their own energy because, strangely enough, the more they used the more there is.

These were my thoughts as I walked with Mark Thomson across

the desolate landscape in the sunshine which could have been any-where and everywhere.

The moment passed and we walked into the last camp of the walk. The field had been lent to us for the night by a man who remembered me leaving. And for our last supper, we cooked a Johann special – tuna fish and cheese triangles with pasta, which had been created one night in a gravel pit in Zaire with the very last of our stores.

Suz and I had a debate over how we would arrive the next day. I had been sickened at how the media had cut out the pictures of the other walkers to head up articles entitled, 'Ffyona walks alone through Britain' and so I wanted us to strap ourselves together, three-legged, and make damn sure we arrived together to send out our message. It would also be something of a joke which I felt this journey was now badly in need of. But Suz felt it would be undigni-fied in some way, so we compromised and decided we'd hold hands as we all walked in.

Nick McDowell and Annabel James arrived to convince me that my refusal to have my photograph taken alone the next day was going to cause some very bad vibes and would no doubt add to the possibility of the 'difficult bitch' headlines none of us could stand any more of. The press were all poised with instructions from their editors to get that one solo picture. We made a compromise: I wouldn't pose alone at the signpost.

By this time, Bruce Henderson had started his journey from London with the ten-foot signpost. It turned out to be an epic, spurred on by the horror of Sara Parfitt getting hold of him if he didn't make it and cutting off his privates. When he finally arrived in camp, Sara asked him if he'd brought it. 'Signpost?' he said.

My parents and Shuna arrived. It was strange to see them there. I wasn't expecting it and when they gave me a four-hooped Russian wedding ring, representing each of my walks and inscribed with them, I forgot to tell them before they left about the plans for the next day. When I remembered, I sent up a note the next morning, asking them that since we'd had our time together in Dover, if they wouldn't mind stepping back as I wanted the photo of the journey to be with Raleigh.

Vaseline had come forward with £60,000 to buy the space on my sweatshirt which I'd offered for sale to swell the Raleigh coffers. It was all due to Sara Parfitt, who remained so frighteningly enthusias-tic about the project and had called on all her marketing skills to bring them on board. She had got a sweatshirt printed with their logo and this she gave me to wear into John O'Groats. We were all very grateful for that money as it meant that many young people from inner cities could have a chance at a Raleigh expedition by funding their places and their support once they returned home.

Before sunrise, the road to John O'Groats was filled with the thrum of many feet as all of us, maybe twenty, held hands for the last three miles, Suz on my right, Sara on my left. I felt tiny amongst them and their rhythm felt so forceful, as though they were frog-marching me to my execution at the signpost. It was ironic really, that what drowned out the sounds of the end was a helicopter, Janet's helicopter, but more importantly, a helicopter. Something had to.

Mine was not the first cry. That came from Suz, just at the point, I think, where she thought I wasn't going to make one at all. We hit the signpost of John O'Groats where I had stood eleven years earlier, alone on a cold windy morning. I looked at all the flashing bulbs and microphones in front of me and heard their questions of, 'What does it feel like, Ffyona?' And of course I had absolutely nothing to say. I didn't know what it felt like to have walked around the world.

Back in Spain at the height of my despair, when I thought they'd find out what I hadn't done, I'd told the BBC there was something I wanted to say at the end. If I got through Europe and Britain without anyone finding out, I wanted to admit it myself. Now Janet pulled me aside and said, 'So, Ffyona, it's all over; but you did tell me there was something you wanted to say at the end.'

'Er, yes,' I thought for a moment. If I admitted it, Raleigh would be utterly trashed and I couldn't do that to them. Besides, I had got away with it. Now that I had a choice, I took the easy path and chickened out. I had to think of something quickly. And then the words of Trevor Paign back in Stanley just popped into my head, words which I'd heard so often from people who'd kept me going along the way. And I figured, I'll just give them back. I looked straight into the lens and said, 'Don't let the bastards get you down.'

I avoided the water. Even though Brent Raymond made a gallant gesture for Canada by stripping off stark naked and dashing into the North Sea despite the dozens of cameras, I stayed well clear. I did not want to dip my toe in the ocean. I conceded to have my photograph taken alone on a bollard. Some said I was very calm sitting there, serene even. No, it was nothing like that.

My father had been trying to get my attention. He carried a bottle of champagne in his hand and seemed to be encouraging the press to gather around him. I tried to tell him please not to. They would snap us together and all there would be, as the final message of the walk, was a picture of a lonely person sitting on a bollard and a man with his daughter. We'd had our time of public reconciliation in Dover; I wanted the public end of the walk to be a salute to young people and what they are capable of. He went away into the hotel and I immediately felt ashamed. When I finally joined them, they'd already opened the bottle and drunk most of the contents.

With them was the manager of the hotel, who told me that he had been the crewman of the Vee Skerry helicopter rescue which I had drawn for the British Airways painting competition. Small world, I thought, but there was something more to it than that: the Vee Skerry painting had been the very moment when the world of my real talents had been penetrated. When I couldn't even get one person to accept me for who I was, I had painted a helicopter, so that I might have some worth.

Seeing my parents and sister sitting in the room, away from the celebrations outside, I felt I had failed them. They'd misunderstood my note. They had supported my need to give the end of my walk to Raleigh but they didn't realise that if we were snapped together by the press, they might use that picture not those with Raleigh. But then my father turned to me and I saw what he'd been trying to do outside. He knelt down in front of me, saying how he commended my efforts of sheer guts and determination and, out of his pocket, he pulled his Royal Marine green beret and he gave it to me.

Not long after, I drove up onto the headland with Tom and suddenly realised what I had just witnessed: my father had given me his highest accolade, all that he stood for, because he believed I deserved it. And he was on his knees to me. I felt a great tearing going on inside me, hot and red, coming back harder and stronger between sobs. I tried to shut it out, block it from being real but the vision of my father on his knees with tears in his eyes kept coming back, demanding I look at it and feel the force of it. I ran for a while, trying to shake it out, trying to find some way to make it all right, to get a grip on it. In some ways I managed it, for about a year.

When I had no strength left to keep the lid down on that vision, I turned to dope to help me. I found the warehouse I had often imagined, 4,000 square feet of empty space and I painted it like the desert and furnished it with driftwood. I slept on the drawbridge outside every night over the Thames below and spent my days trying to find a voice to assume for the book I'd been commissioned to write. But it wasn't time to sit down yet and perhaps the spirits were telling me this because just as I started to write, my back finally caved in. A disc entered the spinal column and was poised to paralyse my legs.

On the day Ken told me I needed surgery, Mark Thomson, who'd come by for a drink several months before and had just stayed, had gone out for a while. I lay on the futon, virtually unable to move. I needed to go to the loo. I rolled onto the floor where I managed to push down my sweat pants and positioned myself over a mug in a press-up position. But the mug was too small and I couldn't stop. I lay in a pool of my urine as it grew dark and chilly in the warehouse. Then the phone rang. I thought it might by my mother and I hadn't told her yet so, very slowly, I moved towards it on my stomach, my clothes mopping the urine ahead of me as I went. It wasn't my mother; it was a vicar whom I'd left a message for earlier.

'Ah, hello Reverend. I'm very sorry but I won't be able to give the talk for your organ appeal next week as I need to have an operation on my back.'

And the very first thing the vicar said was, 'But you can't cancel! We've sold a thousand tickets!'

I started to laugh. I kept a fairly convincing lid on it through the conversation, listening to his panic, demanding dates and simply left him with the words, 'When I know I'll be able to walk again, I'll give you a call.' I put the phone down on his frantic voice saying, 'When? When will that be?' and I just laughed and laughed at the absurdity of this whole situation.

The smashed disc was removed by Mr Stallard, a National Health surgeon, the best in the country and a keen athlete himself. Ken took pictures and had the shreds of disc preserved for me in a jar of formaldehyde. The convalescence was slow. Mark took care of me but when I was on my feet again, he was now the shattered one. He left me to my dope. Orion wanted to know where the manuscript was; they'd postponed it once because of my back. I couldn't write it; I couldn't find the story. I made a half-hearted attempt to leave the country but the dope had slowed me down so much that I considered simply getting off the futon in the morning to be a major accomplishment.

Requests for appearances and talks and giving prizes and red reminders and parking tickets and court cases piled up but I just dumped them in a box. I'd hired the services of Emma Rogers to take care of it all for me. Emma is a mother of three young children, the kind of woman who pulls out all the stops in emergencies – like the time she was riding her horse in the park, was hailed by a stable hand who told her that her son had just been taken to hospital. Instead of dismounting, she turned her horse, gave it a thwack and charged down the high street to get to him.

When I constantly turned down requests, she must have thought me utterly contemptible: here I was with a position of respect and I wouldn't even go out and give a prize to some Duke of Edinburgh Award winners. I felt guilty when I spoke to her. I tried to justify my position with the same kind of trumped-up celebrity rubbish I'd heard from Janet when she refused to walk for a day and it disgusted me. But, I wasn't the person they thought I was and I got tired very quickly of hearing the sound of falling off other people's pedestals whenever I walked into a room.

The questions on their lips had moved on from 'Why?' to 'What are you going to do next?' Hearing that a hundred times an hour, I'd just think, I'm going to get back to the warehouse desert and roll myself a nice fat joint. I managed to go to Canada to give a talk to some young people there and I'd managed to sneak down to Indianapolis and walk westwards for a day. But the demons raged every second, the thought of hearing them every day for four months was appalling.

When I got back, I called Nick McDowell. As a published author himself, I wanted to pick his brains about how I was going to write this book. Not long into the conversation, I just told him the whole story. And Nick said, 'It all makes perfect sense now.'

I told him I'd go and walk across America again one day, but I think we both knew that was unlikely.

I'd left London not long after and moved to Yorkshire to get a manuscript written with a ghostwriter. Being away from London meant cutting off my dope supply, but then the mushroom season started. And then J had come up and offered me heroin. But what was the alternative path I could take?

15

As soon as the seat belt signs were turned off, the girl tried to get out. But I was in the aisle seat. From my footwell, I pulled out a carton of duty frees.

'Oh! You'd forgotten you had them!'

The subtlety was completely missed but I wouldn't let this go. Very softly, so that she had to strain to hear my voice over the scramble around us, I said, 'Nope. I just kept them all to myself.'

Her face turned bright red, the spots lighting up like I'd hit the jackpot on a one-armed bandit. She pushed past me, she pushed past the passenger waiting in the aisle and the one who was struggling with the overhead locker. The last I saw of her was what she left in her wake. But, no matter to her, she thinks she'll never pass this way again.

Out into the teaming arrivals area of late evening flights into the land of the 'happiest, healthiest people on earth'. I hadn't prepared myself for the amount of malnutrition in front of me: so many people could hardly walk, could hardly reach into their bags or even pull their coats on properly. Obesity. I felt a mixture of disgust and pity. They weren't laughing over their grotesque disabilities as I'd seen on the streets of Delhi; they seemed ashamed. I knew I'd get used to it soon like everyone else. I suppose it goes without saying that where there is plenty there is the need for self-denial, but is that a quality of life?

I slept in the airport that night and lent my Thermorest to a travelling salesman whose joviality would have really annoyed me if I hadn't kept reminding myself that the guy was probably just lonely. He told me about his family, brought out the photos and a miniature bottle of Jack Daniels from the plane. But I guess the liquor must have melted the polite veneer because he broke trust and when nobody was around, he tried it on. Not in any physical way, but verbally titillating. He egged me on to ask him how he got his dogs under control. When he told me he jerked them off, I simply asked him, 'You're telling me this because?' He lost it and became embarrassed. I guess he thought he could get away with it. He was, after all, an American travelling salesman.

At 5 a.m. we both waited to check in for our onward flights. I had rarely been in a queue recently, waiting for the same things. I stood out from the others; my hair was in natural dreads, my long jumper was riddled with holes, but at least my black 501s were intact. I distinguished various people from the airport floor by the way they stood compared to those who had slept in a hotel – they were rougher and they stood more erect. But I was surprised when they still took the shit – an effeminate ground steward slipped along behind the check-in consoles and tried to patronise us.

'There's a second aisle open, I don't know why you're all queuing for the first.' The response from the queue was to look down at their feet, trying to disappear. I couldn't help myself; I shouted back with all the sweetness I could muster, 'Where is it? Can you point it out to us please? I mean, we wouldn't want to be standing here if there was another one open.' Nobody turned to stare at me; they stared at the steward. He straightened himself and sorted out papers under his console, he wouldn't look up, he must have known all eyes were on him but after a time, I guess when he thought we'd finally been distracted, his hand darted out quickly and on went the check-in light above him. He looked up as though nothing had happened. But a ripple of giggles went through the queue.

Ahead of me, a sixty-year-old white woman turned and started telling me about her life. That seemed to be the way you do it here; you stand beside people and you start talking about yourself. She lived in a remote village in South America. She told me about the dances and celebrations all night, then she told me they were starving, which makes sense I thought; you don't have such celebrations if you're not living on the edge. She told me about the Bahai faith and how she felt it was her calling to take it to the villagers. By the pause and the slight tilting of her head, I think she expected a very different reaction. I said, 'If I were them I'd look at this woman representing something new and ask myself, "Is she happier, wiser and more content because of it?"' The woman tried to walk away towards aisle number two but I wasn't finished. I called after her, 'What have you seen on the faces of the women? Do they look like you? Do they have an expression like yours? Or are they smiling?'

After I'd checked in, I went outside for a smoke. I turned to see that six people had followed me, not only for a smoke but to smoke where I did. I sat on a railing; they stood quite happily. They even threw their butts where I threw mine. It struck me that by starting to clean my own windows, I was beginning to see out at last and what I saw fascinated me. You can often tell someone's flaws by their mantra in life (as in 'I will walk every step from the Cape and every step to the Med') and perhaps so many American films are about standing up for yourself, because, as I'd just seen, it's their fantasy.

If I'd bought my internal airline ticket seven days earlier, I would have paid a third of the price. I guess the airline companies know that people often have to buy tickets at the last minute so they zap 'em. I found out it's the same with petrol prices – they go up in summer when holiday makers drive long distances and the credit card interest rates go up at Christmas. But those are the rules of the game – you get hit when you're vulnerable and I consider that, like everyone around me who wasn't disputing it, to be absolutely fine. That the strongest survive is a law of nature. But accepting the dog eat dog scenario seemed to contradict something – like, the weak should be protected, that's humanity. But who draws the line here and where?

My first priority was to find me a dog. The morning I landed in Indianapolis I called the dog pound to find that I needed to be a resident to adopt one. In order to get residency I had to marry an American, or invest several hundred thousand dollars in a business and employ scores of people, or do a job no American could do. But I wanted a dog right now. So, I booked into a camp ground, sent myself a letter as proof of my address and sat my driving test. With my local driving licence in hand, I went into the pound.

The screaming noise of them, a lot of them shaking, and the stench, made me want to be quick; but I had to go slow, had to make the right choice. I noticed how the new ones whined. Perhaps they wanted to piddle, perhaps they were holding on, holding on, till finally they just had to shit in their bed. I took out a few of them into the 'meet and greet' room, but they weren't right. I was looking for something specific – a middle-sized dog who looked mean, was young and fit, good natured to me and trainable.

I'd walked past one cage where the registration card on the grate had been turned round. I asked the keeper about it. He told me those were the dogs who'd been in there for eight days and would be put down that day; the dogs on death row. I went back to this dog. He was a young Alsatian cross, a beautiful roan and tan and black; his nose was shiny, he had long ears like a fox and he lay with his head on his paws, just watching me from clear brown eyes without any sign of self-pity.

As I walked him round the meeting room, he was a bit skittish but that was hardly surprising. He sat when I told him to and he liked my treat. His hips weren't sloping down too much and even though he'd spent eight days on the concrete, his paws were in good condition. So I whispered to him, 'Hey boy, you want to go for a walk with me?' The words immediately reminded me of a cartoon I'd seen in a paper. One dog says to the other, 'I had that recurring nightmare again last night.' 'Which one?' asks the other. 'The one where Ffyona Campbell takes me for a walk.'

They kept him that night to give him his worm shots and vaccinations. In the meantime, I went looking for a means of carrying my load. My back was too weak for a pack and I instinctively knew I wouldn't find any hand pushing carts so I went into a department store and asked if they had any prams. It's quite infuriating being misunderstood in a country which speaks your language. 'Prums?' Eventually, after the old miming routine, they led me to the 'stroller' department. They weren't like English prams. The baby faced forwards; none of them had big wheels and none of them looked like they could even tackle a gravel driveway. But then, that's not what they're designed for, more like to be pushed around shopping malls. They were also too small, but I found one for twins which, once I'd folded everything out and down, looked just about OK.

I took my $80 stroller back to the camp ground and set about transforming it into an expedition vehicle without losing too much of its original character. I sewed a plastic folder onto the hood where I could keep my maps in front of me, clipped my essentials bag onto the sides of the pushing bar where I could reach my knife, money, talc, loo paper, zinc cream etc. and found an ingenious place for my water bag which had a tap at the opposite end to the carrying handle: I clipped the handle onto the front of the pram so that the bottom and the tap sat on the plastic foot rest to take the strain and where I could draw water easily. There was a netting area underneath for shopping where my tent, sleeping bag and Thermorest fitted snugly. In the main body of the pram, I arranged each stuff sack - dog bag, clothes, first aid, cooking gear, shoes, laundry and extra bits bag. I sprayed some WD40 into the wheel sockets and had a go. It worked just fine.

I packed up my camp and drove in a hire car out on Route 40. I didn't know exactly where I'd first cheated, but I knew it was somewhere after Indianapolis. Back in May I'd walked on this road from the centre of the city, twenty-five miles out. Now I drove to find the place where I'd stopped that day, but I couldn't find it. Instead, I drove back towards the city, looking for a place to make camp and bring my dog back to. I found the perfect site, a small fishing lake which took campers. It was the first of many perfect camps which just happened to be in exactly the right place. I set up my tent, slept for the night, then stowed everything inside and drove down to the dog pound.

There's nothing quite so wonderful as watching a dog pelting around on the grass in the sunshine after nine days locked in a cage. The staff couldn't tell me where he'd come from, except that he'd been picked up as a stray somewhere in the city. I was a little nervous about how he would behave in all these new situations, but he must have been in a car before, because he immediately curled up in the passenger footwell. At the car hire return place, he obediently waited beside me as I paid the dues, and in the traffic, as we walked to find a cab, he was perfect. He turned heads, too.

The cab driver took us to the camp ground by the lake and here my dog almost shat himself with delight. He nearly choked himself on the food, he was so ravenous. I thought about a name for him and came up with Rumun – rough one – but when I called him I said, 'C'm 'ere Boy', so I called him Boy.

As I walked him down to a local vet, he seemed eager to please, walking well beside me and unperturbed by the traffic. The vet gave him a clean bill of health, put his age at around nine months and gave me some flea shampoo. Boy didn't like this much – being hosed down – but once I'd got him lathered, he didn't seem to mind. He looked so skinny and malnourished underneath that I decided he'd need to break into the distance slowly, walking part of the day, riding in the pram for the rest.

He wouldn't run for the stick, he just bit it and pulled. So, you're a puller, are you lad? He chased the birds and squirrels through the auburn leaves and when he was tuckered out, he fell asleep on a blanket which I'd laid out for him as a bed at the foot of mine. He slept quite deeply for a while, didn't notice the sounds around him, but during the night he woke several times to listen.

I lay awake for a while, soothing him with my voice and stopped to reflect on what I'd done since I'd taken that step towards the computer and turned if off. For months I hadn't actually done any more than get out of bed, walk over to the kettle, down to the corner shop for milk and smokes and back to bed again. It seemed as though I'd been striving for a day without events, a day like being on a life support machine, fed intravenously, plugged into a catheter, staring at a wall. But so many things kept getting in the way of it – like finding my keys and having to go out. I resented these obstacles, as though they were conspiring to obstruct my desire.

If I had to do anything, I did it just enough to get by. I'd started out by doing things one hundred per cent properly, but over the years, as my conscience had begun to grow inside and consume me, I had deteriorated to around five per cent. Why do anything properly if you aren't intending to live?

Lying on the cool, crinkly surface of my sleeping bag with a blue dome over me and a dog at my feet, I wondered how the hell I'd done this. It was as though I'd been taken by the hand, gagged and frog-marched by another side of me. I remembered the feeling and used it many times, 'taking me by the hand' when I was low or tired or frightened. Tomorrow I was going to do something about regaining my self-respect and for the first time I knew why I was about to walk: to find my own truth. I leant down and stroked Boy's head, Alison Hargreaves' words of 'always take the hardest path' had saved not one but two lives already – me and Boy.

As I manoeuvred the pram off the grassy bank of the lake, a little white terrier came to see us off. He trotted beside Boy and me till we reached the main road where he waited and watched us cross to the other side, before turning tail and skipping back to his home. I clipped Boy onto his lead which I fastened on the verge side of the pram and paused for a moment. I asked the spirits for courage to walk well, it reminded me that even though I was an oddity, there was still a code of conduct to follow.

Boy, of course, had no idea of the future; he lived for the moment and right now he was intent on finding out about overflow drains. He barked at these dark holes in the road, giving them a wide berth and straining to look back at them to make sure they weren't following. Once we'd got into the residential area of Plainfield, where the front lawns reached down to our first pavement, I let him off the chain and he darted up to each front door, waiting and looking at me as if to say, 'Is this the place?' I'd call to him and he'd come bounding along, stopping to sniff at black plastic bags along the way.

I had some difficulty manoeuvring the pram up onto the pavements (where they existed) and along them because they were so high and so churned up by tree roots. If Americans ever decided to lend a hand to the environment and walk to the shops instead of driving, they'd need to erect signs along the pavements: Warning – pushing a stroller over this sidewalk may result in brain-damaged babies.

As the miles went by, through the residential areas and small shops with their colourful decorations for Hallowe'en, I felt the bustle around me but I saw nobody walking along the pavement, only across it from car to shop and back again. Sometimes the pram had to be pushed ninety degrees into the air to get the front wheels onto the pavement then heaved up, and after hours of this my back was beginning to pinch. I was reminded of a Vietnam Vet I'd seen in a wheelchair back in Indianapolis, careering down the road against the traffic, in the traffic, his face white with fury, his hands shoving the wheels forward, forcing the cars to get out of the way. At the time, I thought he was just crazy, but maybe he was protesting against the impossibility of mounting the pavements. Would it be too much to ask to put a slipway in all pavements – a completely horizontal slipway, not at a ten degree angle or twenty degree or thirty degree? It uses less concrete, after all.

Though drivers stared at me through their car windows, I didn't feel as though I was carrying that video camera of self-consciousness as on all the other walks because they weren't just staring at me: they were staring at the whole ensemble of pram and dog. I found that the pram protected my front from being bored into and I wondered whether this was why I'd seen African hunters paint their chests: it distracts the eye. Stares have a force of their own, can disarm you of your confidence, can reduce you down.

At dusk and the evening rush hour, a mile before Stilesville, I slipped off the main drag and along a farm road. Boy was curled up asleep in the pram and pushing him up over the hills had worn me out too. But when slightly hungry and physically tired, I felt that sense of grace and strength return, it sharpened my eyesight and hearing, ensuring that I found a secure place to sleep for the night. I pushed deep into a harvested cornfield along the side of a hedge where we were out of sight from either road. I didn't need to disturb Boy because my tent and sleeping bag and Thermorest were in the carrying basket underneath. Once everything was up and up properly, he got out, had a sniff around, ate some food and curled up again on his blanket. I didn't light a fire or that would attract attention to us, I ate a sandwich, packed everything securely away and covered it with a plastic tarp.

By morning the tarp had iced up, mid-October and the winter was coming. We'd only managed fourteen miles the day before; we needed to do twenty-five if we were to avoid the coming snow storms and reach Los Angeles in the three months I had.

I figured we'd rely on gas stations for food and water. My maps didn't indicate where they were, of course, but simply asking at each one before I bought food where the next one west would be, ensured I wouldn't run out. I forgot though, on the second day, that I was asking people who drove cars for an idea of distance and instead of finding another gas station after their estimated five miles, I walked for six hours. By midday, Boy was too tired to walk any more. He was underweight and unused to such distances, so I lifted him up onto his blanket.

I noticed how none of the trucks or car drivers hooted or leered as they'd done the first time I'd walked here. I realised that this pram was probably the best protection from sexual harassment I could have – they thought I'd already been knocked up and they left me alone. However, when Boy sat on the top, he occasionally tried to shag his blanket, turning the whole entourage into a rather perverted advertisement. Before I had time to reach over and smack him, his adolescent convulsions were sometimes so strong they'd jerk him clean out of the pram and he'd find himself on the ground, looking quite bewildered.

At a gas station, while he was quietly dozing, two young girls pointed at him. One said, 'Oh look! How cute! A dog in a stroller.' The other one said, 'What a spoilt animal.' And I said, 'Hey look, Boy, there's a couple of ignorant, judgmental bimbos.'

On the morning of the third day as we set off from Pleasant Gardens, where we had camped secretly behind a school in the playing field, a four-wheel drive Bronco type with blackened windows pulled over on the verge ahead of us. A woman pressed a button and the driver window slid down just at the point when I was trying to separate Boy and another dog who'd run out from a garden. She called out, 'Are you OK?' I called back that I was fine, but she didn't go away. The other dog did and I walked up to her window.

'D'you need a ride or anything?'

'No thanks,' I said. 'We're just out for a walk.'

'Er, Ma'am? I heard you slept behind the school yard last night.' And so I said yes, thinking I was going to get a bollocking, and she went on, 'Do you need some money?'

'What?'

'I have $20. Here, please take it.'

'No! We're fine thank you, put it in a charity box for me.' I pushed on past the car and thought how very bizarre. Still, if the impression others have is that I'm homeless, I'm certainly not going to be robbed either. This pram was turning out to be the best protection I could possibly have.

The next one to stop was a cop. He sidled out and asked, 'Ma'am?'

They're so polite.

'D'you have a baby in there?'

'No.'

He came over and had a look. 'D'you have some kind of ID?'

'What have I done?'

'Well, you're walking down the road.'

'This is a joke, right?'

I gave him my British passport which he took over to the car and radioed in to base with my details. In the meantime, I gave Boy some water and had a smoke break. He came back and said, 'Well, I guess you aren't wanted for anything.'

At a gas station, which appeared, thank God, after six hours' push with no food, I put Boy outside in the shade with some water and went in to get stocked up. As I was paying for my food, I noticed Boy was eating something which looked like bits of meat. I turned to the check-out girl who could see through the window too and asked if she'd seen who'd fed my dog. The other check-out woman said she had. I told her she ought to ask the owner before feeding a dog. She said he looked like he was starving. I said you ought to ask the owner first, because you might be giving him something that's not good for him. She said it was a hot dog.

'But that's garbage.'

'Well that's what I give my dog.'

'I don't give a damn, lady. That's my dog and my dog eats dog food garbage.'

I took Boy over to a lovely patch of grass in the shade of some trees where I laid out his blanket and mine for lunch of tomato sand-wiches for me and Puppy Chow for him, polished off by a nice crispy pig's ear – which I gave to him. I thought about these incidents and I remembered a man I'd once seen in Africa, cycling along with a let-tuce in his basket. I'd asked him where he was going and he'd told me he was cycling for two days to market to sell his lettuce. My first reaction was one of great pity for him but over the days, I passed him several times as he stood chatting with old friends on his way, and I started to see the whole picture: the lettuce was actually a joke, it was simply an excuse to get out of the house.

It was a funny little incident, but now that I had been the recipient of misguided compassion, I began to realise that this happens on a grander scale too. Some aid agencies and missionaries I'd met in Africa might have misinterpreted what they saw in their eagerness to make things better for others. And it struck me that compassion based on pity can be as destructive as greed. I remembered a British water engineer who spent his retirement years digging wells for remote tribal people. He was spoken of back home with great respect, as though others wished their lives could be as useful. But I thought about this some more as Boy spotted a cat and chased it up a tree.

Life revolves around water, the journey every day to get it from the river was the nucleus of village life. The children learned how to carry it, they learned responsibility, they learned how to turn drudgery into fun, they gathered things along the way, they met children from other villages, the adults would trade, swap news and the adolescents would flirt.

But if a well was dug in the village, they would now have a choice as to whether or not to walk down to the river to see their friends. But I always find it's harder to walk to the shops when I have the choice of going in the car and just because they have bones through their noses doesn't mean they are exempt from the temptations of laziness. A well in a village may cut off their life, the kids might be less healthy, less obedient, the adolescents getting stir crazy and so on, like life in the West.

But is progress towards a life without using your body really quality of life?

As far as giving them a choice is concerned, by all means, but surely the true nature of choice is having some idea of the outcome of each course of action? Did the man offering to dig the well actually tell them what might happen? If I am wrong, why is it that some Aborigines, native American Indians, Eskimos, Ethiopians are often considered drunk and lazy and without any desire to live? If it was like that always, humans would have died out years ago. Is life really any better for them because the white men felt compassion to help mop up his greed? Who really benefits, anyway?

Boy's barking had caught the attention of an elderly man in a red baseball cap and lumberjack shirt who now walked towards me over the grassy bank. I stood up to greet him and called out, 'I hope we aren't disturbing you. We just stopped here for a picnic.'

'No, you're not disturbing me Ma'am. I just came out to see what the fuss is all about. Lost a cat recently to the coyotes, run through here like they own the place.' By the third exchange, he told me his wife had died last month. I asked him if he'd like to come and sit on my blanket in the shade. He managed to get down onto the ground and pushed up his cap, accepting the cup of water I poured for him. Boy came over for a sniff, wagging his tail, then darted off again looking for something to bite.

The man had nursed his wife for four years during her illness. She was twenty years his senior and much bigger than he and by the way he spoke of her housebound disabilities, it had taken it out of him. Then he told me about finding God and how they'd both become reborn. I thought this was interesting, so I asked him what it meant to be reborn. He said it meant that he was aware of his sins for the first time. I said, is that a bit like your conscience pricking you and telling you something and you try and cover it up till one day the bubble bursts and you realise who you are and what you've done? He said yes it was just like that, but there was more to it. He said, when you are reborn you are suddenly aware of your good deeds and your bad deeds and you ask for forgiveness. I asked if you were then absolved of it and he said in a way he was. And I asked him about heaven and hell because to me heaven and hell means conscience: you're in hell if you've done something wrong and you're in heaven if you've done something good. He said no, no, no, it's more than that, it's away above the clouds, above the stars. And I said, well isn't that what it feels like when you've done something good; you kind of feel that you're walking on clouds and he said no, it's more than that. But quite honestly, he didn't look like he was tripping in the clouds: he looked empty and forlorn and I couldn't believe he'd really done that much wrong.

I thought, I can sit here and listen to this guy, try to solve his problems in his mind, clinging on to words, but what was he going to do about it? So I said look, when I was studying for my exams when I was a kid I'd be studying all night and weekends and stuff like that, and when it was all over I couldn't remember what I used to do with my time before the exams. So I said it must be a bit like you with nursing your wife: you probably can't remember what you did for fun all those years ago, and he said no he couldn't remember. So I asked him a little bit more about it and he said he used to make knives. He told me more about it and I could see he was getting quite enthusiastic. He also told me how he used to sing in the choir at church and so I said, well, they've probably missed you. Then he got up and shook my hand and he seemed to walk a little more lightly and I think he felt a bit better.

At first, I thought it was strange that he should find the spirits so late in life and to see them in the vein of his failings. But then, Christianity worships the act of sin through the cross. Other people worship the sun, the giver of life every moment and through every action from their infancy to death. I also thought how different he was from the old men I'd seen in the African villages, surrounded by their wives and children and grandchildren, albeit looking fairly hen-pecked sometimes, but not alone. Is it a quality of life to cast out the old? Is this what is meant by being civilised? Is it surprising, then, that the young are not learning from the old, if they only see them a few times a year? Who will teach the young about the spirits? I'd heard back in England they were about to teach morality in schools. But which textbook will they use?

Not long after we'd set off again, a young girl pulled over, got out of the car and asked if I wanted a lift. I told her we were just out for a walk, enjoying the sunshine. She said, 'Well, I hate to see anyone have to walk and God told me to stop.' So I asked her if she thought that one day God might tell her to stop, get out of her car and walk instead so that all his creatures could live? She said she wasn't sure about that, she was just being neighbourly. I asked her why she thought I might need a ride. She said she'd seen people like me on TV. So that's what had raised her conscience? And it seemed that God was her conscience. Are the media now the disciples of God?

I could judge how steep the hills would be by how much of a car roof I saw as it drove up the next one. With the sun on my left, the trees cast their shadows horizontally across the road like a kind of barcode on the hills. After a while, I could look at that barcode and know what I would be thinking as I crossed each line: first set of shadows I'd be thinking, 'Fuck, this is hard work'; second set of shadows I'm thinking, 'Why am I doing this?' third set of shadows, 'Nobody loves me, everybody hates me'; fourth set of shadows, 'I'm going to quit'; fifth set of shadows, 'I can't quit, I'll have to kill myself'; sixth set of shadows, 'I've decided how I'm going to kill myself'; seventh set of shadows, 'I'll just get to the top of the hill and then I'll deal with it!' Then I get to the top of the hill and I'm thinking, 'Wow, this is fabulous!' Because the problem, of course, with going up a hill, is you can't see the downward stretch on the other side. And going down, all you see ahead of you is the next push going up. So, I figured, the world is divided into threes: flat land, uphill land and downhill land. Two good, one bad. But at the top of the bad is the highest feeling, so it's even better than the others.

However, these hills were slowing me down. I'd only managed fourteen miles, then eighteen, eighteen and now eleven into the town of Terre Haute – a name which I hadn't thought to translate. At this rate there was no chance of getting to Los Angeles in the time I had and I still hadn't even started on the Ozark mountains through Missouri and then there'd be the Rockies. The heat and fumes of the traffic with its noise and the wretched pavements all mounted up and I thought right, I'll change my plan. When I walked here before, I missed out a little here and a little there – maybe half. So if I divide the distance between here and LA into half, like around Tulsa, Oklahoma and walk all the way from there, that'll make up the distance. I got fairly convinced by this rationale and I went to a pay phone.

There was a recorded message saying, 'If you wish to speak to the operator, say "operator" now,' so I said 'operator'. But the recorded voice came back with, 'Your request was not understood. If you wish to speak to the operator, say "operator" now.' So I said, 'Aperator.' And I got connected. The operator told me there wasn't a train station in Terre Haute. There wasn't a passenger line nearby, either. My God, this dependence on cars is worse than I thought. The bus company wouldn't take dogs, so I figured I'd hire a car. But the hire car wouldn't do a one-way to Tulsa. So I tried to call 87 and ask if he'd come out and do back-up for me, but his line was constantly engaged. So I thought to hell with it, and started to walk into town. Along the way, I figured I'd call in at U-Haul and hire one of their units. But, during that three-mile walk, I lost the two things which would enable me to hire a car. I didn't lose my purse, I just opened it to find that my Indianapolis driver's licence and credit card were missing. And they were nowhere to be found.

It suddenly dawned on me that something was trying to tell me that I was here now and would be doing the journey properly. Now whether there was or wasn't something arranging this for me doesn't really matter, what matters is that I recognised I was trying to get out of something I didn't want to do. I'd already suffered years of the consequences of my failure, yet I still tried to wriggle out of it now when I had the chance to make it right. So I thought, I've been searching for an edge, I know that's where life exists, I have an edge in front of me and the harder it is the better it will feel. Do I want to feel better? OK, I said, let's do it Boy. Instead of trying to get to Los Angeles, we will simply walk as far west as we can. As soon as I relaxed, my daily mileage increased to twenty-five miles. Take it steady, I thought, and look at what's around us.

When I looked, I felt a sudden sense of comfort – so many adverts on giant billboards told me people cared about me. They wanted me to have a nice day. But then I realised, of course, that it isn't really true: they don't give a damn about me, all they care about is the dollar in my pocket. In a world full of such messages, are we to understand that children are now born with an inbuilt knowledge of how to sort the true from the false? If that is the case, the advertisers will no doubt find a way to convince them otherwise. If not, might it be a little disturbing for them when they realise that their elders are lying to them? Or do we just assume that kids are smarter than we give them credit for? Makes it a lot easier to absolve ourselves of what we're doing to them; it makes it easier to blame the kids when they go off the rails because otherwise we'd have to question the fundamentals, we'd have to question what we took to be true as well.

In the small town of Marshall, Illinois, I stopped to buy more dog food and top up my supplies. This was the first time I'd been into a supermarket on this trip and thought I was in the wrong place – the food looked like toys. The colourful wrappings were the methods used to entice the buyers to a purchase. It was also a place of self-denial and inner conflict. A terrible way to feel about what nourishes you. But that's the American quality of life.

Outside, I gave Boy more water and was just packing away my apples when I glanced up and saw the town notice-board, adorned with flyers. Many of them asked questions like: 'Are you depressed? Are you lonely? Do you feel your life is empty? Then join us at the Church on Sunday.' 'Are you sick of diets that don't work? Do you lack willpower? Then join us at Amy's Gym.'

I remembered the women in Zaire, how they laughed as they pounded their cassava, in rhythm, looking so alive, turning drudgery into fun and so aware of their beauty and then I remembered how depressed they'd looked, as they slouched, waiting in line for the cassava to be milled. With all the labour-saving devices and choices in the West, are we really better off?

But the poster which really killed me was the one that said, 'Lacking motivation? We hold courses in how to identify your goals, how to set obtainable targets so that you can lead the richer, fuller life you've always dreamed of.'

If this is the land of opportunity, why does anyone need to be motivated? Could you sell a motivational course to a Pygmy?

Who is it who doesn't know any better?

By this stage I'd wound myself up a fair bit, but fortunately, comic relief wasn't far away. Boy and I trundled along past a school. The prison-like walls always reminded me that I never had to enter there again but just to heighten my sense of freedom, I looked up at the windows and imagined myself inside, hot and sweating as the sun became an irritation. How can you learn about life if you want to draw the blinds and shut out the sunlight? Just as I was thinking this, the teacher appeared at the window, about to pull down the blinds. She looked at me. I looked back. Then she turned her head and several children came to the window, looking at me. And I suddenly realised what she must be saying. 'Look, children, if you don't work hard, that's what will happen to you!'

I laughed and laughed. How wonderful not to be paraded as super-human any more!

The vagrant young mother disguise worked very well at keeping unwanted attention at bay. But sometimes, older women in cars gave me such filthy looks at how they thought I was treating my baby. So I'd walk over to the pram and start thumping the blanket – squashing down the bags – it brought such wonderful gasps of horror on their faces that they often turned and drove back again to see what had happened to my baby. It being Hallowe'en, I'd picked up an orange plastic pumpkin with black eyes and teeth and stuck it under the hood. However, some of them weren't convinced.

One windy day, Boy and I had our picnic lunch behind a bank of trees away from the road. We were both startled when a man in a white shirt and tie stepped out from behind a tree with a clipboard in hand. He introduced himself as a social worker and had come to take my baby into care. I said I didn't have a baby. He said, but you have a stroller. Take a look, I said. He looked inside and I guess he thought he was too late because instead of some fat little cherub, all he saw was a young Alsatian sharpening his teeth on a pig's trotter.

At gas stations I'd fill up with water and have a smoke break in the shade away from the cars left running while the drivers went in for coffee. They reminded me of shoes left outside the door of a Muslim household: nobody steals the cars either. Some people who were convinced that I was a vagrant would go in and buy something for me, probably enjoying the selection as I had done on the odd occasion for street people in London. But then the moment would come when they had to give their gift and it often made them seem hesitant because they realised they would have to bring their gift of pity into my world of dignity. And it didn't work. Compassion based on pity is very different from compassion based on the corner-stone of sharing.

One afternoon, much further west in the town of Billings, while the cashier was ringing up my purchases, the phone rang and she left the till to answer it. I watched her nodding head till she turned and looked at me and shouted, 'It's for you!' I thought it must be a lazy cop or something so I went over and lifted the receiver to my ear and said 'Hello?'

'Ma'am, are you the lady with the dog and the stroller?' It was a woman's voice.

'Yes,' I said, 'but I'm fine, I'm just out for a walk.'

'I'm standing in Holstein's antique store just across the road from you. Can you see me waving?' I could. 'Do you see that man outside the gas station with the moustache and black hair?' I could. 'Do you know this man?' No. 'Be very careful of him. He was just in my store and when he saw you he went straight out and has been hanging around outside looking at your stroller.' I didn't know if she was being paranoid or if she knew something more about him. I just figured I'd keep an eye on him but she said, 'Why don't you come over here. We'll give each other a big hug outside the store and make out like we're old friends and then you can wait in here till he goes away?' So I bought my muffins and went outside. Sure enough, the man tried to entice me to go home with him with offers of sacks of free dog food. I pushed the pram with Boy on top across the road and he followed me. The woman came out of the antique store and we screamed our hellos and hugged each other. She petted Boy and took us into the shop. The man got in his car and left. We all took down his number plate and the lady asked me if I wanted to stay there the night. I thanked her and we shared a muffin and a cup of coffee, but unless I went out again I would start to be frightened and I had a very long way to go.

I never doubted the size of the American heart but that incident showed me the difference between compassion based on pity and compassion based on the sharing of a common problem.

Through Indiana I politely declined offers of food, money and blankets. It was perhaps the hardest possible test of keeping to the codes of conduct I'd broken so often in Australia. Now I belonged in some way to the street people and, when it got tough, I remembered whom I'd be letting down if I didn't behave well. But in Illinois, they just called the cops. It's illegal to walk along the road – any road – in Illinois. If you've ever tried to rollerskate on gravel you'll have a fair idea of what it's like to push a pram along the grass. They threatened to book me if I didn't. If I'd thought this journey might reveal some of the differences between the America I saw on TV and the real life America, I had forgotten there would be some similarities too. A sheriff pulled over and asked to see some ID. When I showed him my passport he said, 'This passport ran out in the year 2001.'

I couldn't help myself. 'I think you'll find, sir, that it's 1995 at the moment.'

'You trying to get smart with me young lady? I'll have you down to the station for obstructing the course of police doody.'

I have often found it more difficult to take discipline seriously from someone I don't know, no matter what level of intelligence they have. But I remember as a child, when we'd stopped moving once for a year and my parents had come to know the local bobby, one day I was caught shoplifting and he came round to our house and spoke to me about it. I'd never felt more ashamed or embarrassed and I never did it again. But so too with being asked to do something by an employer I didn't know compared to the lengths I'd go to if I did know them. I wondered then about Communism, something I'd never studied at school but, from what I knew of it, it was based on working for the common good. And then I thought about the African village when the corner-stone of their work ethic is also sharing. But it struck me that the stark difference between the two was that one group knew all the people they were sharing with and being disciplined by and the other group didn't. One was a system which grew out of what worked best and the other was an imposed ideal. Perhaps the optimum level at which this can work is where you know everyone in the village.

I didn't know what it was like to live in a small village but when I stopped at a gas station, having walked in the rain for several hours, I was greeted with a run-down of all my actions for the past two days from the cashier who'd heard an update on my progress from her customers. This irritated me somewhat, but she told me, 'Hey, that's life in a small town for you, everyone knows your business.' But then there are gossips for the sake of gossip and those who talk for the sake of looking out for each other and sharing each other's disappointments and triumphs.

These small towns were so quiet. I couldn't hear the sounds of children unless I went into a supermarket. There I heard the screams! The demanding squeals and ear-piercing screams of children denied their sweeties. Is this quality of life? How on earth could the women cope with that noise without smashing their skulls against the side of the grocery cart? Did they think this was the normal sound of a child? Why hadn't I heard this in the Zaire villages? I remembered having this discussion with my old driver G, who had worked with tribal people and had said the greatest shock he had when coming back to Britain was the sounds of the screaming kids.

In the parking lot I noticed a couple of old men, sitting on a wall. They were watching a crowd of women, young and middle-aged. I left Boy for a minute and went to see what these women were all huddled around looking at. It was a newborn baby.

It seems there is a reversal here, of the worth of life: an African baby has less worth than a one-year-old because it may die. A one-year-old has less worth than a five-year-old and so on, till the one who has the most worth is the elder, who has great knowledge and who has lived through so much because of his own strength and his wisdom.

But here in the West, it seems the babies are more important and command more attention than the old. Imagine that! There was no circle of respect around the two old men; the baby drew the attention. Did this give the children an inflated sense of their own importance? Could this have anything to do with why they screamed and demanded?

As I hadn't seen any children playing, I asked a woman about where her children played. She looked at me with my pram full of bags and she hesitated. It told me everything: the children play out of sight because they can be preyed on, by perverts. I noticed the fear of this predator as I walked through a shopping mall on my own because Boy wasn't allowed inside. As soon as I walked alone, people responded differently, groups became tighter, mothers actually picked up their whining kids, people spoke more loudly, but as soon as I fell in time with a group, they put down their kids, milled out and relaxed. I wondered what this fear of something they cannot see might do to the children. Would it be different from pointing at a snake and watching how their father stoned and killed the threat? Or would the children behave like little Bobby and pee in their rooms because he was too frightened to go out to the loo? This pervert stuff must cost the parents a fortune in buying toy warriors for their children to use in dreams, fighting off their dark imaginings. But that's normal, every culture I'd come across has protective dolls.

Sometimes Boy and I would wake in the night and both sit there listening. Two noises might be a falling branch, but a third meant animal. Boy was learning what to be afraid of and what was fine by how I reacted to it. When there were footsteps outside the tent one night in hunting season when the woods were full of men with guns, men who were highly charged, I shouted out, 'Hello outside the tent.' Boy sensed the tensions and stiffened along with me. No answer. I called out, 'If you don't say hello, I'm just going to have to come out with my gun.' No answer. I ripped open the tent flap with a banana in my hand to find a large black bull nosing around the pram. I started laughing. Boy was suddenly playful and chased off the bull.

But there were times when I tensed and Boy did absolutely nothing. Tucked up in my sleeping bag, with the hood over my ears, sounds became exaggerated. I'd think I could hear someone walking, crunching on the ground outside and they seemed to speed up just as my heart raced. I'd pull off the hood to hear more clearly and it would stop. Pull the hood back on and it'd start up again. Pretty frightening, until I reaslied it was just my eyelashes, flashing against the fabric.

Missouri lived up to its name. It poured with rain, making our lives miserable as there was nowhere to shelter and at night in the Ozark mountains it grew terribly cold, dropping down to minus eight. The trees were losing their leaves and the ground we camped on was made up of wet mulch which had frozen solid by morning. Boy started to cotton on to the fun of chasing cars, which was a bit dangerous, so I'd keep him on the lead and hold on to the pram tightly whenever a car overtook because off he went after it, pulling us along behind. It worked a treat up the hills, but downhill was a killer, so I'd put him on top for the downhill stretch.

The deeper we went into the Ozarks, the more coyotes we heard at night. Sometimes they were so close we could hear their yapping. Boy would always pee around the camp to mark his territory and I got into the habit of doing it too: I knew that coyotes would steer clear if they smelt human. He'd always wake at around 11 p.m. and want to go out for a pee. It meant I had to go out with him or he might run off with the coyotes – the bikers of the dog world, wild and free. But there was a good chance they might rip his throat out.

It was during these times of getting out of my warm sleeping bag to protect my dog that I started to understand the nature of 'mother'. I had had nothing in my life before this to prepare me for doing something entirely for the protection or comfort of another. I resented it at first but, if I delayed getting up, Boy would be less obedient than if I got up straight away. If I ever have a baby of my own, it will come as a great shock to me, after so many years of taking care of number one.

I found it irritating to keep mending things like the waterproofing of my tent. I was used to throwing something away if it didn't work. At the age of twenty-eight I owned absolutely nothing which I had nurtured. All my shoes were chucked away when they got holes in them; I was not accustomed to fixing things. And I wondered, if I ever met the right person, what kind of preparation this was for the ups and downs of marriage? If my relationships with boyfriends didn't work, I just chucked them away.

Once more I couldn't help being attracted to the African way of life compared to what I saw around me, but perhaps there was an element of increased want because I knew I could never have it. I saw this tendency in my dog too: if I gave him something to chew on he didn't want it; if I raised it out of reach he leaped for it. But it was the same piece of raw hide. And I wondered whether I was really being objective in my view of the American way of life. But when I spotted an aeroplane trail against the blue dome above me, I knew damn well that I was right not to go for their ways – they were scratching my sky.

I wanted to know why they thought they could get away with breaking the natural laws of the land. I got a hint of this when a cashier in a gas station reached up to the cigarette rack for me and pulled out a packet of Camel Lights. Immediately, another packet appeared in the space. This dispenser told me there would always be more. The bubble gum machine told the little boy the same thing. The natural law of the land says: don't take all the honeycomb or there won't be any next time. But how can you learn this if the supermarket shelf never runs out of honey? If, in fact, the more you buy the more there is. And as far as money is concerned, I spend as much as I have and when I run out I can always rent some. I have no notion that I won't live forever because I've never seen a dead body.

I thought about that a bit more. This notion I have that I'll live forever actually makes me put things off. But if I was more aware that I might snuff it tomorrow, I might start appreciating life today as I'd seen in Bali, under the tuition of Buddhism. I found it an impossible notion, though, because I couldn't dispel this sense of my longevity as my British, middle-class birthright.

The Ozarks were really getting tough: not just the hills; the spacing between the gas stations was now more than a day's walk so I'd have to push enough food and water for four meals, which increased the weight. So I decided to head due south from Vienna on Route 29 to hit Route 66 which ran parallel with the interstate – pronounced 'inner state', which struck me as being quite revealing. My map showed that Route 66 petered out from time to time and I couldn't walk on the interstate, which has the same limited access as motorways. People in gas stations told me it actually ran without a break; but they were motorists. But, faced with another two weeks of mountainous terrain with the bitterly cold nights, I figured I'd risk it.

It was around this time that I started to hear news of another woman with a dog and a cart. Her name was Madge and she'd been walking from Los Angeles, heading for Chicago following Route 66 all the way. But the extraordinary thing about her was that she was a seventy-four-year-old grandmother. The closer I got to 66, the more I heard of her journey. She hadn't made it. Though the stories changed, the most common one was that, 200 miles from the end, her dog Lollipop had knocked over the cart he pulled and it fell on her leg, damaging her knee. She'd gone home and vowed to return in the spring to carry on. She averaged ten to fifteen miles a day. This distance blew me away – the mental side of it after a life of driving a car. And also, that she must have camped out every night because the distance between motels was often two days' walk at my pace of twenty-five miles a day.

It was perhaps this lady's journey which aroused the media to sniff in my direction. The first thing I noticed was a car parked perpendicular to the road in the distance. I recognised the familiar stance of a photographer and simply pulled down my hat to cover my eyes and walked with my head down. As I passed him he called out, 'Just don't give a damn, aye?' The first of the reporters was a young girl who belted out of her car with a microphone, saying, 'Ma'am! Hello! I'm from the *Evening Herald*!' I wanted to say, 'Congratulations', but I just ignored her. Half an hour later, another reporter, this time a man, tried the same thing. I just walked straight past. I stopped at a Casey's gas station, which I'd learned sell the softest doughnuts – the kind you can fold up and put in a matchbox for later. An older female reporter went right in my face with her microphone. I just stared at her and she shrivelled up. I thought this was all so funny. It felt so good: after all these years of having to talk to them to promote my sponsors or the charity, I now didn't have to say a word. I enjoyed being an enigma much more than before because I knew exactly what I was doing and why. It belonged entirely and only to me and there's absolutely nothing selfish about holding on to your own truth.

I had come to be highly selective over whom I stopped to speak to, or 'speak with' I think is the politically correct American terminology which has me gagging every time I hear it. While buying a camera in St Louis I had got chatting with the salesman who, sending his pen like a dart into its container, struck me as more confident than your average cashier. He recognised me as being a traveller and he told me he had run away forty-seven times as a child. We met up for a coffee in the park later and while Boy chewed on everything he could find, Michael Angelo told me his story. There was no need to look for anything sinister in his family because the way he spoke of his adventures, it was obvious he'd done it for the challenge and the danger of seeing how far he could go without being caught. Eventually his mother had given up hope of keeping him in and would simply greet him with the words, 'Hello, dear. What did you learn this time?' He'd finished his college education and felt unchallenged and unstimulated by the scores of opportunities available to him. He'd started to turn in on himself for answers as to why he felt so depressed. I wondered who he had in his life to guide him. There was his mother, but his father had left years before and there were no other close relatives. He was on his own and he felt his failings were his fault. I tried to tell him there was nothing wrong with him; there was simply something wrong with the whole set-up. He said he wanted to come with me, get back on the road, but I told him this wasn't what he imagined it to be. I heard this request a fair amount, especially from girls my age: they thought the idea of setting off with your tent and your dog was terrific, but when I'd broken off from the conversation to say I had to be heading on to find a place to camp for the night they'd recoiled with, 'You're not thinking of camping round here, are you?' Besides, Michael wanted real danger; he wanted to find someone to respect and learn from and he wanted to be surrounded by people who knew him instead of the isolation he now faced, where he was rightly suspicious of others' motives. What Michael needed couldn't be found in the America I saw; he needed something which existed only for those whose parents and grandparents and great grandparents hadn't broken the natural laws of the land.

There were times when drivers tried to hang around me, asking questions which I knew to be robbing me of what I had. They had no intention of sharing anything of their knowledge with me; it seemed like they wanted to take a piece of me and run off with it. Once, I would have enjoyed this attention, seen it as my group of sympathisers and wrung every ounce of pity out of them by being 'nice'. But now, now that I had some self-respect, I saw them clearly for what they were: highwaymen on the road of strength. I am not a missionary and I am far from being a saint and who wants to be Cliff Richard anyway. Once I was sure by the second or third exchange, I'd tell them to get lost. I didn't consider this to be a breaking of the code: by facing my own failings I saw others' behaviour more clearly. If they didn't know they could get up themselves, nothing I could say could do it for them. They had to do this entirely alone. If something bad happened that day I made sure I did not connect the two incidents as pay back on me.

The only time I ever asked a stranger for help was on the evening of the second snow storm. You instinctively know when you've cocked up on your choice of camp. I'd passed a good place before entering a very steep ravine. Stupidly I thought it would be wonderful to camp down at the bottom by the stream with the rocks; stupid, because cold air sinks. As I went down, I realised this but the hill was too steep and I was too tired to turn back again. The light in the ravine was failing and a car pulled over to ask if I wanted a lift. I knew it was a very dangerous place to stop and as I screamed out to the driver to move on, another came round the corner and there was the most godawful screech and stench of tyre rubber as the second car narrowly missed me. Past the bottom of the ravine, all the fields were fenced in with padlocked gates. I put on my fluorescent orange hat in the failing light and pushed on up the next hill but I couldn't find anywhere off the road to camp. I saw a farmhouse and figured I'd ask if I could camp in their field or perhaps on the leaside of the barn.

The old man who opened the door shut it quickly in my face and told me to go away. He said I couldn't camp there, it wasn't his farm and repeated for me to go away. I restrained my urge to say something rude, thinking, well, he has the right to refuse me and turned back down the gravel driveway. It was now almost dark and Boy was being difficult because he was tired and hungry and kept pulling and tugging on the lead, knowing we should be in camp by now. Fortunately, I spotted the entrance to another driveway which was out of sight of the house and high enough from the road not to be seen. We slept there the night and Boy woke to a magical day of snow, which he loved to bound around in. I wondered whether the man who had refused me shelter felt some remorse this morning and maybe that would be his punishment, more than any bad words I said to him.

But if I had been rude to him, my luck would change. It would come back at me very quickly and whenever I tested it, the system never failed.

Once, when being followed by a guy in a car towards the end of the day, I saw a sign for a Kampground of America and felt it would be safest to get to this camp. I asked a woman at the gas station how far it was and when she couldn't understand me I got quite impatient with her, quite sarcastic in fact, implying that she was stupid. She said it was four miles away. I set off for it and sure enough the sign said four miles. After four miles I got to another sign which pointed in another direction saying two miles further. After two miles and by now highly wound up, there was another sign saying one and a half miles further. I apologised in my mind to the woman: I realised my patience was being tested and at the end of that sign was the camp ground.

I thought about this a fair amount the next day as I walked, wondering whether or not I had actually moved the camp ground by being rude. But I figure it didn't really matter, just as long as I thought I had and so didn't do it again.

The snow storms weren't too much of a problem during the day as long as I kept an eye on the cars as we went around the corners in case they skidded into me. These corners, with their camber designed for a car driving at a certain speed, were a pig for me because I had to fight against the force of gravity on the pram. My left arm and shoulder muscles were often painfully knotted after the hundreds of miles of this and it threw out the right side of my back in compensation. At night we were so cold, my bones started to ache and my muscles would stiffen. I curled around Boy and he curled around himself. I made sure I kept his water bowl inside the tent or it would freeze solid.

The tent was not one hundred per cent waterproof. Even though it was a top of the range, made by one of the best manufacturers in America, you had to waterproof them yourself. I can't have done it properly and my sleeping bag was often sodden by morning. If the sun shone during the day I would lay out all the kit to dry during our picnic, but after a while the constant damp irritated my joints. It started to get to me and, after one storm too many, I headed for a motel.

The motel, though, wouldn't take dogs. So I took out all my cash and laid out $100 on the counter. 'If there's anything wrong with the room in the morning, keep the money. As you can see, I can't afford to lose this but I assure you my dog won't mess the room.' It worked.

The scenario of being out in the cold with a long way to go and then suddenly finding a door and stepping into absolute comfort, warmth and security had always appealed to me even as a child. To me, that was the very height of a home: to be the complete opposite of everything outside, a capsule you suddenly come across when in dire need. When I looked at the people in cars driving to their houses, I knew they couldn't appreciate them as much as I appreciated this motel room and I wondered whether that's the kind of exasperation some parents have when they say, 'I've worked all my life for you kids so you can have what I never did and you just don't appreciate it.' Of course they don't; they weren't the ones without in the first place.

I shut the door. Security! Privacy! Boy loved it too, sniffing around, wagging his tail, then zonking out for a couple of hours till he'd be up again looking for something to chew on. I carried a variety of raw hide bits with me but I never came across a meat counter in a supermarket which actually had any bones.

I had a bath for the first time in weeks and pulled off a few ticks. 'Tick patrol' had been a daily routine with Boy, usually at lunchtime while he was dozing or he wouldn't stay still long enough for me to hold an alcohol-soaked cotton wool pad on for long enough to kill the sucker.

Then I turned on the TV and watched a chat show. There was a line of teenagers and their mothers. The teenagers were blank-faced and sulky, the mothers were trying to get through to them. One of the teenagers was pregnant and the point was raised that she was not old enough to deal with adult problems. But I thought, no matter how old she is, if she hasn't had the experiences along the way, how could she possibly have the knowledge of an adult? At twenty-eight, I had only just become, for the first time in my life, able to take care of another life. And it happened quite by accident; it wasn't as though I had a multitude of guides to make sure I experienced things to prepare me for obstacles along the way. And nor, it seemed, did this teenager. Her body was mature enough to have a child. It wasn't her fault that she hadn't received the guidance along the way to deal with it. If my dog behaved badly and was disobedient, would you blame my dog?

I felt sorry for all of them. None of them understood each other, perhaps because they didn't share the same pain. Each generation born in the West is experiencing a life which has never been lived before. Nobody had been there before them, nobody can really say how the isolation of computer games can affect them in later life, nor how to reassure a young man of twenty-five who finds out he's sterile because of the oestrogen in the water. Is it surprising that young people don't listen to their elders if they know their elders haven't experienced the same problems? It's not that they don't want people to look up to; they're crying out for them. How can we possibly blame them for behaving differently from us when it was us in the first place who set up the 2.2 household, invented computer games, manipulated their minds through advertising, showed them life as make-believe on TV and directed them towards a pot of gold at the end of the rainbow without telling them it's actually a crock?

Further towards Oklahoma, I hit the Trail of Tears. Though nobody could tell me what it was, I knew of it from reading Forrest Carter's *Little Tree*, which Raymond had given me. This was the route taken by the Cherokee Indians in a forced eviction from Georgia to the new Indian lands in Oklahoma after a series of con-artist treaties. It was called the Trail of Tears, some said, because of the thousands of men, women and children who died along the way through the winter. Others say it was because the white settlers who saw them dying were the ones who cried. As I walked on their path, I thought of what they were walking into and it struck me that Indians are made of pretty tough stuff, but that's when they had hope. I felt it must have been the lack of hope which killed them in the end. Perhaps they couldn't see any way out of it.

I don't want that to happen to our young people.

We broke the natural laws of the land because we got away with it. Just one more factory won't matter. Now that it's about to come back on us, perhaps the sound of Armageddon will be the adolescents putting their parents on trial for breaking the natural law of taking without giving back. Somehow, I can't imagine what else it would be fought over. I expect, though, that we will be saved from some of the punishment we deserve because they'll know how beautiful and exciting the world was once, before we wrecked it.

Thanksgiving was coming up soon and I asked people along the way to tell me about it. So they told me they thanked God for providing food for them. They said when the first pilgrims came over from England their crops failed and they were starving. Then the Indians showed them how to hunt and gave them seeds to plant maize and the following year after their first harvest they had a huge feast to thank God for their salvation. But hang on, I said, it wasn't God who saved them, it was the Indians. Well, they said, they did invite the Indians over. So I asked them if that is what they do now, invite the Indians. No, they said, it was just a family thing. Well, I guess they had to twist the story over the years to be an act of God, because how on earth could they face the shame of what they then did to the Indians?

Somewhere near Grand Lake O, I came across a buffalo ranch. I'd been told of this place the previous morning, that it had been set up about forty-five years ago by a woman who still runs it. I was quite excited at the prospect of meeting a wise one; perhaps she would be like a white Maya Angelou.

As I opened the trading post door at the buffalo ranch, I spotted her straight away by the way she held court to a group of visitors, sitting on a chair composed of dozens of buffalo parts.

'Come in,' she said.

'Thanks. I've put my dog on the rail out there. I see you've got peacocks and ducks and things. Is that OK?'

'Why yes, that's fine dear, and where are you from?'

'I'm from England. Are you the lady I've been hearing so much about who set up this place?'

'Did you see me on TV last night?'

'Oh, were you on TV?' one of the visitors asked. It was 3.00 p.m.; she must have waited all day for someone to bring up her celebrity.

'Half-hour special and then they ran my ad.'

'More like five minutes, but it seems like a long time on TV,' said the guy behind the counter.

So she told me how she and her late husband had come here forty-three years ago and brought buffalo from Texas because nobody had seen buffalo.

'Were they here originally?' I asked.

'Oh yes,' she said, 'but the Indians killed them all.'

'I'm not sure about that,' I said.

'The white folks killed them all,' corrected the guy.

'The white folks, that was it,' said the old lady. 'Got onto their tongues, a delicacy, and chucked away the rest.'

I wanted to get on to how the Indians tanned their hides, as Raymond had taught me brain tanning and how each animal has just enough brains to tan its own hide.

'Yes, I believe they used the skins,' said the old lady.

'Did they brain tan them?'

'Brain tan them? Ooh, how disgusting,' said the old lady.

'I wonder if you could tell me about the Trail of Tears.'

'Oh, I don't know nothing about that,' said the old lady.

By now I could see she was getting quite cross with me, so I asked her about the kinds of buffalo she had, as one of them I'd seen was called Watusi.

'That's African,' said the old lady.

But she didn't know any more, didn't even know if it was from East Africa or anything about the blood and the milk they provide that feed the tallest people in the world. So, I tried to ask her about something she might know.

'No, Ma'am, I don't know what the Oklahoma symbol means.' Old queen buffalo wasn't too pleased. She turned back to her newspaper and no doubt would have to be massaged a fair bit to get her to come out again. So I said it must have been an almighty struggle when she came here forty-two years ago . . .

'Forty-three years ago,' she corrected without looking up.

'During the dustbowl years? Did your nearby friends have to pack up and move to California?'

'Oh no, it wasn't like the book or the movie of *The Grapes of Wrath*. Very few people actually went and most of them were Chinese and just migrant pickers anyway, they weren't inhabitants of Oklahoma.'

I didn't believe this, but I asked about the Indians who lived around here. The girl serving behind the counter told me about the Indians' blood card, which indicates the degree of Indian blood that you have, and she showed me hers. She had blond hair and I would never have known that she was part Indian. I asked her, 'Was it your parents or grandparents?' But then I looked more closely at the card and it said she was one five hundred and twelfth part Indian. She didn't even know which ancestor it was. She said, 'I think it was my great-great-great-great-great – how many?' She looked over and asked the other lady. 'About four or five greats or something. Yeah well, she was full blood but anyway, it gets me free college education.'

I walked away feeling really disappointed. I'd been looking forward to meeting a strong and intelligent and curious and passionate and humble old woman, but instead I found an egotistical, self-centred old grouch. Where are the guides?

Walking on Route 66 again, through the towns of Depew and Stroud and Chandler, I began to think of Steinbeck's *The Grapes of Wrath*. OK, as one story goes, thousands of families had packed up and left this area during the terrible droughts of the dustbowl and, inspired by flyers they saw of work in the west, they had gone in search of a better life in California where they could pick grapes all day in the luscious valleys. But, because so many people were willing to work, the conditions deteriorated and their wages were not enough to live on – another story of American history being based on what people were told, only to find that it wasn't all it was cracked up to be.

'Work hard and all will come to you,' I found was actually true. But it depended on what you worked at.

Late one afternoon, quite tired with the headwinds which now replaced the hills as the form of push but which were more tiring because they buffeted me and I couldn't see when it would stop, I thought stuff it, we'll knock off early. We camped in a crappy place but I couldn't be bothered to go further on. The next morning, after five miles, which was my previous day's target, I came to the most perfect camp I'd seen yet, a natural spring lake in the sandstone. A clean area, free from grass and bugs. So, the next time I felt like knocking off early, I remembered this and pushed on and the places I found to camp were always the best. Not just because I was tired and glad to get off the trail; they were unique, as though I couldn't have planned it better myself. Now whether I make these things by what I do, I don't know. All I know is that's how it works out and, besides, it encourages me not to be lazy.

I thought of this some more. Perhaps it is a natural law of the land too, that if it wasn't so hard it wouldn't be so good. If it weren't the case, surely none of the animals would be bothered to do anything either. If you don't get rewards for what you do, why do them? Do I help someone out because I think the good will come back at me? Yes, partly, because it could be me one day. The Tuareg taught me that. But somehow, it gets messed up with guilt. Who messed that up in my head? Somebody religious, I think, somebody saying it was selfish. It seems to me there is some confusion here over the gifts of life.

Oklahoma City, and I was reminded of the bomb that went off

there last year. I didn't see the place because I didn't want to walk down to it: there were too many pavement edges for my back to take. Boy hated the cities too and there was a fair chance we wouldn't get out the other side to camp before night fall. So we went over the top and down to 66. Along the way, I thought of the images I'd seen on TV of the flowers, teddies and so on which had been placed there. It was said to be out of respect, but I think it was something slightly more than that.

To me, it's as if when something evil happens, we instinctively rush in to mop it up with goodness. Like the weather: high pressure rushes in to low pressure. Our emotions do charge the air around us, but I wondered what happens to that energy? What does it change into? Somehow I knew I wouldn't find the answers on Route 66, I needed to go to a place of wisdom and whilst the signs for Cherokee trading posts caught my eye, when I saw the symbol of a teepee and knew they didn't live in teepees, I figured this was not the place.

But I did meet a young family who gave me a great dose of inspiration as well as an insight into a moral problem I'd been pondering. I'd been told there was a gas station seven miles further on and so I hadn't stocked up with food or water for the night. But there was nothing after two hours' walk. After four hours, by now quite worried and quite wound up in the onslaught of voices telling me how stupid I was and what I couldn't do, I saw the shape of a gas station ahead and finally Boy and I pulled in. It was also a camp ground so I decided we'd stay there the night.

I let Boy off the lead and within a few minutes, the two young boys who lived there were chasing around him, laughing and shouting over to me, 'Hey, hey! Look what we can do!' I suddenly realised I hadn't heard that phrase or the sound which went with it for so long.

I went into the gas station and got chatting with their grandmother, Carole, whose thirty-five-year-old son David owned the place. She'd come up to help him over the winter because his wife had run off with another bloke. She told me that David's spine had started to crumble at the neck but because he couldn't afford to pay out $300 a month for medical insurance before this happened, he was having to pay for the treatment himself and he couldn't get anyone to insure him now. Each pain killer he took cost $60. He was already in debt to his father to the tune of $150,000 for an operation. They knew there was more treatment he could have which would help, but they couldn't afford it. So, what it boiled down to was that health was based on money.

I thought about this the next day as we set off again with a bag of chopped steak from Carole because the coyotes had made off with Boy's bag of food as we slept inside the store. Even in Britain, where we have the National Health Service, treatment can be refused because it would cost too much. Survival, it seems, is based on the most financially fit. Since the N.H.S. is the system we know and believe is right, I suppose it's only natural that we want to impose it on other people. The question has been raised: how can we refuse our medicines to others in Africa, for example, if we are enjoying them ourselves? But that's only half the question. The real question, I think, is are we right to accept that money decides who will live and who will die – that money is God? Is this more right than nature being the one who decides?

It was a beautifully peaceful stretch of road, sometimes a little cracked where the surface had been pushed up by weeds and I could tell a car was coming by the clip, clip of the wheels on the edges of the concrete sections. But it was getting a little boring, that is, until I started to be followed. I recognised a car which had passed me several times and now it was waiting up ahead, partially hidden by the trees. American car number plates are only required to be on the back of the vehicle – a stupid policy as far as I was concerned because it meant I had to go round the back of his car to get its number. I held my Dictaphone in my hand as I ignored the driver who was beckoning me to go over to him and I read out his number and car description into my pretend police radio.

'Hey! What do you think you're doin'?'

'More to the point, what do you think *you're* doing?'

He sped off and I never saw him again. I did this several times a day now that I was getting into the more remote areas of Oklahoma. But there was one guy whom I spotted as a problem when I walked out of a gas station. He just didn't look as though he was there for petrol. I saw him again further into a town, then I saw him in a cash point booth, staring at me. It was getting late and I'd intended to walk through town and out the other side to camp. But this guy was trouble. So, I turned round and walked back the way I had come, actually having to stop for him as he pulled out from a side turning. I found a motel but they wouldn't accept dogs. I put $200 on the counter but this woman wouldn't have anything to do with me. I wanted to tell her I was being bothered but something told me that was my problem. There was one other motel, two miles to the north. Though I didn't want to walk so far out of my way, I thought it best.

They took dogs and, just as I was walking to the room, the local sheriff pulled me over. He said I should be very careful around here. He said he didn't think I'd get through alive. 'Oh, pooh!' I said, but thanked him anyway. I put Boy in the room and went out to put laundry in the washing machine. Suddenly, the guy who'd been following me appeared at the motel in his car. He wound down the window and said, 'D'you want to go somewhere?' It wasn't a threat, but I didn't want him hanging around as I walked the next day out on the lonely highway. So I said, 'Oh! There you are! The police have been looking all over for you!' Before he could drive out of sight, I had his licence plate and he knew it.

But a hitch-hiker at a gas station wasn't going to be dissuaded by that course of action. Boy wouldn't go near him, which was unusual as he was often embarrassingly friendly. I figured the best policy was to be friendly, not to show any sign of being intimidated and so I shared my coffee and asked him where he was going. He said he was going to California to drive trucks, that he'd been living in the woods for four years since his wife and five children died in a fire. Then he said I should be careful of the people around here. I ignored this last line and said, 'Are you a praying man? Because I've heard there's a lot of comfort to be found in the words of the Bible.' He said he wasn't much into that. So I wished him well in finding what he was looking for and repeated what he'd said to me: 'Watch out for the people round here.' And Boy and I headed off.

Sometime later, on a road which was empty of traffic and dotted occasionally with rundown shacks, I saw this man in the wing mirror on the pram. He was some way behind but he was walking quite quickly. I gently let Boy off the chain and hoped to God he wouldn't think a confrontation was just another silly game. I had often helped hitchers to get lifts but I couldn't do that now; I wouldn't want this guy in my car so I had no business suggesting anyone else did. But I had to get him off my tail. And then, just as it had been for many before me, the sign for Lucille's truckstop came into focus. No neon, you'd easily pass it if your eyes weren't sharpened by need. I parked the pram under the canopy knowing that if the crazy one approached, Boy would bark and I'd be right there.

The glass door had a black paper blind pulled down behind it and a dusty 'Open' sign sat on the window ledge. As always I felt the old ritual of hope for it to be open, expecting it to be closed, and tried the door. The free movement of it without the half-expected restriction of a bolt and I knew I was safe. Inside was a narrow black shop with a counter on the right and just enough space to stand in the corridor which led back to a small room. An elderly lady dressed in black pulled off her glasses, pushed herself up from the round table and moved towards me. This is her ritual, I thought. 'Well, now, what can I do for you?' I was going to say I wanted to wait up for a bit until this guy who was following had passed on but more tactfully I said I'd read about this place and stopped by to say hello.

'Where did you read about it? Have you seen this book?' she asked and picked up a large coffee-table glossy. 'This one's German,' and she flipped to the page, 'wrote about me – all this and this and this' – like a six-year-old indicating her first story. 'Have you seen this book?'

'No, actually I'm not German, I'm English.'

'Well, did you see this one? Another book, paperback?'

'No, I saw you mentioned in the Cruiser's Guide to 66, a small grey effort,' and she cocked her head, 'written by Tim Ross.'

'I think I know it.' And I'm thinking, yeah, I know this ploy. You make out like you don't know where you appear to be a bigger deal than you really are. I know, I've done it. I wanted to check on the crazy one so I said I'd get the book for her. He wasn't outside. Either he'd been picked up or was waiting. I came back in. 'And where are you from?'

'I'm from England.'

'Then you must sign the visitors' book,' and she pushed the thick foolscap binder towards me.

'Ah, nobody gets out of this place without signing the book,' I quoted. 'Tell me a story, Lucille, and I'll sign your book.'

'What kind of story do you want?' She excused herself a minute and walked back to the table and picked up her glasses.

'Well, back in the forties, when you first set up, were folks still leaving for California or coming back?

'Well, now,' she positioned herself in front of me, black hair, black turtle neck and gold pendant. 'I came here in 1941 just before the Second World War broke out. Folks were still heading west for the fruit picking in California and many of them got jobs in defence factories and when the war was over the factories shut down and the folks came back, many of them to the land they'd left behind.'

'What were they like when they left?'

'Pretty beat up. By the time they got here many of their cars and trucks broke down. I'd buy them, had a whole yard of trucks out back.'

'But where did you find the money?'

'Somehow. I guess the Lord showed me the way to help these people make it to the west. But then some of them were so broke they pawned what they had. One time this cabinet,' the cabinet she was leant on, 'was full of watches, clocks, dentures, all kinds.'

'I think it's ironic that those people whose farms were destroyed by the dust were probably sitting on a gold-mine of oil. When did they discover the oil?'

'Oh, that's been going on for years, but I was born and brought up on a farm. We always had plenty to eat.'

'But farming's risky business isn't it? These people suffered year after year.'

'Well, all I can say is my Daddy raised haooghs [pigs] and we planted what we needed in the garden and times were tough but all we needed was money to buy soap and lard and flour.'

'Are you saying these people were lazy?'

'I'm saying that we always had plenty to eat.'

'So what about the Indians who lived here? When everybody left they stayed?'

'Well, I've known Indians for forty-five years and they're lazy.'

'Well, maybe lazy doing white man's stuff. If they'd been lazy before they'd have died.'

'If the white man hadn't come the Indians would have died. They'd have killed all the buffaloes, they didn't know nothin' about farming.' She pushed her glasses firmly up against her face. 'Indians are bone idle and they want beer. They'll do anything for it, pawn anything. One time I had a guy trying to pawn a bag of groceries he'd bought on welfare.'

'But the women are strong,' I said, 'and they must be keeping things together?'

'Well, I don't know about that. I have my daughter, we had to make ends meet and when the highway pulled through, that's Interstate 40, they cut us off, I took to selling beer to make ends meet. I got a reputation for the coldest beer in Oklahoma.' I thought it was rather ironic that the gas station called Phillips 66, which was now on the interstate, was killing old Route 66.

'So how far is it to Wetherford?'

'Seven miles.'

'I'd better get moving then to get there before night.' It was 3.30 p.m. I needed two hours' walk to get there and buy food before sunset at 5.05 p.m. I paid for my T-shirt and collected up the pen she gave me and the postcard I'd bought and when I reached for the

Cruiser's 66 she took it from me. I froze at the thought of losing it to her pile; I needed it. She opened the cover and signed her name. Nice meeting you, Lucille.

Again I felt let down, but I suppose she was telling me what she knew from her experiences and yet I couldn't get out of my mind how hard it must be for the coming generation to find their way back to our real teachers if our elders speak of them like that. She couldn't see why the Indians were drunk and lazy and she was ignorant to think that the Indians would have died without the white man. If they were heading so quickly for extinction, why would they bother to spend so much time decorating themselves and their cooking pots? If they were so miserable and drunk and lazy, why were they dancing? If she was so perfect, why wasn't she?

Into Texas and the snow storms returned. As it turned out it was one of the coldest winters on record: the East coast experienced total shut-down and New York had four days without crime as everyone was snowed in. The police had a field day catching criminals who were holed up in motels. They said the snow was like a white flag, that people helped out strangers who were stranded. Perhaps New York was experiencing its first change from compassion based on pity, to compassion based on the sharing of a common problem. But after four days, when the food started to run out, survival of the fittest began and those people who'd never broken the law, now began to steal.

As for us, it was pretty hard going. Especially at night in temperatures of fifteen degrees below zero. My bones ached all through the days too but the biting headwinds reminded me that this was nothing compared to walking across the Arctic. I started going to motels, which wasn't a good idea because getting warmed up meant the next day would be worse. It also meant I started to whinge for the first time on the journey and Boy got depressed too – he wanted to run around at the end of the day, not be locked inside a room with me asleep on the bed. The headwinds were sometimes so strong that it would take me seven hours to walk ten miles instead of the usual two and a half to three. This meant that I had to carry more food and water, making that weight even harder to push. Boy pulled a fair bit for me but he'd get irritable being on the lead and I'd let him off, envious of how easily he ran around. I heard a very major storm was coming in within two days and I knew we had to get to Amarillo and find a motel to hole up in. At times when I felt the onset of the 'poor me's I just took me by the hand and said, 'What's the alternative?'

I saw a signpost for the Big Texan restaurant and motel, fifty miles away, and I remembered that Brian and I had been there all those years before. This became the incentive and finally, after long days and nights, we got there.

There was the temptation to rush inside this motel room out of the cold, but I always remembered when I had my hand on the handle to say thank you, to remember what I'd been through to get there and it felt much better when I opened the door.

I felt the sense of grace when I'd pushed hard and in the Big Texan I remembered how Brian and I had laughed. But it was a surface kind of laugh. Like the shallow breaths you take when you're unfit compared to the deep ones I could take now which seemed to reach into new chambers, invigorating them. Though I knew I could never put right what I had done wrong, by giving it a 'sequel in the future', as Sartre would say, this was the closest I could get. I thought I'd had the choice to bury the deceit, but I hadn't really. It wouldn't stay down and let me hold my head up at the same time and I missed that. But my confidence was definitely coming back because during the night, I actually told myself a joke in a dream and woke up laughing.

The storm lasted for two days, freezing the snow on the roads, but the outlook was now OK for the next few days. We had to be moving on. On the far side of Amarillo, I stopped in a mall to buy a balaklava and was taken aback by the attitude of the shoppers. It was a week before the biggest celebration of their religion – Christmas, the birth of their saviour, the guy who'd spent his time saying people are more important than things – and yet the shoppers were irritable, tired and there were posters all over the place advertising the services of support groups, asking if you were miserable or lonely. It seemed as though these shoppers were engaged in an endurance test, as though this wasn't a celebration, more like a time of renewing their vows to the Almighty Dollar, like the final race of the year to see if they could still compete. And with every Angel face and re-run of *It's a Wonderful Life* I got a sense of how sinister and hypocritical its competitors really are. I had this terrible image of a Christmas tree in a living room with an angel on top and the arms of the branches reaching down to cuddle the children to suckle underneath at the presents, and they were ripping them open and when I looked at their faces they had blood on their mouths. It was like lion cubs at their first carcass, the kids being given their first taste of materialism.

Still, they weren't all like that of course, that was just my imagination.

Towards the west of Texas we were too cold now to sleep out much at all. There was absolutely no chance of reaching LA and my only desire was to get as far West as we could. We walked from one motel to the next but unfortunately they were badly spaced for us – some only sixteen miles apart when I was aiming for twenty-five. But we couldn't do thirty-two in one day against the strength of those headwinds. The day before Christmas Eve we had stopped in a motel on the outskirts of Vega. I called ahead to the town of Adrian to the motel there to see if it would be open on Christmas Eve. They said they would be, but only after 6 p.m., which was an hour after dark. Since Adrian was only fourteen miles from Vega and would take no more than four hours to walk to, I asked the Vega motel manageress if we could stay a few hours longer before setting off and of course I'd pay extra. But she was a bitter-faced woman, who had been pretty rude to me when I'd checked in and now she said no. I said, 'And a Merry Christmas to you too.'

The picture of her face and my desire to smash it against the counter kept me going pretty fast for that fourteen miles. I was expecting there to be a gas station as we were completely out of food – Boy's and mine. But the gas stations were all closed. In Adrian they were all closed too, with signs saying they would be open in two days' time. I wasn't so concerned for myself, but Boy couldn't go that long without food. But I shouldn't have worried because this was cowboy country.

Not only was I given a lift back into Vega to stock up on supplies from the Allsops gas station, I was treated to a delicious lunch the next day and a tour of the local characters by Billy Meldon and Kirk Garrison who lived there. Their grandfathers had pioneered this land where the water table is as much as 600 feet below the surface of the ground. And I couldn't help thinking that if so much could be achieved by people with such spirit, there's hope for us yet.

Billy told me the service road which ran along the interstate was about to run out. Though I'd called ahead to each department of transport to make sure I wasn't going to find myself in the middle of nowhere with no road to walk on, their information wasn't correct. He drove me up ahead to see where it ran out and where it started up again. There was a gap of twenty-five miles where I'd have to walk on the interstate. I had another idea: I'd walk on the desert floor; but I couldn't push the pram on it so we took the pram to a disused gas station at the beginning of the next road section and hid it. Billy took us back, and Boy and I set off. There would be two full days' walk without food or water top-ups along the way.

For the first stretch, on the desert floor, Boy suffered terribly from the thorns. We'd come across some before and I'd got him some boots to protect his feet but he refused to wear them. Now he'd writhe in agony, thrashing around, trying to get the thorns and cactus out of his paws. He'd rip them out with his teeth then let me get at them, but five minutes later he was in the same state. The snow provided a numbing effect for him but we had a good eight hours of this ahead of us and I was glad Boy didn't know it.

He made no noise when he was in pain like this, perhaps some leftover instinct to protect him from predators. He didn't whinge when tired, he just knuckled down and got on with the job. I often thought I'd been looking all over for a guide and yet here was one right beside me and he was more loyal and more brave than any human I'd ever met, just like my donkey.

I wonder where we got the notion that to be animal is somehow a derogatory and degrading term. My dog didn't shit in his food trough like my kind. Perhaps one day, when the next dominators of the earth take over from us, they'll look back at humans as the ones with 'pea brains'.

I got a sense of this when, during the night, Boy knocked over the water bag and I hadn't closed the nozzle shut. I woke up to a cracking sound and realised the water had seeped into my sleeping bag and had frozen around us. It was 1 a.m., four and a half hours to go till daylight. And then, of course, we had no water. During the next day, I stopped to light a fire and melt some snow. There, under the only trees I'd seen for a couple of days, I found a perfectly round stone. I picked this up and held it in my hands, its smoothness and the weight of it felt very comforting in my hand. I carried it for the next day, intending to take this back to Nan but, when we finally pulled into the small town of San Jon, I met a woman who was leaving for California to say goodbye to her father who was dying. I gave her the stone to carry with her.

Another two days of isolation through another snow storm as we headed down Route 209 to hit Route 60 because there was now no side road to walk on. On New Year's Eve we found ourselves in the thick of a wind storm. The tent pegs wouldn't hold in the sand so I laid all my kit around the inside of the tent to keep it down, but the wind caught underneath and I spent the night lying spreadeagled, clinging on against the cracking, whipping of the fabric. It was just about bearable till I wanted to pee.

At those times, if I'd stopped and realised where I was I might have panicked. Instead, I put on the blinkers because it's frightening to be aware of the enormity of the danger. If I had been, I'd just go to pieces. And you rein in, and put one foot in front of the other and this is something that the critics just don't understand – the hard edge of this isn't during the pretty mountains, it's the dangerous times. Instead of pretending I am smaller than I am so that others don't feel inferior, instead of apologising for it, I see this now as a very positive attribute I possess.

When it happens, I get that certain strength, a calming voice, a relaxing of my facial muscles. A core growth and I can feel it in the pivotal part of my body, my lower back, in my abdomen, a strength which reaches up into my neck, my arms and my shoulders and I feel like mother, capable of taking care of anything. That's what I know is the beginning of my true self and my own strength. And that is the nature of woman.

By the time we hit Melrose, Boy was shivering from the cold. Fortunately, though, the sun came out after another storm but the headwinds kept up as we inched forward for another four days in the desert till we would get to a town.

There were six days to go until my visa would run out and by this time I was getting fairly concerned about finding a home for Boy. I didn't want him to have just any home, I wanted him to be with another dog for company, I wanted him to have a territory to defend and masses of exercise. But now there weren't even any farms. I knew I couldn't leave without making sure he was OK, he'd taken care of me not just by protecting me from possible hassle, but by giving me something to take care of, which had replaced the soul-searching. His attitude of searching for the fun in everything had lifted my spirits so often, just as Pete had done in the Sahara. Yet where was I going to find someone who would take care of him here in the middle of the desert?

Seventeen miles before we reached the town of Fort Sumner, where Billy the Kid is buried, a Chevy truck pulled over. I was about to say I was just fine and didn't need a lift when I saw who was driving it – a great big man with his son or grandson beside him. He had soft, gentle eyes and when he asked me if I wanted a lift, I asked him if he wanted a dog. He got out and had a look at Boy. Yes, he said, he'd be interested, he needed a guard dog. But I wanted to see his place before I'd make up my mind so we drove to his ranch just outside Fort Sumner. There, his dog and his horses were clean and well looked after. He said he wanted a dog to help him round up the cattle and by the way he treated his other, older dog, I saw he could train Boy well. The man's name was Pete, ironically enough, and he was a rcdeo champion, breaking and training horses to ride at competition level.

I spent the day with them, making sure Boy would fit in. He seemed delighted with his new friends and I couldn't have imagined a better place for him. He had his own kennel outside, next to the other dog, and I laid his blanket in there. I would have to leave for England for four months to write this book. I'd be back then, I whispered to him and, if things didn't work out here, I'd take him with me as I carried on to Los Angeles. He just licked my hand and rested his head on my knee.

Sitting alone on the bus to Albuquerque that night, I felt a bit choked up but each time I reminded myself that he now had what he'd always wanted: another dog to play with, a firm handler and a job to do.

Back in London as I started on the book, I looked over the notes I'd made on paper of that first American journey and I came across the point where I had started to walk again properly after the abortion. It was twenty-two miles before the town of Fort Sumner. I had forgotten this place. But the spirits had not. They knew when I'd walked far enough the second time, so they sent me a good man to take my dog at seventeen miles before Fort Sumner. This place had been marked back in 1985 by a man who had come out of the desert to give me a red rose. I now understood that he brought me that gift and the note of thanks that went with it, not for that time, but for this one.

EPILOGUE

It was time to tell my father.

I hadn't spoken to him for nearly a year, ever since I'd visited my parents and the re-run of Live Aid had been on TV. My father had expressed his disgust at the music. He refused to accept it was a way of communicating and I wondered if he noticed what kind of argument we were really having. In the end, when I couldn't get through to him, I smashed several plates and left.

Now I pulled up outside their house in the sunshine, unsure of what to expect. I turned off the engine and heard my father tinkering in the garage. He came out, saw me and opened his arms.

'Hello! Hello! What a wonderful surprise!'

He welcomed me into the kitchen, then went in search of my mother who was engrossed in the garden, nurturing her very first cucumber. I heard her squeak and saw her running up the path, running towards the hug which would mean the end of her own ordeal. For eighteen months she had kept my secret safe. I wanted to tell him myself, when the journey was done, but it was a selfish request. When she knew I was out in America, walking alone, she had woken many times in the night with that mother's intuition that her child is in danger, but could ask for no comfort. Now it was over for her and for me, bar this final ordeal.

In the sitting-room, alone with my father, I set the green beret on the table between us and said there was something I had to tell him.

'I'm listening,' he said.

I watched him closely for any signs as I told him the story, the whole story, but he gave nothing away and he asked no questions till I'd finished. Then he said:

'Are you off the drugs now?'

'Yes,' I said, rather surprised. 'It was them or another walk.'

'I'm very glad to hear it. I commend your honesty over this.' He rubbed the bristles on his chin for a while and then said, 'I've been doing a lot of thinking too and I wanted to talk to you, but you've been away for so long. In fact,' and he leaned forward with his face suddenly open and receptive, 'I find I want to talk to you all the time.' Communication. At last.

I wrote this book because the truth is hard enough to live with, but deceit is even harder. The lie I was living had got under my skin and infected my core and, like the bacteria, throwing its waste to the centre, it began to consume me.

I should not be remembered as the first woman to walk around the world. I leave that accolade for another. When I cheated, I broke the unwritten rule of the Guinness Book and though I made up the distance by walking that stretch again – re-walking one-third of the width of America – it is not enough to secure the purity of that title and nor should it be. But what's in a title when I see how much I gained instead?

In the early days of the walk, I had been influenced by the opinion of my father. I had been a mimic of him and the walks had been his. But when I cheated, I made the decision myself, as myself. It became *my* skeleton and therefore *my* shape. Like a broken bone which has now mended, I am stronger there. But before I admitted my deception, the world around me was an alien and mystifying place in which I could not belong. It questioned me, it praised me, it criticised me and I judged it all from my isolated position of deceit. But once I admitted it, and set about putting it right, I was no longer afraid of failing.

I don't have to pretend anymore. There's nothing left to cover up or to be ashamed of. I can see out now and I am the one asking questions.

The opportunity I was given, to make good what I did wrong, is not always there for everyone. But whatever those situations might be, I know the native Americans would say that you cannot heal others unless you have been wounded yourself.

I went back to America to walk on my own from Fort Sumner to Los Angeles, just for the hell of it. Boy was delighted to see me and we set off together. He was in fine health but after three days in thirty-five degrees centigrade heat, I knew he wasn't going to make it. Pete and his wife Mary-Ann wanted him as theirs, but when they came to collect him, Boy ran out to greet them, then ran back to me. As we sat in the motel room, he rested his head on my lap, then looked up at me for a while as if to say, 'I love you very much, I love you because you found me a home.' And with that, he got up and went over to Mary-Ann and lay down beside her.

I crossed the treeless deserts of New Mexico, Arizona and

California at the hottest time of the year. At midday, when the temperatures reached fifty degrees centigrade, I found good shade in the flashflood drainage ditches under the road. The wind had swept them perfectly clean and I would lie down for several hours, reading stories of the Hopi Indians or reflecting on my own journey. When I had stood at the apex of that V in Yorkshire and was tempted by J to take the easy path, I asked myself if I really wanted to live anymore. But the spirit of Alison Hargreaves had guided me then, showing me the hardest path which was the only way out, as no doubt she will often do when people are lost on *their* mountain. And when I chose it, I was no longer unsure of who I was. I became a woman then.

Women are the keepers of morality. Men will find meat today with their physical strength. But women, with their inner strength, will ensure there is meat tomorrow. Perhaps our role in the west is confused because the morals we once kept – taking only what we need, giving back what we have taken – are no longer deemed important. It is thought possible to live without them and so the keepers of morality have been made temporarily redundant.

As the end of my journey drew near, I, as a woman, wondered what I have that I can give back to the world I've walked around.

The answer struck me as I descended into the Los Angeles basin, with its brown rim of pollution like a filthy lavatory bowl. Drivers pulled over to offer their pity that I was on foot and to tell me it wasn't possible to walk a few miles in the heat to the next gas station. At first, I thought my gift might be to show them that it *is* possible to walk down to the shops, but when I told them I walk because I believe that cars pollute the environment, I saw terror in their eyes. And it struck me that they've been robbed of something much more serious than just their belief in what they are capable of.

A squad of Australian soldiers once challenged the Aborigines to an exercise in survival. It took the form of a race across the desert. Both groups would go on foot, carrying everything they'd need. The soldiers were loaded down with water and food, navigational equipment and camping kit. The Aborigines were naked and carried just three sticks each – their spear, their woomera and their hand drill for making fire. Who reached the finish line first? The soldiers, of course, despite being exhausted, dehydrated and barely on speaking terms. The Aborigines had kept up pretty well until, three-quarters of the way into the race, they gave up. The promise of some wild honey growing many miles off their route had lured them away and they were found, several days later, happily munching on honeycomb in the shade. When asked to explain themselves, the Aborigines revealed why they were the winners of the exercise in survival: 'Sugarbag,' they said, 'properly-big-feller-good-time.'

Our physical ability is not the only thing which the engine, the milling machine and the matches have robbed us of.

The waves of the Pacific Ocean marked the end of my own captivity. I knelt in the sand and drew a circle around me, turning anticlockwise till I came back to the beginning. But I did not close the circle to form a ball that I could bounce away and begin my life afresh. Instead my finger continued on past the start, forming the beginnings of a spiral which I will keep with me, adding to as I grow. Along this line I laid mussel shells as symbols of what I had struggled to overcome, and the oval shapes of their open halves shone with the iridescence of butterfly wings as I stood up in my spiral and said to myself:

I am free now, I am animal and I'm going home.

POSTSCRIPT

Temptation is the oldest story in the book. It comes when we are offered an easy way. The Western Way is the easy way. This is the gift some believe we must take to other nations – disguising the temptation to break the natural laws of the land by calling it 'development' or by calling it 'choice'.

Survival
for tribal peoples

THE 'PYGMIES'

In the forests of central Africa live the peoples who are generally known as 'Pygmies', though they dislike the name since it is often used as a term of contempt, rather than just a description of their short stature (their average height is about 4' 8" or 1.5 m). They number about 250,000 altogether, and they live in all the central African countries: Zaire, Congo, Cameroon, Gabon, the Central African Republic, Rwanda, Burundi and Uganda.

The different Pygmy peoples live far apart and speak different languages, but all are united by the same deep relationship with the forest which is their home. They see the forest as a personal god, fruitful and kindly: they live by gathering the wild produce of the forest and hunting its animals, and have a system of exchange with the villagers who farm in the forest clearings: the Pygmies provide the villagers with meat and honey from the forest, or work on their farms, and in return they get the farmers' produce such as manioc and palm wine. Though they may seem to be like servants to the villagers, they are free to return to the forest at any time; it is their skill in living from the forest which makes them independent.

The Pygmy people live in small bands, which can move easily through the forest. Quarrels and disputes are worked out within the band by humour and ritual – they have no 'chiefs' or formal system of government.

Today the independence and culture of the 'Pygmy' people are in danger, above all because of the threats to the forests, which are being cut down to provide timber, or cleared for farming. For instance, in the Central African Republic, ninety per cent of the forest has already been allocated to European logging companies. Other parts of the forest have been turned into national parks or wildlife reserves, which generally means the Pygmies and other forest people being turned out. The nation states in which the Pygmies live do not recognise that they have any legal right to the forest lands that are their home, although international law recognises such claims. Unless their right can be recognised, all the Pygmy peoples may end up where the Twa Pygmies of Rwanda and Burundi are – as landless labourers and beggars.

© *Survival 1996*

THE TUAREG

The Tuareg people have their home in the Sahara and the Sahel regions of Africa. Living in one of the earth's harshest environments, as nomadic herders or mixing herding with farming, the Tuareg have developed a highly complex and sophisticated society. Formerly they were the masters of the region, controlling the important caravan trade across the desert.

'Tuareg' is an outsiders' name for them. They call themselves by various names of which the most inclusive is *Kel Tamajak* (or Tamasheq): 'speakers of the Tuareg language'. Tuareg lands are today divided from one another by the borders of five nation-states: Niger, Mali, Algeria, Burkina Faso and Libya. Estimates of the total number of Tuareg vary from 1–3 million, of whom perhaps 1–1.5 million live in Niger and probably half a million in Mali.

Most Tuareg follow the Islamic faith. They have a rich heritage of poetry and song, which is handed on to new generations by singers accompanying themselves on the drum or lute – but the songs of today speak of war and exile.

Formerly the Tuareg had a complex social hierarchy, reaching from nobles to slaves. (Slavery was practised not only among the Tuareg but throughout West Africa.) Clan membership and family property were usually inherited down the female line. Women had – and have – great freedom, and used to take part in the decision-making processes of their communities while these were still independent. Many women are musicians and singers, and it is generally mothers who teach the ancient Tuareg alphabet, *tifinagh*, to their children.

The Tuareg fought the French invasion of the 19th and early 20th century with ferocious tenacity. In the end, however, they lost the use of much of their territory, and their political organisation fell apart.

Since African independence, the division of the Tuareg people between separate states means that they are dominated by the majority populations of each, most of whom are settled farmers; and they have become ever more impoverished and landless. This has driven them to political militancy and finally to form armed anti-government movements, some of which aim for secession and a Tuareg state. Since 1990–91 there has been a long and bloody conflict in both Mali and Niger. Entire camps of women and children have been massacred. The result is a refugee crisis of which Algeria, Burkina Faso and Mauritania have borne the brunt.

Recently there have been peace initiatives in both Mali and Niger – but only time will show if the Tuareg are yet destined to find peace in their own land.

© *Survival 1996*

THE ABORIGINES

The Aborigines first came to the Australian continent 40,000–60,000 years ago. In time there came to be about 500 different peoples each with their own language and territory, and each made up of several clans. Today many people think of the Aborigines as nomads living in the desert. In fact most of them lived in farming communities along the coast, where food was more plentiful.

In the inhospitable deserts of the interior the Aborigines adapted the harsh environment to their needs. They burned the undergrowth to encourage the growth of green shoots (the food of the game they hunted) and they were experts at finding water.

Land is crucial to the core both of Aborigines' spiritual life, and their physical survival. Their concept of land is rooted in the Dreamtime – a time long past when the earth was first created. One Aboriginal man explained it like this: 'By Dreaming we mean the belief that long ago these creatures started human society, they made all natural things and put them in a special place . . . In many places the great creatures changed themselves into sites where their spirits stayed. Aboriginals have a special connection with everything that is natural.'

Like so many other indigenous peoples, the Aborigines were devastated by invasion and colonialism. Their population plummeted from between 300,000 and 1,000,000 when Captain Cook landed in 1770, to just 60,000 in 1900, as a result of new diseases and massacres. The government tried to integrate those who survived by taking children from their parents (often by force) and giving them to white families – so that Aboriginal ways would die out. Luckily this policy failed, but it caused unimaginable suffering – something which is only now being addressed by Australians.

Today, the Aboriginal population is about 250,000. Roughly half of all Aborigines live in towns, often in 'fringe dweller' camps where housing and health conditions are very poor. The fact that the infant mortality rate for Aborigines is three times the national average, and their suicide rate is six times higher, shows just how bad the Aborigines' situation is. Only since 1992 has the Aborigines' right to own their own land been recognised nationally – secure control over their land is the most important Aboriginal demand. Many Aborigines, such as the Martu in Western Australia, are now presenting 'native title' claims in an effort to get legal title to their land and prevent outsiders from occupying it or destroying their sacred sites.

SURVIVAL – A UNIQUE ORGANISATION

Survival is the only organisation of its kind. Started in Britain in 1969 in response to massacres in Amazonia, Survival now has supporters in 81 countries and works for tribal peoples' rights through campaigns, education and funding. We work closely with local indigenous organisations and focus on tribal peoples who have the most to lose, often those most recently in contact with the outside world.

Our work, from Siberia to Sarawak, Canada to Kenya, brings real change and many successes. For example, one campaign forced the government of Brazil to recognise Yanomami land; and Botswana's government halted plans to evict Bushmen from a game reserve within weeks of Survival issuing a bulletin.

Campaigns are directed at governments, companies and others who violate tribal peoples' rights. As well as letter-writing – which generates thousands of protests – we use many other tactics: from embassy vigils, to lobbying the powerful; from putting cases to the United Nations, to advising on new laws; from informing tribes of their rights, to headline-grabbing stunts. All our work is rooted in direct contact with hundreds of tribal communities. We believe that public opinion is the most effective force for change: it is already making it harder for governments and companies to oppress tribal peoples.

We set out to demolish the myth that tribal peoples are relics, destined to perish through 'progress'. We promote respect for their cultures and explain the contemporary relevance of their way of life. We also produce material for children, the conscience of the future. We enable tribes to talk directly to companies invading their land. We point out the threats, giving them the information they need to make *their* voices heard.

Survival also ensures that humanitarian, self-help, educational and health projects get funding. One example is the Yanomami medical fund, which succeeded in virtually eliminating malaria in some Indian areas.

Survival is the only organisation of its kind which refuses money from governments – ensuring our freedom of action and making us stretch our resources to the limit.

Since 1969, the world's attitude to tribal peoples has changed. Then, it was assumed that they would die out or be assimilated, now, at least in some places, their experience and values are considered important. Survival has pushed tribal issues into the mainstream. This, perhaps, is our greatest achievement, but there are many barriers of racism, tyranny and greed still to overcome.

Tribal peoples need your help. Please write or phone for more information, or use the form to join us.

Stephen Corry
Survival International

membership form

I wish to join Survival

Name

Address

Country

Postcode

at the annual rate of £/US$

and / or make a
donation of £/US$

Total £/US$

Standard £15/$30   Donor £50/$100   Unwaged/Over 60 £5/$10

Life £250/$500   Family £25/$50

☐ I enclose my cheque (£ or US$) payable to Survival

☐ I wish to pay by Visa/MasterCard/JCB/Switch/Delta (delete as appropriate)

Credit Card number   Expiry date

Signature   Switch Issue No.

Date

Please detach this panel, enclose payment
and return it to: **Survival**, 11–15 Emerald
Street, London WC1N 3QL, United Kingdom.
Tel: 0171–242 1441. Fax: 0171–242 1771.
Charity number: 267444

Survival
for tribal peoples